STEPPIN

STEPPING STONES

Edited by Christina Baxter

Consultant editors:
John Stott and Roger Greenacre

Hodder & Stoughton
LONDON SYDNEY AUCKLAND TORONTO

British Library Cataloguing in Publication Data

Stepping stones.
   I. Church of England —— Doctrines
   I. Baxter, Christina   II. Stott, John R. W.
   III. Greenacre, Roger
   230'.3   BX5131.2

   ISBN 0 340 41598 3

Hodder and Stoughton Editorial Office: 47 Bedford Square, London WC1B 3DP.

CONTENTS

FOREWORD
by the Archbishop of Canterbury

It is sometimes claimed that there are such diverse and dynamic forces operating within the Anglican Communion that its eventual disintegration is inevitable. It is heartening, therefore, to find a group of Anglicans set out to work with each other over several years. Nor is this the first time that Catholics and Evangelicals within the Anglican Communion have co-operated in this way. Other instances of such endeavour are mentioned in this volume.

Their critics have sometimes accused them of entering into 'unholy alliances' simply on grounds of expediency. Such indictments are robustly refuted here and the claim is made that Catholics and Evengelicals are united instead by a concern for theological principle, candour and a distaste for deliberate ambiguity. If this is the case, it should be welcomed on all sides.

This book is itself an exercise in constructive theology. It shows remarkable convergence on several important theological issues, based on a recognition of the validity of the traditional Anglican emphasis on Scripture, tradition and reason as the essential resources for theology.

The chapters on the Church are nicely balanced. We are reminded that Anglicans are part of one, holy, catholic and apostolic Church. A reminder of the Church's oneness is also, of course, a reminder of tragic divisions. Here the provisionality of Anglicanism is emphasised. Anglicanism does not (or should not) exist for its own sake, but as a witness to the reconciliation that is possible among Christians of various persuasions.

It is my hope that convergence among Christians of different kinds in matter of belief will lead us all to a common confession of the apostolic faith within the communion of a reunited universal Church. Could the comprehensiveness of the Anglican Communion, based on an acknowledgement of the authority of Scripture, tradition and reason, be a witness to and a catalyst for the dawning of this great vision? I hope and pray that it might be so.

ROBERT CANTUAR
April 1987

PREFACE

'There is no sight of – or even any evidence of interest in – any internal Anglican agreement between Anglican Evangelicals and Anglo-Catholics on this vexed subject of grace and justification.' So wrote Clifford Longley in September 1986 in *The Times*. He called the lack of integration he perceived between the two groups 'the internal Anglican dis-ease'.

Our own perception of ourselves and of our mutual relations is different, however. To begin with, Evangelicals and Catholic Anglicans have always been united in their strong commitment to the Nicene Creed, interpreted according to its plain and natural sense. We recognise that its 'natural' sense is not always 'literal' as opposed to 'figurative'. For example, the statement that 'he sitteth on the right hand of the Father' is evidently as metaphorical in the Creed as it is in the Bible. At the same time, it is equally evident that he 'was incarnate by the Holy Ghost of the Virgin Mary' and 'the third day he rose again' are statements intended to be understood as historically as 'was crucified also for us under Pontius Pilate'. The great majority of Catholics and Evangelicals in the Anglican Communion, although aware of a spectrum of different opinions within our ranks on some other issues, are firmly united in upholding the traditional understanding of the virginal conception and bodily resurrection of Jesus.

As for the doctrine of salvation, which the Creed does not expound, it is a mistake to regard the truth of 'Justification by grace alone through faith alone', issuing in good works of love, as an exclusively Evangelical conviction, for Catholic Anglicans hold it too. In 1960 Michael Ramsey, at that time

Archbishop of York, answering the question how the Anglicanism of 1889–1939 stood in relation to the Reformation theology of the sixteenth century, wrote:

> There was for all typical Anglicans, not least those of the Anglo-Catholic school, no hesitancy on the cardinal convictions of the Reformation: that works cannot earn salvation, that salvation is by grace alone received through faith, that nothing can add to the sole mediatorship of the Cross of Christ, that Holy Scripture is the supreme authority in doctrine.[1]

We therefore welcome the newly published agreed statement of the Second Anglican-Roman Catholic International Commission, entitled *Salvation and the Church*, which helpfully clarifies the theological questions involved in the debate and clearly affirms that salvation is a 'pure unmerited gift', which is 'due solely to the mercy and grace of God' expressed through Christ's 'definitive atoning work'.

The coming together of Catholic and Evangelical Anglicans on doctrinal, moral and ecumenical issues has sometimes been regarded by others with deep suspicion. It has been perceived as 'an unholy alliance', that is, a political strategy of 'co-belligerence', in which two groups have together opposed certain ideas and proposals, although for different – and even mutually contradictory – reasons. A recent example is the way in which some Catholics and some Evangelicals felt in conscience bound to oppose the Anglican-Methodist Unity Scheme in England and so contributed to its defeat in 1969. Their alliance was not 'unholy', however, for they were united by a concern for theological principle, a commitment to integrity and candour, and a consequent distaste for what seemed to them to be deliberate ambiguity.

The following year, a small group of them felt challenged to explore and to publish their shared positive convictions. Thus, *Growing Into Union*, subtitled 'proposals for forming a united church in England', was produced. Its four authors, two Anglican Catholics (E. L. Mascall and Graham Leonard) and two Anglican Evangelicals (C. O. Buchanan and J. I. Packer), described themselves as 'all four committed to every line in the book' (p.19). What was remarkable about it was not only its outline proposal of an alternative union scheme (based on solid theological accord, involving one stage instead of two, multilateral, and encouraging gradual development at the local level), but its opening theological section which revealed an unexpected degree of accord (alongside continuing tensions) in the four controversial areas of 'Scripture and Tradition', 'God and his Grace', 'Church and Sacraments' and 'Episcopacy and Ministry'. For example, in the chapter on grace (pp. 40–9), which is described as 'free, unmerited, unsolicited love, taking the initiative to rescue the undeserving and enrich the unlovely', all Pelagianism ('the doctrine of self-salvation through self-sufficient self-reliance') is firmly rejected as 'among the profoundest of heresies', and eight theses are then developed in relation to God, Christ, faith, justification, sanctification, grace and the Church. Inevitably, *Growing Into Union* was criticised by some on both sides, and to be sure some paragraphs were less clear than others. Nevertheless, it was a brave, innovative book, whose authors saw the quest for visible unity in truth 'as a matter of plain Christian obedience' (p.11).

During the 1960s and 1970s both groups were seeking (and to some extent experiencing) a renewal of faith, worship and life. On the one hand, there were the National Evangelical Anglican Congresses at Keele in 1967 and Nottingham in 1977, and on the other the first Catholic Renewal Conference took place at Loughborough in 1978. Each group's assembly was attended by observers and/or consultants from the other group, and each expressed the desire for deeper mutual understanding and fellowship.

In consequence, during the 1978 Lambeth Conference at Canterbury, Dr Eric Kemp, Bishop of Chichester and President of the Church Union (CU), and John Stott, Chairman of the Church of England Evangelical Council (CEEC), discussed the desirability of promoting dialogue between theologians representing the Catholic and Evangelical traditions within the Church of England. The signatories of this Preface, with the active encouragement of CU and CEEC, then convened a small group, consisting of four from each side. We first met in 1980 and have continued to meet regularly twice a year. We have explored such fundamental areas as 'Authority in relation to Scripture and Tradition',

'Nature and Grace', 'The Cross', 'Eucharistic Sacrifice' and 'The Lima Text on Baptism'. As a result of our meetings and exchanges, we have grown in mutual understanding, respect and affection. In spite of some residual disagreements, we have found ourselves in substantial accord in many areas.

When the main themes of the 1988 Lambeth Conference were announced, it seemed to us that we should attempt to speak to some of them together. Not that we have planned one essay for each theme or sub-theme. Instead we have chosen those major topics of debate in which we believed we could speak with one voice, namely Anglican identity, Christology, the Church, ministry, family and mission. Each essay carries the endorsement of its two authors, in each case a Catholic and an Evangelical. The copyright is with CU and CEEC, the parent bodies of the dialogue, although naturally they do not accept responsibility for the opinions expressed, any more than does the group as a whole. In any case, several of the contributing authors are neither members of CU or CEEC, nor of the original dialogue. We are especially grateful to Christina Baxter for accepting the difficult task of co-ordinating and editing, to Canon Sam Van Culin for encouraging us in our enterprise, and to the Archbishop of Canterbury for his Foreword.

Lambeth 1988 will be of critical importance for the Anglican Communion; indeed, some observers, by no means all of them cynics, are prophesying its collapse and distintegration. While we do not make any extravagant claims for this volume of essays, we do sincerely believe that such a venture at such a moment is timely and significant. Catholic and Evangelical Anglicans have much in common. Paradoxically, not the least important is the combination of a deep love for our Church with a sharp awareness of its fragility. In consequence, we dare not be uncritical, but must constantly weigh what is said and done in the name of Anglicanism against those more fundamental loyalties to which we as Catholics and Evangelicals owe allegiance. Professor Stephen Sykes, who would not want to be identified with either of our traditions, has said that nobody's loyalty to Anglicanism should 'be more than strictly penultimate'.[2] So we cannot accept as either fair or accurate other Anglicans' view of us as 'parties' within Anglicanism. Anglicanism at its best is not the pursuit of moderation for its own sake; it is rather the fruitful and positive interaction of our two traditions, and its dynamic is the hope of their final and total reconciliation. We reject the accusation that our two traditions are essentially negative, narrow or sectarian. Indeed we affirm the contrary. Catholicism by its very nature is inclusive of all truth, however diverse the means by which God teaches it and we receive it. Evangelicalism by its very nature is concerned to point prophetically to the overriding priorities of the gospel. These two emphases are not antithetical; rather they need each other and call for each other. A Christianity that is not in this sense both Catholic and Evangelical is in the end neither Catholic nor Evangelical.

While we have often found ourselves drawn together by opposition to certain so-called 'liberal' trends in theology, we acknowledge with respect the serious contribution to the life of our Communion which many who have stood in the liberal or 'Erasmian' tradition have made by their honest and questioning spirit. We are nevertheless convinced that the two traditions which have the widest and deepest significance, and which have given our Church its greatest saints and its greatest leaders, are those called 'Evangelical' and 'Catholic'. It is not too much to claim that the future of our Communion will depend on their closer unity, and that this closer unity will also contribute powerfully to the healing of the Reformation schisms.

It is in this spirit and with this hope that we recommend to our fellow Anglicans our collection of essays and the dialogue out of which it has grown. In the process of pre-Lambeth discussion throughout the Anglican Communion, in which many thousands of ordinary Church members are expected to be involved, we trust that these essays will help to stimulate, clarify and unite their thinking and their action.

Roger Greenacre
John Stott
February 1987

---

1 A. M. Ramsey, *From Gore to Temple* (London, 1960), p. 166.
2 S. Sykes, *The Integrity of Anglicanism* (London and Oxford, 1978), p. ix.

1

ON DOING THEOLOGY

1   THEOLOGY AND THE NATURE OF FAITH

Why do theology at all? Do these questions of doctrine actually *matter*? 'He can't be wrong whose life is in the right' is a popular and attractive philosophy, and anyone worrying about 'forms and creeds' probably deserves to be written off as a 'graceless zealot'. Theology, organised and sustained reflection on Christian life and language, may be a (fairly) harmless hobby, but it can't be an enterprise central to the life of faith.

In response to this attitude, this essay suggests a definition of theology which would bring it a good deal closer to the heart of Christian experience: theology is an expression of *responsible faith*. 'Responsible faith' here means not just faith prepared to give an account of itself, but faith aware that it exists as a *response* to something: it is an answer to some call or initiative beyond itself, and so is always 'answerable', as we say, to something other than itself. Its authenticity or integrity is not to be judged simply in terms of the intensity of an individual experience: it is open to being judged and challenged by its own origins in a summons, a moment of creative newness in the human world. And theology is important as being one way in which that challenge can be kept before the present experience of believers. As such, it is an activity in which every believer can and should be involved – not a specialist activity for the few.

Of course there are other ways of thinking about faith: you could lay the emphasis on present feelings, or on the acting-out of a loosely defined inspiration – a hope or purpose fired by the memory of Jesus – or on a listening for your own innermost truth, trusting that this will lead you to fulfilment. None of this is in itself wholly wrong or foolish; but the Christian understanding of faith insists that feelings and inspiration and truth to yourself only become part of a really *transforming* process when seen in the light of something more far-reaching (and more disturbing). In the New Testament, 'faith' is the name of that condition of life created through the death and resurrection of Jesus; it is the rebirth that lies on the far side of an entry into, a 'yielding' to, this mystery. It is first that simple trust that Jesus in his ministry asks for, trust in himself and in his Father; but only after Easter can the full scope of that trust be grasped, because only then do we see the full dimension of what God promises in Jesus. We are called out of the emptiness and nothingness of our struggles for self-sufficiency by the revelation of God's inexhaustible mercy and his sovereignty over death and hell; we lose our familiar and safe (but illusory) selves as we give ourselves over to the kingdom present and active in Jesus, and so share in 'a death like his'; and we are given back ourselves, renewed and absolved, and open to unimagined possibilities, made alive in the 'spirit of him who raised Jesus from the dead'. If we want to understand what Paul and John in particular mean by 'faith', it is no use looking for accounts of mental attitudes, or feelings or aspirations. Faith is the whole of what comes into being in us when God is allowed to interrupt and transfigure our lives in Jesus; and so it is not to be separated from the fact of the Christian community – the body of those marked off from the parent community of the Jewish people and from the pagan world around by baptism, the enactment of dying and rising, loss and rebirth with Jesus Christ.

Faith, in this sense, is not a replacement for knowledge of a mere 'ordinary' kind, not a set of answers to questions or a bundle of bits of esoteric information. Some of our long-standing worries about 'faith and reason' seem to arise from the odd idea that they are two rival ways of getting to know things; whereas faith in the New Testament context is more a way of seeing myself and my world afresh, and a resource for hoping, choosing, and acting. It relativises the whole issue of 'wanting to be sure' independently of changing my whole life, it questions the deep alienation of mind and heart we are so used to, and suggests another kind of understanding from the reductive and functional approach we commonly bring to the world. Justification by faith is also a justification in 'unknowing', the learning to live with what exceeds our grasp: more, perhaps, like learning to swim than learning to drive a car? an attunement, not a mastery.

Commenting on Genesis, Luther wrote of Abraham that he hid himself in the darkness of faith and therein found eternal light.[1] This entry into darkness means that faith is God's *creation*, the act of God in cutting across our self-despair, our recognition that we cannot bring ourselves to truth, to real life, acceptance, salvation, all that is meant by the 'righteousness' of Paul and the Reformers. This is the 'alien righteousness' which Luther speaks of, a state radically foreign to what moral effort, spiritual exercise or pious reflection can achieve. In his creation of faith, however, God also transforms us; he gives himself to us in love and so draws us into fellowship, indeed *union*, with himself. Because he speaks to us and with us, he makes us partners in his everlasting life.

'Responsible' faith today remains faith conscious of having been created, almost *forced* into being, by God's entry into the world of women and men, conscious of its character as a following not a beginning. Believers, aware of living in a new climate in their relations to each other and to God, look with some wonderment at the complex events at the root of their present condition; and as they try to explore and see more fully the distinctive newness of that condition, they will inevitably seek to think through and make more fully their own those generative facts. If they were not awed, bewildered and overjoyed by this newness, there would be no questioning – and no sense of a risk of forgetting or betraying. 'Christian theological thinking is thinking rationally in the wake of the act and word of the living God'[2] – a thinking that doesn't seek to master but to be mastered by what it reflects on; or, better ('mastery' being so corrupted a metaphor in a world of real enslavement), seeking to be one with, immersed in, 'owned' by its source and stimulus, the hidden drawing of God's love.

2   FAITH AND THE NEW CREATION

To talk about God 'interrupting' our world needs more clarification. The Christian Church exists as an identifiable community dating its origins at an identifiable moment; and this suggests that its existence can't be seen properly as *just* a dimension of continuing human experience. The Church – as its very name, *ekklesia*, proclaims – believes that it is there because it is called to be there, and that it is a place where the final and decisive truths about human beings are uttered and enacted so as to summon the whole human world to *judgment*, to summon the world to answer for its life, its failures and hopes. Thus God's coming among us is seen by the Church as, at one basic and important level, a negation: it relativises and apparently overturns existing attempts to make total and satisfying sense of our existence; and it offers 'to make its own sense' of us. There is a Church at all because the experiences focused upon Jesus so profoundly disturbed the religious and social 'sense' of the day, and could not be contained within these available patterns. The Church doesn't appear as a carefully planned and organised phenomenon.

So the sense of discontinuity in Christian origins cannot be evaded.[3] Jesus is not seen as offering useful illustrations of existing types of experience: what happens in and around him *constitutes* new possibilities of experience. But this also means that the negativity, the rupture and the novelty of Jesus doesn't simply say 'no' to our humanity, and leave it there. It says 'no' to the humanity, the world, we invent and organise for ourselves, in our own various and warring interests, 'no' to our consoling images of ourselves; but it says 'yes' to (and enables us to say 'yes' to) us as we fundamentally *are* – creatures of God, objects of his love, called to fellowship with him: 'a quicknesse, which my God hath kist'.[4] The negation does not annihilate us, but remakes us, re-forms what we can say and do, feel and imagine. And by bringing us back to what we most deeply are, it points to a continuity beyond the initial rupture: what seemed most strange (Jesus, and the new identity he offers us) is at last seen to be most natural, most homely, answering our most central and strong desire. We are not by nature sinners, posturing, manipulating, fantasising, trying to 'create' ourselves in despite of God and at the cost of each other, but we are chosen by God, called to share his freedom, before ever we turned from him. What happens in Jesus is new; yet, as Paul and his followers constantly remind us,[5] the hidden truth, the 'mystery' of faith, is that it is also older than all human struggle and drama. The 'foolishness' of God, his coming into our world so much at an angle to our expectations and ideas, is the Wisdom in which he made all things. The Word which is Jesus, Jesus rejected and slaughtered, is in the beginning with God.

The events of Jesus's life, death and rising thus give us knowledge both of God and ourselves, a knowledge grounded in the reality of a new *relation* to God and ourselves. And, as the Church seeks to share this converted vision with the whole world, convinced of its urgent pertinence to all, it is bound to go on reflecting on the inner logic of all this. The sense of a recovery of our real identity as creatures, and the pressure towards universal mission – these things pose for the believer the question, 'What must be true of Jesus for this to be happening and for this to be intelligible?' and the instantly related question, 'What must be true of *God* for this to be intelligible?' These are the foundational theological questions of Christian belief, arising as they do directly out of the corporate experience of absolution and renewal, and the impulse to mission; they do not arise out of speculative guesswork about Jesus as an isolated historical individual, and they do not arise at all where the twin roots of new life and missionary urgency are absent. 'Responsible' faith is faith beginning to explore and respond to the events of its formation in praise, thought and action – constantly aware that its response stumbles far behind the massive and disorientating work of its author, and so constantly self-critical and not disposed to take itself, *in* itself, too seriously.

3   THE AUTHORITY OF THE CROSS

In this light, all Christian theology must be first and foremost a theology of the cross, acknowledging the disturbance caused by the *particular* living and dying of Jesus, and not subsiding into generalities; a theology for baptism, articulating the loss and re-creation that constitute our entry into faith. First God must be before us as hidden and strange, for only then can we learn to see ourselves in his light, when we realise that he is not to be seen or grasped in the light of what we think we are. Without this discipline, the believing community risks slipping into forms of speech or action that are self-indulgent and self-protecting.

If anyone wants to know why theology matters, they should study that archetypal crisis of the Church in our century, the struggle between the Confessing Church and the 'German Christians' in the 1930s.[6] Here – as the Barmen Declaration proclaimed[7] and as Barth and Bonhoeffer tirelessly repeated – is the parting of the ways between a true Church, responsible to God's act in Jesus Christ, and a pseudo-Church, answering only to the pressures of the age. The theology of the cross can be and is properly a theology of resistance to a world that enslaves human beings to idolatrous and oppressive models of what they may be – and to a Church blind to this enslavement. If there is a Christian social and political ethics, its grounds are not in culture alone or in a diffusely benevolent humanitarianism, but in the judgment passed in Christ upon the prince of this world, and upon the self-serving delusions which that prince sows in the minds of men and women – the delusions that foster racial exclusivism, sexual domination, military expansionism and whatever else. As many have discovered and are discovering, a theology of the cross which is a theology of judgment and resistance lies close to a deeper *participation* in the cross – from Bonhoeffer in his cell to the camps of the Soviet Union, or the detention blocks and interrogation centres of Johannesburg or the back streets of Santiago. 'Responsible' faith, *theological* faith, is faith called to answer for itself before courts and rulers, in the face of idolatry maintained by violence.

Faith in such circumstances is authoritative: it presents what (by the grace of God) it is to the world, and to the rest of the Church, in confidence. If faith can on occasion confront the world in judgment, and pay the price, it testifies to its awareness of having been entrusted with something solid and precious. 'Freely you have received, freely give': the authority of the faithful in (not over!) the world is bound up with gratitude for the transforming reality of what has been received. And so the blood of the martyrs is occasion for the Church's celebration because it is from them that we learn what it might be to give thanks with the whole self, and thus learn the dimension of a gift that can so 'demand my soul, my life, my all'. How then can we undervalue or apologise for it? A theology looking in this direction, then, has the job not only of bringing criticism to the Church's life and speech, but also awakening the Church to *this* kind of authority – a transparency to the gift and promise entrusted to it for the life of the world. Theology is not there just to issue challenges to the Church (certainly not in the name of its own expertise); its essential critical activity should be inseparable from its role in helping the Church's thankful articulation of the gift that lies behind and empowers all Christian activity. Theology should empower the liberating preaching of the Church in its full authority as it recalls the Church to judgment and dependence.

4 THE AUTHORITY OF SCRIPTURE

If theology, then, exists to help the Church to be what it is called to be, if for this end it involves a steady and radical exposure to the foundational events of Christian faith, it will necessarily accord central and decisive importance to Scripture, since Scripture is the unique witness to those events. This does not mean, however, that we are to imagine the theologian (the reflective believer) sitting down to study Scripture as if it were nothing but a historical report or a moral programme or a textbook of doctrine, and rising up to deliver definitive pronouncements. No, the Bible continues to be of unique significance because without it we should not have any understanding at all of faith itself. It has this significance not simply because it speaks to us of God's active presence in history, but because it speaks of this by being itself a response to God, rather than merely by detached 'reporting'. Of course, the Bible is not all praise and thanksgiving; it is also law and narrative and argument. It is not just a list of examples of human response to the call of God; it presents to us the story and the content of that call, indeed presents the call itself and enables our response to it. And what gives it unity and integrity is the fact that it speaks in and *to* the life of communities (Old and New Israel) that define themselves in terms of God's call. All that is said in Scripture is within the context of trustful response to a summons, a summons continuously alive and powerful in the memory and the prayer of a community. We should not know how God's act is liberating and transforming if we did not hear it spoken of in liberated and transformed language, the language of a converted people. In its whole tenor and context, Scripture defines faith for us; what we find to say about faith is to be tested by this norm.

The Reformation appeal to Scripture (which all Anglicans, Catholic or Evangelical, are bound to recognise at the heart of their heritage, and which is enshrined in our classical and contemporary ordinals) assumes that the person reading Scripture is not engaged in a mere literary exercise, but is being dealt with by God. In this text, which relates and witnesses to the call of God to prophets and apostles, God continues to call his people now. To quote Luther again: 'He who merely studies the commandments of God [*mandata Dei*] is not greatly moved. But he who *listens* to God the Commanding One [*deum mandantem*], how can he fail to be terrified by majesty so great?'

Perhaps we do not think often enough about the authority of Scripture in relation to the way it teaches us *wonder* (which is so much a part of faith). The Bible presents the primary and classical response of self-forgetful thanksgiving for God's coming among us. Behind both Old and New Testaments is the dread, the bewilderment and the incredulous delight of people caught up in the unexpected and re-creative work of God. 'Behold, I am doing a new thing'; 'I am God, not man';

'fear fell upon them all, and they glorified God, saying . . .
God has visited his people'; 'they said nothing to anyone, for
they were afraid'; 'my Lord and my God'. No accident that we
can find so many powerful examples of this in the resurrection
stories.

The essential test of a theology claiming to be 'scriptural' is
whether it begins and ends in this sort of wonder; and the
possibility of theology of this kind depends a lot on whether
the theologian is consciously part of a community *aware* of the
newness of its life, aware that the gospel is surprising. Not just
the availability of Scripture as a text, nor the individual
holiness and insight of the theologian, but the life of a Church
concerned to be converted, testing its own faith by its
continuity and congruence with what the language of Scripture shows – this is a necessity for creative theology. This is to
say in other words that the theologian's reading of Scripture
depends for its fruitfulness on the action of the Spirit, the
Spirit which is the power making present to us now the event
of God's acting in Israel and in Jesus. Or, in other terms
again, you can't be a 'scripturally-minded' theologian in a
Church wholly devoid of saints: at best, you might be a
learned repository of biblical lore, which is *not* the same
thing. The theologian is there to help the Church be the
Church through his or her attention to the classical witness of
faith and conversion; but that attention is itself in turn
enabled by the degree to which the Church is truly a
fellowship of the Spirit. The relation of holiness in the Church
and the critical service of theology is subtle, an interpenetra-
tion at many levels.

5 LISTENING TO TRADITION

This consideration reminds us that no reflective believer can
read the Bible as if no one had ever read it before. Scripture
can and must address us as new, as surprising, teasing,
challenging, but its address will still inevitably be heard as it is
reflected through a history of reading. Others have been here
before; and if they have really heard the summons and the
challenge of Scripture they will help to flesh out for us the

definition of conversion and faith set down in Scripture. Their discipleship is part of what nourishes ours, and we have a certain kind of responsibility to them as well as to the bare text of the Bible. If the Bible shows what it is like to be converted by God's interrupting of the world, the history of faithful reading of the Bible shows what it means for the *converted* speech of Scripture to be also *converting* speech for the generations after.

The history of reading as a history of discipleship is a central aspect of what theologians mean by 'tradition'. 'Tradition in its primary notion is not the revealed content, but the unique mode of receiving revelation, a faculty owed to the Holy Spirit.'[8] It is not the uncritical and uncriticised memory of the Church, but the memory of the Church's struggle for faithful understanding of scriptural revelation, and so of its own true nature in the purposes of God. The Church returns to Scripture to be converted, to test its present life and witness against the primary proclamation of the gospel. Tradition as bondage to what has been said and done just *because* it has been said and done has nothing to do with theology: the tradition that is important for theological method is the story of a Church thinking and living in confrontation with the primary challenge of God and its classical testimony. This is why tradition can itself be a critical and renewing factor in theology ('Tradition represents the critical spirit of the Church . . . made acute by the Holy Spirit'),[9] a creative recovery of the past in the context of an idle, banal or corrupt present. The Reformers, the great Anglican divines, the Wesleys, Newman, Barth – all owe their renewal of immediacy in relation to the fundamental revelation to a recovery of 'tradition', a vitalising memory which reassures us that the present doesn't exhaust our possibilities. And perhaps one distinctive insight of a Reformed theology is that 'tradition' includes the memory of deep discontinuities, moments of 'recovery' (or 'retrieval', as modern philosophies of interpretation like to say) that represent a painful breach with prevailing fashions and assumptions – an insight that should at least offer some hope to theologians inclined to pessimism in the face of an uninspired present. The great seduction, of course, is to misread this as meaning that theology's future lies in a revival of the past; but this would be a *capitulation* to the past, a retreat into memory as an inner and static vision, not a conversation with it that encourages us to believe things might become different.

In any good conversation, we discover what we never realised we wanted to say: we become more articulately ourselves as we allow ourselves to be probed and discovered by another. For the theologian, this should mean an abiding wariness of our tendency to that kind of historical snobbery that assumes superior skills in some areas to be a guarantee of more comprehensive insight overall. We unquestionably possess a more nuanced awareness than previous generations of how the Bible as a collection of texts came into being and of the diversity of style and genre within those texts. This may or may not assist our skill in 'faithful' reading; and it does not automatically make us better readers and interpreters (for theological purposes) than an Augustine or a Luther – or the modern exegete still operating unselfconsciously in a 'pre-critical' intellectual world, the African catechist or the Orthodox monk. *Nostalgia* for a pre-critical world is a pointless and dishonest response to our situation. But we have everything to lose in failing to take these alternative readings seriously – i.e. in relation to their understanding of a faith and a discipleship we claim in some measure to share.

6   THE USE AND ABUSE OF REASON

Attention to tradition emphatically does not mean that we are condemned to repeat the past; and relativising the present moment and its seemingly total claims does not mean pretending that it doesn't exist. We cannot make our starting-point other than what it is – what is given in the historical contingencies of when and where we happen to be. We can *listen* to the voice of a pre-critical age, but if we pretend to *speak* with that voice we delude ourselves (and deny the reality of genuine dialogue and challenge in our relation with the Christian past). So the questions we put to Scripture and the history of reading Scripture arise from both the problems and the skills we have as persons of our own age and context. It is probably misleading to speak of a 'responsibility' to this context in quite the same sense as our having a responsibility to Scripture and tradition – yet it is not completely wrong. God calls us as and where we are; and his converting revelation does not make sense for us, does not become intelligible and *communicable*, utterly independently of the ways in which we now try to 'make sense' culturally and intellectually. So long as we use the same language in our general intellectual life and in our theologising, we cannot totally separate them, even if we acknowledge the error of simply transposing the canons and conventions of the one on to the other. Our responsibility here is to make sure that, as far as possible, what is said in theology can be *heard* as a proposal for 'making sense' in the world as it is, not just as the dialect of a ghetto.

The problem is that in every culture, but especially in one as fragmented as ours, 'making sense' is not reducible to a single method. What some people call the 'tyranny of rationality' or 'rationalism' arises where we suppose that 'reason' is a technique of argumentation applicable in exactly the same way, across the board, to all sorts of speaking and acting. In fact, reasoning is a vastly diverse thing; the natural scientist makes sense with one kind of language – more dependent than we once thought on imagination and controlled 'fantasy' (certainly in the further reaches of physics); the social and political scientist works through the creation of models and stories of the interaction of groups or individuals – and points out how easy it is for some to have their 'sense' made by others who have, or wish to have, power over them (ideology as a tool of control); the artist works to make sense of the uncompromisingly local or specific – *this* narrative, *this* canvas, *this* stone or wood, *these* musical relationships. All are 'reasoning' – arguing, persuading, pursuing conclusions, resolutions, adequate statements; all are searching for consistent utterance and integrity of vision.

Theological reflection cannot set aside considerations of what counts as 'reasoned' integrity in a culture; and to allow this is not to impose an alien rationalism upon faith, for there is no one scheme or 'grid' to employ. And it is certainly not to suggest that there is any mileage in the myth of an omnipotent and objective faculty, 'Reason' in a sort of degenerate eighteenth-century sense, that can discover a passive object called God, and map out what he can and cannot do. What we have called 'making sense' is as flawed and limited as the rest of human activity.

At first sight, though, this confronts us with a daunting agenda: no one area of our intellectual life is going to provide us with an abstract methodology for doing theology, and theology must learn to be at home with an immense variety of styles of thinking. We may note and develop a striking parallel with some bit of scientific or social-scientific or artistic method, but we should beware of claiming that such overlaps deliver to us *the* key for doing theology now. Making theological sense in relation to all this is bound to be a fragmentary and unsatisfactory matter: there can be no *summa* for this age, or perhaps for any readily imaginable future age. Theology cannot claim either to give decisive endorsement to any *one* kind of contemporary reasoning, or to offer a general intellectual synthesis. It can only attend to and struggle to speak with the plurality of reasonings that it confronts in specific settings, in the hope that, as already remarked, it can demonstrate an at-homeness and suggest an overarching context of living, perceiving and acting, in which the varieties of human searching and human integrity might find a place.

This implies, too, that theology must sometimes show that it can bear the disturbance and uncertainty, even the pain, of such exploration without seeking to impose a neat intellectual solution drawn from its own conceptual repertoire. Many of those who try to do theology will know the experience of emerging from engagement with a novel, play or film with a richer but far more confused or tormented awareness of human possibilities. God forbid that we should try to come up with the sort of 'Christian response' that attempts to remove the tensions, or even to exploit this experience as a quarry for 'illustrations' of doctrinal argument. We are required rather to wait and see what resources in our Christian vision are touched or awakened or challenged by this; to let the artist's statement and our own commitments work on each other. In such a situation, the good theologian needs patience, a deep suspicion of theoretical reconciliations, the 'contemplative' capacity to stay with a work of the imagination for what it is in itself, and the strength to live with a degree of inner conflict and unfinishedness. We have already noted that in good conversation we learn what we distinctively have to say for the first time; this is true for the theologian in dialogue with Scripture and tradition, and it holds, too, for the theologian's encounter with the contemporary imagination. Here especially, a distinctive and individual voice reveals itself under the pressure of an alien questioning; and a sensitivity to the variety, the ironies, tragedies and non-resolutions of the imagination may save the theologian from a captivity to trivial optimism in theology and lying cliché in his or her response to the contemporary world as a whole.

7   THE PRIMACY OF SCRIPTURE IN THE LIFE OF THE CHURCH

Scripture, but not as a textbook; tradition, but not as a museum of conventions to be repeated; reason, but not as an abstract and uniform technique: the threefold cord of traditional Anglican theological method is an almost inescapable pattern in thinking about theology at all, even in our 'post-critical' time, once we grant that theology has to do with response and responsibility in our faith. But if we are to restate and reclaim the validity of this method, we must avoid any suggestion that the theologian is a detached individual working on three separate repositories of truth, and seeking to weave their data into a system, a religious theory. There would be no Christian theology without the community of faith, and no community without the anchorage of scriptural witness to its origins, to the power that creates and preserves the faith from which the community lives. The order and relation of the three aspects of our method matters enormously: the nature of our response and responsibility to 'tradition' and 'reason' must be determined by our response to the creative events witnessed to in Scripture, as we return constantly to the question of *faith* and its meaning.

This 'determining' role of Scripture, however, will operate

in different ways. Sometimes it is immediately evident, in a theology beginning with the exegesis of the biblical text. But it may also appear more obliquely in the course of our dealing with tradition or 'reason'. That is to say we may discover it as we attempt to trace the characteristic methods of some saint or doctor; or as we become aware of what we need in resisting the pressures of some secular or pseudo-religious contemporary tyranny; or as we return to the angular puzzles of the gospel narrative from some encounter with the difficult particularity of modern imaginative narrative. Testing ourselves in the processes of encounter and understanding, we are repeatedly brought back to the central question of the foundation of trust or hope in us, which is God's self-disclosure to his people; and this means being brought back to the testimony of those first summoned to be God's people, and, ultimately, to the focus and embodiment of God's summons which is the person of his Son. The primacy of Scripture needs to be recalled whenever theology looks like becoming generalised religious reflection; but it is not a principle that can operate meaningfully abstracted from the community of believers assembled through the ages around Christ and from the concrete questioning arising now from the theologian's history and context.[10] Theology is about the roots of faith, and so of present choice and action, not about patterns of ideas – even 'biblical' ideas (as I have suggested, Scripture is not best read as a collection of ideas). Its criteria are not to be reduced to fixed abstractions; they are always to do with the author and the perfecter of faith.

8   THE LIMITS OF PLURALISM

What about the problem of the 'professional' theologian's autonomy and the 'pluralism' of theological discourse? All we have said takes it for granted that the theologian does not ask to be heard or understood independently of the community of faith, and that the theologian as such does not determine the boundaries of that community. What power the theologian *does* exercise in the Church should depend on the closeness of his or her work to questions affecting the particularities of life and faithful witness now; though these should not be defined simply as the questions that a majority of Christians in a particular time and locality happen to find interesting, but those that might be shown to affect what the Church essentially is. Theologians who claimed autonomy in the sense of asserting a right to be heard *in the Church*, quite irrespective of their awareness of such questions, would be (to put it mildly) making a rather eccentric claim; they would be defining their own commitments in some detachment from the commitments of the Church as Church. And in so far as theology is necessarily a committed reasoning *within* a committed community, such a situation blunts the *freedom* of theology to perform its role for the Church: it imprisons itself within a set of private preoccupations.

On the other hand, that freedom depends on theology's agenda not being set for it by either an ecclesiastical establishment or a consensus of popular devotion. Its role requires it to be in some degree unpredictable, and its responsibility is not simply to the expressed needs of the empirical Church (a point which, once again, a Reformed theology ought to grasp). What makes the theologian's autonomy a problem is that many in the Church do not distinguish between criticism of the empirical Church and criticism of the gospel, and that some theologians do not seem clearly enough to appeal to an authority other than scholarly expertise or contemporary fashion in challenging convention-al versions of ethical or dogmatic positions. The suspicious Church member needs to learn a certain detachment from comforting but provisional or partial schemes of understand-ing; the theologian has to show an 'obedience' and attention to the general Christian commitment to faithful responsive-ness when confronted by the divine interruption. And to the degree that some theological positions appear to evade any element of being constrained by the unmasterable initiative that calls forth faith, they weaken or undermine the essence of the community itself, and cease to be recognisably *theology*: the Church is justified in a critical retort to or repudiation of them. To take an obvious instance: if it is claimed that the particular identity of Jesus is utterly immate-rial to the beginnings of the Church, or that the Holy Spirit is simply a metaphor for divine immanence in world or Church, it becomes impossible to make sense of commitment to and in a community that baptises, makes eucharist, nurtures a certain understanding of prayer and contemplation that is closely related to the paschal narrative, and reads the Scriptures. Such claims have ceased to be 'in conversation' with concrete ecclesial faith, past or present, and have next to nothing to do with the ideas of responsibility and responsiveness we have been trying to outline.

This is not a licence for heresy hunts or any other paranoid defence of orthodoxy: at one important level, the truth looks after itself – if we believe that the ministries of Word and sacrament enact for us the indestructible presence and *givenness* of God's promises. But it is a reminder that in some circumstances those who have some right to speak for the worshipping Church have the right to say of certain ideas that they have no claim to be called Christian theology because they are at odds with the very *conception* of the Church. Such a 'right' is not a limitation of intellectual freedom, a hierarchical tyranny, but the recognition that the 'grammar of commitment' presupposed by the very activity of theology does not admit of flat self-contradictions. And – whatever unease may be felt about aspects of this or that theologian's explorations – it is probably only rarely that a whole set or system of views can be characterised as essentially anti-theological. Furthermore, for this to be feasible requires a profoundly self-critical and 'responsible' Church in the first place, a Church that is actually concerned for its integrity, and so is prepared to endure some heavy theological questioning – not a Church that retreats into the repetition of formulas as soon as awkward questions are raised.

Nor does this threaten the proper multiplicity of theological 'styles'. 'Formal' and 'informal' dogmatics,[11] philosophical and methodological work, political theology, theologies tending to the intellectual, theologies tending to the affective or intuitive, all these are and always have been called out by diverse circumstances, according to how the question of what faith and the community of faith mean. A Bernard and an Abelard, a Segundo[12] and a von Balthasar,[13] a Karl Barth[14] and a David Tracy[15] represent spectacularly different understandings of this question; but the Church and its leadership are not called on to pronounce on the relative priorities involved (which is why generalised condemnations of liberation theology, for instance, seem so misplaced), so long as the question remains one about *faith*, and is asked with the urgency appropriate to that responsibility basic to Christian faith itself.

All these generalities inevitably suggest a far more easily controlled and stabilised relation between theologian and Church at large than is ever the case. In practice, theology *is* difficult and the occasion of difficulties for those who aren't full-time theologians. But the intellectually and spiritually disturbing dimensions of theology, the harshness of its questioning, rest upon the nature of the Church as the triumphant creation of a gracious God. If the Christian way were simply an experimental spirituality loosely inspired by a dead foreigner, we should no doubt be spared a lot of trouble; we should also be spared the transformation of the human world by God's mercy in Christ. As it is, theology remains hard, for theologians and for their public, but the fact itself indicates the occasion for unstinted gratitude, celebration and – as we have seen – wonder at the sovereign work of grace. 'The wrath of man shall turn to thy praise'; so, too, should the complexities and the turmoil of theology.

NOTES

1 WA, X:3, pp. 352–61.
2 This is how Karl Barth, perhaps the greatest theologian of the century, defines theology; for an elaboration of this statement, see his book on Saint Anselm, *Anselm, Fides Quaerens Intellectum* (London, 1960), esp. pp. 46ff.
3 Even a book like E. P. Sanders' recent *Jesus and Judaism* (London, 1985), which heavily stresses Jesus's at-homeness in the Jewish world of his day, points eventually to the inescapable novelty of the free offer of God's kingdom to the wicked (see chaps. 6 and 10).
4 From Henry Vaughan's poem, 'Quicknesse'.
5 As in the opening chapters of 1 Corinthians and Ephesians especially.
6 Perhaps best set out in Eberhard Bethge's classical biography of Dietrich Bonhoeffer (London, 1970).

7 Translation in A. C. Cochrane, *The Church's Confession under Hitler* (Philadelphia, 1962), and in J. W. de Gruchy, *Bonhoeffer and South Africa* (Grand Rapids, Exeter, 1984).

8 From the Russian theologian, Vladimir Lossky, *In the Image and Likeness of God* (New York/London, 1974), p. 155.

9 V. Lossky, op. cit., p. 156.

10 This is perhaps why the 'biblical theology' movement of the 1940s and 1950s, although it nurtured essential insights about the *unity* of scriptural language and imagery, proved too difficult to sustain in the face of the onslaught of the radicalism of the 1960s. A new biblical theology will have had to have passed through these fires and been strengthened in the process.

11 The distinction is drawn by Barth in volume 2, part 1, of the *Church Dogmatics* (E.T., London, 1957), p. 277.

12 Juan Luis Segundo, prominent Roman Catholic liberation theologian, author of *The Liberation of Theology, Theology for Artisans of a New Humanity*, etc.

13 Hans Urs von Balthasar, Roman Catholic expert on early Christianity, author of a fine study of Barth and of a large number of works on the interrelation of art and contemplation and theology, including *Prayer, Engagement with God*, and the multi-volume *The Glory of the Lord*; critical of many developments in the Roman Catholic Church since Vatican II.

14 The foremost defender of a theology based entirely on revelation and grace; a Swiss Protestant deeply critical of liberal protestant ideas, author of the huge *Church Dogmatics*, and the more accessible *Evangelical Theology, Dogmatics in Outline* and *The Humanity of God*.

15 Liberal Roman Catholic philosopher-theologian, concerned with the role of the theologian in society and university as well as Church; author of various studies on the foundations of theology, including *The Analogical Imagination*.

BIBLIOGRAPHY

Hans Urs von Balthasar, *Engagement with God* (London, 1975). *A brief meditation by a leading Roman Catholic theologian on the nature of vocation and covenant in Scripture.*

Karl Barth, *Evangelical Theology* (London, 1965). *The most easily accessible introduction to Barth's thinking.*

D. W. Hardy and D. F. Ford, *Jubilate. Theology in Praise* (London, 1984). *This argues that all theology arises from and expresses the praise of God as drawn forth by the acts of God.*

Inter-Anglican Theological & Doctrinal Commission, *For the Sake of the Kingdom. God's Church and the New Creation* (Anglican

Consultative Council, 1986). *The first report of this Commission, drawn from all parts and all traditions of Anglicanism; deals with the basic assumptions of theology, and the problem of Christianity's relation to culture and politics.*

Dietrich Ritschl, *The Logic of Theology* (London, 1986). *A sophisticated but not too technical discussion of theological principles by a rather unusual German theologian who has spent many years in pastoral ministry, and has taught in the USA and the Third World.*

DISCUSSION QUESTIONS

1 Do you think of yourself as a theologian?

2 Do you expect theology to be any use to you and your fellow Christians? If not, why not?

3 Why do you think that Anglicans have said that nothing can be *required* Christian belief that cannot be found in the Bible, at least implicitly?

4 What sort of associations does the word 'tradition' have for you? How do these connect with what the essay says about it?

5 Does religious experience have any authority in theology? If so, what kind of authority?

2

JESUS – GOD WITH US

1 INTRODUCTION

Christology has been at the centre of much of the theological
debate of recent years, and rightly so, because the credibility
and relevance of Christian faith in the modern world depend
on the credibility and relevance of the Christian claims about
Jesus. In England, the long-running debate about the validity
and interpretation of the doctrine of the incarnation has been
succeeded recently by discussion of the historicity and
significance of the virginal conception and the empty tomb – a
discussion which has brought little theological light into the
darkness of widespread misconceptions. There is a serious
danger that such debates may simply pit traditionalism
against innovation. On the one hand, there are strident
polemical assertions of orthodoxy, which seem to assume that
orthodox belief can be preserved merely by being repeated
with authoritarian sanctions. On the other hand, there are
attempts to make Christian belief credible and relevant in the
modern world, which seem to assume that credibility and
relevance are achieved by diluting the faith until it resembles
the best sentiments of secular culture.

But orthodoxy and relevance are not opposites. Since the
real value of orthodoxy lies in its faithfulness to God's
revelation of himself, it is genuinely preserved, not by
defensive authoritarian repetition, but by being continually
rediscovered as something newly meaningful for every age.
The credibility and relevance of Christianity reappear when
the attempt is made to repossess the full meaning of orthodox

faith at the points where it touches, illuminates and pene-
trates the reality of human life in our society today. Orthodox
belief is not a fragile inheritance from the past which needs
careful protection if it is to survive in the modern world. It
recovers its own meaning and power and relevance when we
put it back where it belongs: on the spiritually creative edges
of the Church in its contact with the world in its contemporary
spiritual need. The present chapter is no more than a
preliminary attempt to rediscover the point of orthodox
Christology from such a perspective.

2   PARTICULAR HISTORY – UNIVERSAL SIGNIFICANCE

If there is one key Christological question, around which
most other Christological issues, including those which have
been so much debated in recent years, revolve, it is the
question of the *universal* significance of the *particular* man
Jesus. The man Jesus, about whom all Christological claims
are made, was a specific historical individual, who lived at one
time and place, about whom can be said all kinds of specific
things which can be said of him and of no one else, just as any
other historical individual has many features quite specific to
him or her. As is well known, the early Christian creeds insist
on this specific historical identity of Jesus: born of Mary,
crucified under Pontius Pilate. But from the beginnings
of Christianity the basic and characteristic Christian claim
about Jesus, however varied the forms in which it has been
put, has been that this particular man has universal significance for all men and women. How this can be – how one
man can have ultimate religious significance for all other
men and women – and, if it can be, why it should be *this*
man, out of all the billions of human beings who have ever
lived, who has such significance, are the key Christological
issues.

In dealing with them the first Christians, who had the
temerity to assert the universal significance of an unknown,
crucified Galilean peasant all the way from India to Spain,
had in some ways a harder task than modern theologians,

whose task is in part to understand how Jesus has in fact *proved* to be of religious significance on an extraordinarily large scale, his influence crossing barriers of time and culture to a greater extent than that of any other figure of religious history, so that to a greater or lesser extent even the other great world religions have increasingly taken account of Jesus's significance. But contemporary Christology has also the task of continuing to understand Jesus's significance for secular or pluralistic societies, some of whose representatives – not even excluding Christian theologians – are inclined to suppose that in them Jesus's significance is at last confronting uncrossable limits.

In attempting to understand the universal significance of the one particular man Jesus, it is essential that Christology resist its perennial temptation to make Jesus's significance intelligible by reducing his particularity. The universal significance of Jesus is to be found *in* his specific historical identity, not despite or outside it. If Jesus is abstracted from his particular history, made into some generalised notion of ideal humanity or divine presence, Everyman or God-Man or God-in-Everyman, if he becomes interchangeably Jew or Gentile, black or white, male or female, ancient or modern, then paradoxically *his* universal significance evaporates. Jesus has proved universally significant *not* as a universalisable myth, but as the particular first-century man Jesus of Nazareth, who lived and taught and died as that man lived and taught and died – and rose.

It is important at this point to mention the resurrection, because there is a sense in which it is this unique feature of the history of Jesus which universalises him. Certainly it was the resurrection of Jesus which made his universal significance most obvious for the early Church. It meant that he had entered on the final destiny of all humanity ahead of all other human beings. As the one man who had already risen he must have a unique role in God's purpose for the rest of humanity. He had been raised to God's right hand in order to be God's agent in the fulfilment of his eschatological purpose for the world. Thus, for the first Christians, the resurrection gave Jesus a kind of finality and universality in God's purpose, conferring on him the unique status of ruler of the universe and coming judge of all humanity. The risen Jesus gained the universality of divine status.

But it is important to remember how tenaciously the early Church retained the conviction that the exalted Christ was *Jesus of Nazareth* crucified and risen. The exalted Lord in his universality by no means replaced the particularity of Jesus of Nazareth. He did not become a generalised divine symbol but retained the specific features of the man Jesus. For the early Christians, to say that Jesus was Lord of heaven and earth and judge of all was to say precisely that Jesus of Nazareth, whose unique story they told and whose teaching they remembered, was Lord of heaven and earth and judge of all. Against every tendency to forget that, Paul always insisted on the cross as the mark of Jesus's specific identity and the evangelists wrote Gospels which, for all that they proclaim the living Christ, do so by telling his earthly history. Apocalyptic and Gnostic Gospels with purely post resurrection settings, in which a Christ of heavenly glory but no specific human features conveys oracular utterances of artificial timelessness, lost the battle for the early Church's faith with good reason.

In that case, the risen Jesus cannot simply have universal significance conferred on him despite his particular human history, as though a man who would not otherwise have been of universal significance became so in his resurrection. The resurrection of Jesus must be understood as validating and implementing the universal significance already inherent in his earthly history. The universal significance of his particular human identity as the man Jesus of Nazareth must still be identified. Our suggestion is that Jesus transcends his particularity in the only way any individual can transcend his particularity without losing it: in his relationships. Jesus's universal relevance is to be found in his relationships, as a particular individual, to God and to other human beings. On the one hand, Jesus enjoyed a unique relation to God: as the unique son of his Father, Jesus identified himself unreservedly with his Father's will, and so embodied God's presence in his life, deeds, words, suffering and death. As the one who was uniquely identified with his Father, Jesus spoke and acted with unique authority, commanding the demons, forgiving sins, declaring his Father's will.

But as well as, in this way, representing God's authority over his people, Jesus also identified with other people. His relationships of identification with other human beings are perhaps not so easily labelled unique as his relationship of identification with his Father, but they are certainly characteristic of him as the particular man he was. He showed a loving identification with other men and women, by which we mean not simply an abstract identification with humanity in general, but a concrete identification, as Jesus's loving concern reached specific people, as he sided with them, lived his life for their sake and in the end suffered for identifying with their cause. Jesus's loving identification with men and women was with actual men and women, and in that sense limited, but because it called a halt at no limit it was in principle unlimited and potentially universalisable, so that Paul, whom Jesus never knew, could speak of 'the Son of God, who loved me and gave himself for me' (Gal. 2:20). Jesus in his earthly life displayed a potential identification in love with all humanity, but he showed it in the way in which a particular historical individual can: by concretely identifying in love with those people he actually encountered. This potential universality becomes actually so by means of his resurrection and his post resurrection presence in the Spirit.

Jesus's unique identification with his Father's will and his potentially unlimited, loving identification with men and women make him the one who embodies *God's* loving identification with *all* humanity. The essential point here is that this makes Jesus a man who is unique in his universal significance *without abolishing his particularity*. On the contrary, it is precisely *as* the particular man who lived his particular history that Jesus embodies God's loving identification with all humanity. His universality is found in the actual ways in which he communicated God's loving presence to men and women. It is found in his dealings with Peter and Martha, the paralytic and the Gerasene demoniac, the high priest's slave and the penitent thief, and no generality can replace the stories of these concrete relationships. It is found in the stories Jesus himself told, of the good Samaritan, the persistent widow and the labourers in the vineyard, for which no generalised instruction can substitute. God in his love reaches out to and identifies with all humanity, not by some mere doctrinal statement of the fact nor by some mere religious symbol of it, but concretely in the form of Jesus's particular human life and most concretely of all in its end in Jesus's death on the cross. This particular life history is not simply an *illustration* of God's loving identification with all humanity, it is actually the way in which God brings his love for all humanity into actual human lives.

However, this last point requires an explanation of the way in which the potential universality of the story of Jesus becomes actually universal. How does it realise its universality beyond the circle of those who encountered Jesus of Nazareth in his earthly life? Again, it is important to understand this in a way which does not simply *replace* the earthly Jesus by the risen Jesus and his presence in the Holy Spirit. It is through the universal presence of the divine Spirit that the exalted Christ can be encountered by Christians today, but still the one who is so encountered is the one who is known from his story in the Gospels. He is encountered only as the universal significance of his earthly identity as a particular man is realised. As a way of summarising what happens in the Church's experience, we may say that Jesus's universality achieves actuality as the Gospel story of Jesus is told and remembered and *intersects* with the equally concrete and particular stories of other men and women in other times and places. The points of intersection will be different in different cases, and so just as Matthew told the story differently from Luke, so we may tell the story differently from the way it was told in the tenth or the sixteenth century, and we in Britain may tell the story differently from how it is told in Peru or Hong Kong, and one of us may tell the story differently from the way the other tells it. Hence the Church in different times and places has relatively different images of Jesus, which arise because the points of intersection between the Gospel story of Jesus and those of the Church and the world at any particular time and place differ, and so different aspects of the Jesus of the Gospel story come to the fore at different times and places. But these different ways of telling the story of Jesus – which was already in the New Testament told in a variety of ways – are various *angles* on the one particular man who, because he lived for God and for all of us, both has and achieves his universality in this way.

Recognising Jesus's universality in his loving identification with others frees us from a certain kind of problem about the universal relevance of Jesus which constantly recurs in Christology, but is perhaps best illustrated today by the argument of those Christian feminists who find Jesus's maleness a problem. How can Jesus as a man be the human figure of supreme religious relevance to *women*? But Jesus's maleness is only one aspect of his particularity. There are comparable problems in the fact that Jesus was a Jew and not a Gentile, an unmarried man who had no knowledge of sexual or parental experience, a person with no physical or mental handicap, a young man who died before experiencing old age. How can Jesus be the figure of supreme religious relevance to Gentiles, married people, parents, handicapped people, elderly people? If Jesus's universal significance for all men and women has to mean that he lived, in his own human experience, all the diversity of human experience, then he must cease to be a particular human person.

A desire for *this* kind of universal relevance in Jesus can make him only a kind of symbolic Everyperson with whom everyone can identify because he/she is *specifically* no one. Jesus himself dissolves into a mere symbol. But if Jesus is universally relevant through his loving identification with others, then his particularity is no problem. Jesus practised the love which transcends all barriers between people and all the varieties of human experience and really identifies with the experience of others. Specifically, as the particular man he was, Jesus gives the lie to the claim which sectional groups are inclined to make: that only they can understand themselves. The evidence of Christian history is that people of both sexes, all ages, all races and cultures and conditions, have experienced Jesus's loving identification with them. In himself, Jesus is male, not female – but (we might say) he is female *by identification*. In himself, Jesus is Jewish, not black

– but he is black *by identification*. And so on. In this way we do not need to reduce Jesus's particularity in order to make him universally relevant, but can find his universality in his particularity.

3   JESUS AS GOD INCARNATE

This understanding of the universal significance of Jesus's particular humanity can serve to safeguard the real meaning of the doctrine of the incarnation against the misunderstandings to which it is prone. Jesus, we have said, is the particular man who embodies God's loving identification with all humanity. The doctrine of the incarnation means: Jesus is God's own particular human reality by which in his love he identifies with all humanity. The doctrine of the incarnation, therefore, presupposes the story of Jesus and cannot be a substitute for it. It presupposes the particular human history of Jesus and identifies it as *God's* human history. It claims that there, in that specific history, God is present in the world for all of us.

The doctrine of the incarnation therefore loses its real point whenever its reference to the actual story of Jesus is forgotten. When it comes to mean: God became man – rather than: God became *this* man – its Christian meaning is lost. The Christological statement of the Council of Chalcedon – that Jesus is one divine person in two complete natures – proves misleading whenever its intended reference to the particular man Jesus is forgotten. If we use the name Jesus for a general idea of God in human nature, then he becomes a mere religious symbol and incarnation really is, in the proper sense, myth. Jesus may then attain the universality of myth, but he loses his own real universality, which his actual historical relationships with his Father and with other people in his specific history give him. But the function of the doctrine of the incarnation, properly understood, is not to abstract Jesus from his human history. Its point is quite the opposite: to point to God's utter involvement in Jesus's human history. It means: that particular history is God's own human history.

For the same reason the doctrine of the incarnation should never function to reduce the real humanity of Jesus to any extent, though it can be misunderstood in this way, as though Jesus could only be God incarnate by being less than fully human. Properly understood, the doctrine of the incarnation requires us to conceive Jesus, not grudgingly but wholeheartedly, as absolutely and thoroughly human. Only when we are sure we are talking about a man who is as human as we are, human in every way that we are (except for sin) and no less human in the specific way that was unique to him, can we correctly say, and know what it means to say, that he was *God's* human existence in the world. Only as the wholly and particular human being he was is Jesus God. Then incarnation gives God the specific, human and thisworldly reality which he has for Christian faith in Jesus. Otherwise a doctrine of incarnation deprives Jesus of reality and lifts him into the realm of myth, which believers would sometimes prefer to inhabit, or the realm of ideas, which theologians often prefer to inhabit.

This discussion of the proper function of the doctrine of the incarnation may help us to answer the question, which has been forcefully posed in recent years, whether we actually need such a doctrine. Might not the significance of the story of Jesus be as adequately or even better expressed in other ways? After all, the early Church used other ways. The doctrine of the incarnation was not part of the Church's proclamation or teaching from the beginning: Peter did not preach it on the day of Pentecost. The doctrine developed in the course of Christological reflection in the early Church. Can it therefore be essential to Christianity?

One way of responding to this question is to see the doctrine of the incarnation as a kind of synthesis of four elements of Christian belief and practice which *were* there from the beginning of Christian faith and which are arguably essential to what Christianity has always actually been, throughout its many historical forms. The doctrine of the incarnation developed as a way of summing up the combined significance of these four essential features of Christianity. Together they led the Church to formulate the doctrine of the incarnation: it depended on them and in turn became, as a consequence of theological reflection on them, the necessary theological basis for them. The four elements are:

(1) Belief in the universal definitiveness of God's action in Jesus for human salvation.
(2) Belief that God himself has unreservedly involved himself in Jesus's human history for human salvation.
(3) Belief in Jesus's living contemporary reality as the one whose own person is humanity's access to God.
(4) The practice of the worship of Jesus.

The first two points have been sufficiently discussed in section 2, and reference has already been made to the third. There was never a Christianity in which it was Jesus the dead prophet who had opened up the way to God. From the beginning, Christian access to God was through Jesus the living person, whose message could not go on without *him*. All three *beliefs*, it should be noticed, were closely connected with early Christian *experience* of God through Jesus. Not that the experience produced the beliefs, but that these beliefs about Jesus's significance and role were validated, for early Christians, by that fresh experience of the Spirit which seemed eschatological in its novelty and which came to them through faith in Jesus.

The fourth element – the worship of Jesus in religious practice – has a special significance for the understanding of the origins of the doctrine of the incarnation, since the full implications of the three beliefs become especially clear in this religious practice. It is significant that even within the earliest Jewish Christianity, Christians accorded Jesus religious worship as a natural, spontaneous response to the role which Jesus played in their religion, as summarised in our three elements of Christian belief. If Jesus is God's definitive act of salvation for all, in whom God has unreservedly involved himself in human history, and not a figure of the past but in person the living way of access to God, how could early Christians not worship him? This religious practice of the worship of Jesus expressed the religious attitude to Jesus which was inherent in the earliest Christian faith. The significance of this religious attitude must be assessed within the context of Jewish monotheism, which it is not too much to say was *defined* by worship. What it meant for the Jew to believe in one God was that only the God of Israel might be worshipped. The practice of the worship of Jesus by Jewish Christians who clearly had no intention of abandoning Jewish monotheism makes it clear that Christians in fact regarded Jesus as God even before they said so or had any satisfactory conceptual means of including him in the being of God. But to Christological reflection the practice of worshipping Jesus crystallised a religious attitude which was either, for Jewish-Christian monotheism, idolatrous or else required theological grounding in a doctrine of divine incarnation in Jesus.

In the period of the Fathers, when the doctrine of the incarnation was debated and formulated, the focus was on elements (2) and (4), whereas (1) and (3) were taken for granted. Nowadays (1) and (3) are also real issues in theological debate, and it is reservations about these, as much as about (2) and (4), which frequently lead to the view that a doctrine of the incarnation is no longer appropriate today. Virtually all those who today regard all four elements as fundamental to Christian faith find an incarnational Christology desirable and appropriate. Those who do not are usually questioning one or more of these four elements, but it should be recognised that in doing so they are questioning not simply one way of expressing Jesus's significance, but the fundamental shape of Christian belief about Jesus from the beginning.

Seen as a necessary synthesis of these four essential elements of Christian belief and practice, the doctrine of the incarnation does not, of course, *replace* them, so as to make them redundant, any more than it replaces the story of Jesus, which the four elements themselves presuppose. The doctrine of the incarnation is not the only Christological claim to be made, nor will it in every context be the most appropriate Christological claim to make. Its function is to be the doctrine which, when the other important things about Jesus have been said, safeguards their full significance. As such it is not, of course, the gospel, and not a test of saving faith, but it remains the test of an adequate Christian theology.

4   THE DOCTRINE OF THE INCARNATION AND GOD

The doctrine of the incarnation cannot be understood simply as a doctrine about Jesus. It is pre-eminently a doctrine about God, and here lie both its real difficulty – in the age of the Fathers when it was formulated and in our own time when its validity is again being questioned – and its real potential to illuminate the way in which Christian faith finds the particular man Jesus the key to the universal reality of God.

The problem for the Fathers was a Platonically influenced doctrine of God which made God metaphysically wholly other than and religiously wholly remote from this world. God *defined* as the opposite of all that this world by definition is – the immaterial, immutable, impassible, immortal reality contrasted with this material, mutable, passible and mortal reality – could have no direct dealings with this world, least of all could he become incarnate as physical human reality in it. The Platonic definition of God made a real incarnation of God himself inconceivable. But the Fathers, discovering through theological trial and error the extent to which the gospel ran counter to their ideological environment, insisted that Jesus was really God himself incarnate. They asserted this without explicitly abandoning their philosophical definition of God, but by asserting it they implicitly relativised that definition and so to an extent Christianised it. It was only in thus challenging the thought of their age that they met its real religious need. The remote God was found to be near in Jesus. The God who was otherwise a philosophical abstraction towards which the mind could aspire only in abstracting itself from this world was found in Jesus as a concrete, particular reality in the midst of this world. In other words, in Jesus God could be known.

The particularity of the story of Jesus, so alien to the Hellenistic quest for philosophical and religious meaning, was precisely the way in which the Christian gospel made the universal reality of God real for the people of that period, as it has done in all subsequent periods. In so far as the patristic doctrine of the incarnation may sometimes have functioned to obscure the particularity of Jesus and lift him out of his thisworldly history it was an accommodation to the philosophical environment which did the gospel a disservice. Its real thrust, however, was otherwise: it identified Jesus as God's own particular, thisworldly identity, and so as the form in which God can be encountered and known. The modern Western religious situation is not so different from that of the Fathers, except that the God of philosophical abstraction has become the absent God of atheism. The difficulty in believing in the incarnation today is that God has become remote to the point of absence. But, conversely, it is only if he has a concrete identity in our world that God can be encountered afresh. The modern Christian task is to discover where the story of God's historical presence in Jesus intersects our modern story of his absence from an atheistic world devoid of religious meaning.

What the doctrine of the incarnation has to say to us, as to the Church of the Fathers, is that in Jesus God particularises himself. He remains, of course, the transcendent mystery which can be known only as the unknowable beyond the limit of everything finite. Jesus himself, as God's own existence in the world, still points beyond himself to the unknowable infinity of God. Otherwise neither Jesus nor God would be God. But in Jesus God also comes out of his mystery and gives himself a particular, thisworldly identity. Jesus is the visible image of the invisible God. As such he is the icon which protects us from and smashes all our idols. He is God's provision for the religious need to specify who God is and to form a concrete image of him, in order to relate to him. From this need arises the inveterate human, and even Christian, tendency to idolatry, in which we project a fantasy God, God as we would like him to be, or very often God as we think we would like to be ourselves, or even God as we fear he could be. To remember that God is the transcendent mystery beyond all our images of him is an essential safeguard against idolatry, but not sufficient because it does not meet the real religious need to identify God. But the doctrine of the incarnation points to God's *self*-identification of himself, where in the life and words and deeds of a particular man God makes himself concretely present to us. More specifically, his *love* becomes concrete in Jesus in contrast not only to all concepts of God as other than love but in contrast to all the false concepts of divine love which we so easily entertain.

Once again it is the particularity of Jesus which is so important here. Jesus as a generalised divine symbol is no more use than any other such religious symbol. It is as the particular man, Jesus of Nazareth, that Jesus is God's specifiable identity in this world and the remedy for all our religious fantasies.

5   JESUS AS GOD'S SOLIDARITY
WITH THE WORLD

How can we describe God's love as it becomes concrete for us, as he enacts it for us in his own human history? Perhaps the best summary – given that the summary cannot replace the stories it summarises – is that Jesus is in person God's solidarity with the world. God's love in Jesus is not the mere benevolence of a God who holds aloof from us, but a love which he enacts in Jesus's life of loving identification with men and women. Jesus therefore did not direct people to find God in abstracting themselves from the life of this world, but made God concretely present with them in ordinary, this-worldly life. God's love reaches people as Jesus enters their villages, sits at table with them, goes fishing with them, lifts children on his knee, tells stories of farmers and housewives, weddings and unemployment. This is why God's love enacted in this history can reach all people as Jesus's story intersects their own stories of thisworldly life.

God's love enacted in Jesus's particular history holds aloof from no one. Jesus associates with outcasts of all descriptions, touching lepers, who were outcasts in one way, and socialising with tax-collectors, who were outcasts in another way. He treats women, the second-class citizens of his time, with exceptional respect, and seeks out the demoniacs, who seemed no longer human at all. But lest we think his attitude simply one of reversed discrimination, he dines with Pharisees and counts a rich aristocrat among his loyal friends. Thus he concretises God's love as solidarity with people in all conditions, even those denied all human solidarity. His solidarity is no uncritical endorsement of lives and attitudes opposed to God's love: it includes his confrontation and critical dialogue with the religious and political leaders of the nation and his prophetic woes on the cities which rejected his message. But these features of his ministry arise from a sympathetic concern for the true good of those who refuse to see it themselves, so that he weeps even with those who cannot weep for themselves. Without condoning sin, he associates with sinners, and so his Father's love reaches them, not as distant benevolence, but as loving identification.

Finally, this identifying love of God is concretised as sacrificial love in Jesus's suffering and death, which are God's ultimate act of solidarity with sinful humanity. Again, the particularity of the story of Jesus makes all the difference to our understanding of the doctrine of the incarnation. In fact, this is the most important point at which Christology must never forget who Jesus particularly was: that in the end he was the crucified Jesus. The general idea of God become human – undisturbed by the identification of God as the *crucified* Jesus – is much too comfortable a notion. It panders, like so much idolatry, to our wish to believe that the human project is remarkably good and successful, an achievement which God himself crowns by becoming the perfect man, the summit of the race. The incarnation can thus seem to be God's seal of approval on the world as it is, but only because it is overlooked that God became *that* man, the crucified Jesus, identified with humanity in its godforsaken fate under the judgment of God and with humanity subject to the injustice and brutality of human affairs. God identifies himself for us not in identifying with humanity in the heights of our proud achievements, but in identifying with dehumanised humanity in the depths of our weakness, condemnation, misery and despair.

Of course, Christology is here inseparable from the doctrine of the atonement. The *particular* form which God's love takes in Jesus – in all of Jesus's practice of loving identification with people, but finally and especially in the cross – identifies God for us *and* precisely because it takes this particular form transforms us in the way that the gospel of Jesus Christ transforms people. The potential universality of Jesus's loving identification with others becomes actual as his story intersects with ours, and this universality, which in his ministry derives from the diversity of aspects of the human condition with which he identifies, takes the form, in his death, of identification with the underlying truth of the human condition of all men and women. To find the cross the final point of intersection between Jesus's story and ours, and to encounter God's love in his solidarity with us *there*, we have to abandon all our pretensions to goodness and success and see ourselves as those with whom Jesus in his godforsakenness was identified. God's love particularised in the crucified Jesus is not a smile of approval on the success we have made of our lives, but his solidarity with us as we really are, in our failure. This is why it affects us and transforms us. The aloof benevolence of the God who cannot become incarnate and the smile of approval from the God who becomes merely ideal humanity simply confirm us as we are. Theirs is the love of the false gods we project for ourselves. But the self-emptying, sacrificial solidarity of the God who is with us as the crucified Jesus reaches us, changes and transforms us.

An additional note on the virginal conception and the empty tomb

The preceding discussion may help to provide a context in which the two particular Christological topics of the virginal conception and the empty tomb can be better appreciated. Some special consideration of them is appropriate here because of the recent debates in the Church of England, to which the House of Bishops' statement on *The Nature of Christian Belief* was a response. Some confusion in these debates has resulted from the tendency, in the popular mind and in the media, to *equate* the virginal conception with the incarnation and the empty tomb with the resurrection of Jesus. The bishops' statement rightly makes clear distinctions here. Only in the light of a clear understanding of the primary doctrines of the incarnation and the resurrection can we hope to see the significance of the secondary doctrines of the virginal conception and the empty tomb. Also, in our view, regrettable is the desire to see the virginal conception as the *necessary means* of incarnation and the empty tomb as the *necessary means* of resurrection, as though the primary doctrines logically require the secondary doctrines. This is too theologically ambitious and speculative, and goes beyond the witness of Scripture. Probably more satisfactory is to attempt to understand the virginal conception as a God-given *sign* of the incarnation and the empty tomb as a God-given *sign* of the resurrection.

The virginal conception is the more difficult of the two signs to understand, as is clear from the considerable variety of ways in which theologians have tried to understand it in the past. We must frankly admit that, whereas (as the Creeds testify) the Church has always held the belief that Jesus was born of a virgin, there has never been an agreed understanding – still less an orthodox doctrine – of the theological *significance* of this belief. The only respect in which Christian teaching on this point has been consistent has been a negative one: that the miraculous *manner* of Jesus's origin in no way reduces his fully human *nature*, as *homoousios* with us, sharing our human nature as a full member of the same human race. This negative point is of great importance as delimiting acceptable interpretation of the virginal conception. By the standard of orthodox incarnational Christology, an interpretation of the virginal conception which reduces Jesus's real humanity is much more seriously heretical than is a denial of the virginal conception on the grounds that it must reduce the real humanity of Jesus. Controversies about the virginal conception always tend to bring to the surface the sadly common popular misconception that Jesus could only be divine by being less than fully human, and that therefore the virginal conception was required because, by restricting his humanity, it, so to speak, made room for his divinity. Against such a misconception, it needs to be clearly stated that, *if* the virginal conception is understood to imply that Jesus was less than fully human, then denial of it is more orthodox than belief in it. Failure to state this clearly indicates that orthodox statements are being treated as shibboleths rather than as means of understanding the faith. But, of course, Scripture does not suggest and orthodox theological tradition has never accepted that the virginal conception does imply that Jesus was less than fully human.

In section 3 above, we said that only as the wholly and particular human being he was is Jesus God. His virginal conception, like his resurrection on the third day, is one of those unique features of Jesus's human history which make him the particular, unique human being he was and is. But, again like his resurrection on the third day, it is not simply a unique feature of the same kind as those which distinguish every human being from every other. It is not, in this sense, a *relatively* unique feature, as, say, his physical appearance is. It is an *absolutely* unique feature, in the sense that nothing of this kind has ever been the case for any other human being. It is this, of course, which gives rise to the objection that it makes him less than fully human. But, so long as we exclude the genetic misinterpretation of it, which makes Jesus a divine-human hybrid, there is no reason why the virginal conception should make Jesus less than *homoousios* with us. Belief in the incarnation commits us to the view that Jesus was *both* wholly human *and* absolutely unique among human beings in that he is God's own human existence in the world. In his case alone, his particular human identity is *God's* human identity. It would therefore make sense to see it as including absolutely unique features which distinguish Jesus from all other human beings, and such a feature at his point of human origin would be particularly appropriate. The virginal conception would thus be a sign of the incarnation.

But why should the sign take this form of virginal conception? Here it may help to revert to our understanding of the incarnation as God's solidarity with the world, especially as this understanding – expressed in the name 'Immanuel' – is implicit in Matthew's application of Isaiah 7:14 to the virginal conception (Matt. 1:23). As God's act of solidarity with the world, the incarnation means that God graciously identifies with us human beings: not that he simply is one of us, but that he chooses in love to become one of us for our sake. Solidarity is not being willy-nilly in the same boat, but voluntarily identifying with the situation of those one loves. It is of the nature of loving solidarity to be gratuitous. So, as God's solidarity with us, Jesus is God's self-gift to us. This is what the virginal conception indicates. It is a form of human origin in which human initiative plays no part. Its point is not so much that it dispenses with the male role in reproduction, but that it dispenses with the sexual act and so with all human initiative in bringing about conception. Mary, in Luke's narrative, is a *willing* recipient, but precisely a willing *recipient* of the divine act. She initiates nothing. Hence the sense in which every human child is a gift of God is in this case, by the miracle, heightened and made absolutely and unambiguously true. Jesus is sheer, absolute gift of God. He is not a mere product of human history; he is the humanity of the God who graciously identifies with us and shares our human condition. No less human for that, for God's solidarity with us requires his full humanity. But human *as* God's self-gift to humanity, as 'Immanuel'. We cannot say that the incarnation as God's solidarity with the world *required* the virginal conception, but we can see the virginal conception as an appropriate sign of it.

The appropriateness of the empty tomb as a sign of the bodily resurrection of Jesus can be perhaps more readily appreciated on the basis of our argument in the preceding sections. In section 2 we noticed how important it was that the early Christians, in recognising the universal divine significance of Jesus on the basis of his resurrection and exaltation, did not allow the risen Christ to *replace* Jesus of Nazareth in his particular humanity. The risen Christ was not a generalised divine symbol but precisely *Jesus of Nazareth* crucified and risen. Jesus's particular humanity as God's solidarity with us was not dissolved at the end of his earthly life, but glorified as God's permanent solidarity with us and as the promise of our resurrection to glorified humanity like his. Hence Jesus's personal identity, as the same human individual, through death and resurrection, is essential to what his resurrection means, and this human personal identity involves, of course, *bodily* resurrection. Fully human individuality can only be embodied personality. So the risen Jesus is not an attenuated spirit, which would be less than fully human, but, as risen into new bodily life beyond the reach of death, more fully the same human person.

This understanding of the risen Jesus's personal, bodily humanity is what preserves Christianity from relapsing into other-worldly spiritualism. In Jesus we know God in his solidarity with us in this worldly, bodily reality – not temporarily, in order to transport us out of it into the realm of pure spirit, but permanently, in order to redeem and transfigure precisely this worldly, bodily reality. The contrast which sometimes arises between, on the one hand, a 'worldly' form of Christian discipleship, following the earthly Jesus and practising his loving solidarity with all men and women, and, on the other hand, an 'other-worldly' faith in the risen Christ, with its hope set on that human destiny beyond death which is promised in his resurrection, must be really a false dichotomy because of the personal, bodily identity of the risen Christ with the earthly Jesus of Nazareth. This makes Christian hope not a reason for detachment from this world but a reason for involvement in it. It does not undermine Christian solidarity with the world, but strengthens it, making it solidarity in hope, solidarity, therefore, even with the dying.

We cannot say that the empty tomb was logically necessary to Jesus's personal, bodily identity through death and resurrection. However we understand this bodily identity, it cannot *depend* on the continuity of *matter*. Already in the New Testament, Paul clearly recognised that our own risen bodies will not need to be continuous with our present bodies in material composition (2 Cor. 5:1), while we now know that even in this life the matter of which our bodies is composed is completely replaced every seven years, so that in this life continuity of bodily identity does not absolutely depend on continuity of matter. We cannot therefore say that Jesus's resurrection to newly – eschatologically – embodied life *could* not have left his earthly corpse in the tomb. But the apostolic testimony of Scripture is that as a matter of fact it did not. This fact of the empty tomb, while it did not by itself give rise to faith in the resurrection of Jesus, was and has always continued to be a powerful *testimony* to the reality of Jesus's bodily resurrection. Indeed, it is hard to see how the reality of Jesus's personal, bodily identity in resurrection could have been adequately perceived by his disciples and communicated by them to others, had the tomb not been empty. In that sense the empty tomb is the appropriate, God-given *sign* of Jesus's resurrection.

BIBLIOGRAPHY

Richard Bauckham, *Knowing God Incarnate* (Grove Spirituality Series 6, Bramcote, Notts, 1980). *A booklet which expands on the theme of knowing God in the* particular *man Jesus.*

James D. G. Dunn, *Christology in the Making: An Inquiry into the Origins of the Doctrine of the Incarnation* (London, 1980). *An authoritative (and fairly technical) account of the origins of incarnational Christology in the New Testament.*

Jürgen Moltmann, *The Crucified God*, tr. R. A. Wilson and J. Bowden (London, 1974). *A modern Christological classic in which the themes of identification and solidarity are prominent: difficult but rewarding reading.*

Gerald O'Collins, *Interpreting Jesus* (Introducing Catholic Theology 2, London, 1983). *A useful, up-to-date textbook on Christology.*

Klaas Runia, *The Present-Day Christological Debate* (Issues in Contemporary Theology, Leicester, 1984). *A fair account and critique of contemporary options in Christology.*

John Webster, *God is Here! Believing in the Incarnation Today* (Basingstoke, 1983). *A readable account, for a general readership, of the relevance of incarnational belief.*

DISCUSSION QUESTIONS

1 Do you find helpful the idea of Jesus's universal relevance through his *loving identification* or *solidarity* with all people? Try to select some particular stories in the Gospels through which Jesus's loving identification can reach (a) you yourself in your own experience, and (b) people in the society in which you live.

2 Do you find it difficult to think of Jesus as *both* fully divine *and* fully human? If so, think about why this is so.

3 If you did not believe in the incarnation of God in Jesus would your understanding of and faith in God be any different?

4 In the cultural situation in which you live, do people find it difficult to believe in the virginal conception of Jesus or the bodily resurrection of Jesus? If so, why do you think this is? What would you say to such people?

3

MINISTRY, MINISTRIES AND THE MINISTRY

INTRODUCTION

The theory and practice of Christian ministry are more debated now than ever before. Even if the Reformation be excluded from this general claim, it could be argued that the present debate is in part at least the continuation of the discussion which began then. There are, of course, important differences of which account must be taken. The protagonist churches all exist within a very different social, economic and political milieu, while the philosophical climate and world of ideas and learning have changed almost beyond recognition. In short, all the (Western) churches are minorities now, and this if nothing else must influence the way in which they approach what divides them. Interdenominational conflict and antagonism have largely given way to ecumenical dialogue and in questions of ministry, as of much else, debate has now for most people the declared end of reconciling conflicting positions. Catholic and Protestant alike are now disposed to seek, and hence are more likely to find, common ground, and to recognise truth and Christian integrity in the convictions of erstwhile adversaries.

A further important development in recent years has been the drawing of the Orthodox churches into the debate, with the effect of a new perspective on the hitherto largely domestic Western conflict of the Reformation. A consequence of these developments may already be seen in the emergence of an increasingly common expression of the Christian faith concerning the ministry as well as other matters of dispute between Christian communities. This process is bound to be problematic since it inevitably requires the reassessment of some aspects of the confessional histories and stances of all the churches. Clearly, then, the ecumenical consideration of the ministry imposes a strain upon the internal cohesion and sense of identity of all participating bodies, and perhaps for none more than for the Anglican Communion, the fragility of whose own unity has been cruelly exposed.

It is not difficult to see how the changing situation of the churches and their increasing quest for unity have forced questions about the ministry to the centre of the stage. It is, as Anglicans know only too well, the difficulty of satisfactorily resolving such questions that has so frequently led otherwise promising unity schemes to founder. It may in part be a reaction to this that some have suggested that ministry is a so-called 'second-order' issue, presumably implying thereby that it is a matter of relative indifference and should be left to be resolved along with many other purely practical difficulties once the really substantial matters of theological dispute have been settled. This solution has a certain superficial attractiveness. After all, the ministry scarcely compares in importance with the fundamental realities of the nature and existence of God and of the economy of salvation which it is intended to serve. Such a view does however fail to take account of the difficulty (which is theological as well as practical) of distinguishing clearly between first and second order questions. More seriously, moreover, it forgets that it was precisely because of its intimate connection with theological and soteriological concerns that the Reformers challenged received patterns and theories of ministry. The ecumenical difficulties surrounding the ministry arise not only from the practical divergences of structure and pastoral pattern, but also from different understandings of the relationship between Scripture and tradition, of justification and sanctification, and hence of the Church and sacraments. They also arise from the persistent denominational and confessional Christianities which identify themselves not merely with reference to their own positive affirmations, but also by denying the authenticity of other Christian churches and ministries.

The modest essay which follows does not attempt to discuss all these issues. We have approached this subject with a very genuine concern to represent the distinctive contributions made to the doctrine of the ministry by the 'Catholic and Evangelical' wings of our Communion. As we struggled together to face up to the challenges, conflicts and hurts of past divisions in a spirit of mutual respect and trust, so we saw emerging lines of convergence and points of agreement which are expressed in this essay. We do not claim that we shall have satisfied everyone by our method or our conclusions, but we have satisfied ourselves that we have done more than merely affirmed each other's right to belong to a body which has for long asserted its comprehensiveness. We think that we have also discerned a common faith lying at the heart of that comprehensiveness and making it not only possible but even a necessary characteristic of the fullness of the Christian Church.

1   THE MINISTRY OF JESUS CHRIST

Christian faith proclaims that it is only through Jesus Christ that humankind has access to God. This assertion rests not only on the work and teaching of Jesus of Nazareth but upon the conviction that this Galilean carpenter is the Word made flesh, the second Person of the Holy Trinity incarnate, the Son of God, and that throughout the course of human history the Holy Spirit enables men and women to enter into fellowship with God through him and through their union with him. By 'ministry' Christians intend the means whereby this mystery is administered, human beings hear and receive the good news of the kingdom of God and are enabled to grow in faithfulness to it. Ministry is fundamentally, therefore, the initiative and work of God himself, having its origin and power in the will of God for the salvation of the entire world and being inseparable from the person of Jesus Christ and the activity of the Holy Spirit.

When Christians speak of ministry they have in mind above all the confession that 'God was in Christ reconciling the world to himself'. Reconciliation, indeed, is at the heart of

Christ's ministry. His first reported words in Mark's Gospel are 'The kingdom of God is at hand; repent, and believe the gospel'. Reconciliation, then, entails the preaching of 'good news' which is intended to bring humankind back to God. Jesus saw his own task as essentially one of obedience to the Father's will, and declared that the Son of man 'came not to be served but to serve and to give his life as a ransom for many'. The whole of his earthly life was devoted to the proclamation of the reign of God, its reality and imminence, its demands upon people and the possibility of admission to it. He exercised this ministry in word and deed, by his existence as well as by his activity, in his death as much as in his life. Through his life of obedience Jesus glorified his Father and opened for his brethren a new and living way of salvation. It was a life entirely given to God for the sake of humankind, and we should not draw false distinctions between the various aspects of his ministry.

Nevertheless, the sealing of his life of self-offering by the death that he died, made it inevitable that Jesus's death should come to be interpreted in sacrificial terms, and to be identified most particularly and more intensely than any other aspect of his life with the divine work of restoring fellowship between God and humanity. When this identification of the work of Christ with the death of Christ is made all but exclusive, serious problems follow for many aspects of Christian faith and life and, of particular significance for our present purpose, for the doctrine of ministry.

In view of this it is especially important to bear in mind the many-sidedness of the ministry of Jesus. This many-sidedness is clearly illustrated by the richness of John 17, the so-called high-priestly prayer. If it be argued that we appear to be bringing the discussion to focus not on the ministry of Jesus as a whole but more precisely on his priesthood, we would reply that to sharpen the distinction is to perpetuate a false antithesis which has already done too much damage. It may well be, for example, that the sacrificial interpretation of the death of Jesus was the original impetus, carried further in the wake of the destruction of the Temple and the cessation of the old sacrifices, for the ascription of priestly language to him, but it is no less clear that from an early date this was not the only relevant factor. Jesus describes himself as having completed (already) the work the Father had given him to do on earth. This includes revealing God and his will to the disciples, sharing his own joy with them, protecting them; it must moreover be understood in the light of the whole gospel with its series of signs through which Jesus's glory is seen and his disciples are moved to faith – signs which are themselves the disclosure of God's own glory.

Perhaps we should infer from this that the ministry and the priesthood of Jesus should not be set off against or even alongside each other, but that each should be seen as part of the definition of the other. The concept which unites the humanward and Godward aspects of the ministry of Jesus is self-consecration. 'For their sakes I consecrate myself.' This cannot of course be separated from his forthcoming death, any more than the claim by Jesus to have completed his work can be separated from his final cry of triumph, 'It is finished'. But the significance of neither is exclusively limited to the cross. The relation should more properly be seen in terms of Calvary's sealing the self-consecration that was the essential characteristic of the whole of Jesus's earthly life.

The priestly ministry of Jesus, his self-offering to the Father and his love for his brethren in life and death alike, is perfect. Christians are agreed that it cannot be added to, repeated or reproduced in any way. The total self-offering of Jesus is, moreover, salvific in a more than exemplary way, precisely because he is the incarnate Word of God. The way in which this effects atonement between humankind and God has been variously understood, however, and has not been made the subject of dogmatic definition. This is in keeping with the scriptural evidence which authorises a certain agnosticism about what might be called the 'mechanics' of atonement, while speaking consistently of the *fact*, of the uniqueness, sufficiency and efficacy of the salvation wrought by God in Christ. Salvation too has been understood in a number of ways, and although it must never be reduced to any purely human or worldly vision of prosperity or maturity, it should equally never be radically separated from the physical, social and historical aspects of human life in the interests of some supposedly 'spiritual' salvation. Just as the ministry of Jesus covers the whole of his being and activity, so, too, its effects concern the whole of humanity.

We have asserted that the atonement means the many-sided reconciliation of man with God. This reconciliation is effected by the mediation of the incarnate Christ, through whose humanity we have access to God, and whose interces-sion is eternally trustworthy. We should therefore avoid another false distinction, namely that between the work the Father gave Christ to fulfil on earth and his eternal priest-hood. In the letter to the Hebrews we read that 'he ever lives to make intercession for us'. The Revelation of St John tells us of the celestial liturgy in which the victory of the Lamb and the salvation of his people is unceasingly celebrated. At this point it is well to remind ourselves that it is not just 'everything in heaven', but also 'everything on earth and under the earth and in the sea' that joins in the responsive song:

> To the one seated on the throne and to the Lamb
> be all praise, honour, glory and power,
> for ever and ever.

In John's vision there is an integral connection between the eternal worship of heaven and the praises of the creatures of earth. If 'God was in Christ reconciling the world to himself' it was so that the world might attain its proper end in the purpose and plan of God, become what it was created to be beyond the constraints and the frustrations of sin.

This raises acutely the question of the relation between the earthly life and work of Jesus and the continuing history of the world and the judgment of the gospel. Any presentation of the ministry of Jesus must offer an answer to the question 'What is Christ doing now?' One answer, which cannot be denied, is that which, appealing to the witness of Hebrews that 'he took his seat', asserts that there remains nothing for him to do. On the other hand, the sovereignty of Christ over all powers and generations has still to be disclosed, has yet to be realised, and we must seek to understand how what Jesus Christ has already achieved in time can be applied in time during the remaining course of human history. In other words, the priestly ministry of Jesus Christ involves *both* an unrepeatable 'full, perfect and sufficient' self-offering, characteristic of his whole life and sealed and summed up in his death, resurrection *and* his eternal intercession. Jesus himself said to his disciples, 'I have overcome the world', but he also said 'in the world you will have trouble'. In the world, that is to say, in the remaining course of their existence in the history of the world in which sin retains elements of power, there will be trouble for the disciples of Jesus.

This, of course, means taking seriously the aspect of 'already/not yet' which is at the heart of Christian life and ministry. On the one hand, the finished work of Christ results in the undiminished joy and confidence of Christian people throughout the ages because the decisive victory of Jesus means present power. But, on the other hand, we are the suffering pilgrim Church awaiting the fullness of our salvation and at every moment dependent upon the eternal high priest who is the Lord of the ages. Day by day his sovereignty is being disclosed in and through individuals and situations. His sovereignty is not new, but it is new *in them*, and through the Holy Spirit it is the same Jesus Christ, whose self-offering brought together time and eternity, who achieves this work.

2   THE MINISTRY OF THE HOLY SPIRIT

Jesus told his disciples that the Holy Spirit would be sent by the Father to lead them into all the truth and to remind them of all that he, Jesus, himself had taught them. This Holy Spirit will be the counsellor/advocate/intercessor/protector (all implied by the word *paracletos*) and will be the constant companion of the disciples of Jesus as they continue to live in the midst of a world which does not acknowledge him. In other words he will be both the confidence of Christians and the condemnation of the world. Moreover, this same Holy Spirit will come upon the disciples of Jesus with power, enabling them to perform mighty works.

This clear emphasis in the gospels on the work of the Holy Spirit after the glorification of Jesus Christ is reinforced by the awareness of the early Church of the Spirit's constant guidance and power. It must not be forgotten, however, that

Jesus sent his apostles out during the days of his earthly life as well to witness to the kingdom and to perform mighty works. He also assured them that when they were called to account for their discipleship of Jesus the Holy Spirit would give them the words to say. In the Old Testament the outpouring of the Spirit had been seen by the prophets as characteristic of the age of the Messiah. In understanding this pouring out of the Spirit on all flesh the chief New Testament event is the descent of the Holy Spirit upon Jesus at his baptism and his abiding with him. Pentecost and the Church's consciousness of the presence and work of the Spirit must be seen in relation to this.

The experience of and testimony to the Holy Spirit in the new covenant should be seen as the fulfilment of prophecy and also as the more explicit disclosure of signs and indications throughout the Old Testament and indeed in history and existence generally. The prophets not only spoke about the Spirit of Yahweh, but were reckoned by Old and New Testament writers alike to have been inspired by him.

In all these ways, however, it is Jesus Christ who is the central point of reference. From any standpoint within history the Holy Spirit always acts in integral relationship with the work of the second Person of the Trinity, and as such has always a reference to the Word of God incarnate, Jesus Christ. From the Christian perspective, talk of the Holy Spirit always either anticipates or applies the work of Christ, points to him as the ultimate fulfilment or as the active agent drawing all things, people and ages into union with him. It is against this background that we should look at the specific question of the work of the Spirit in relation to the problem of ministry in the Church.

Ministry, as we have already said, means primarily Christ's own work in reconciling humankind to God. *Ministries* refers typically to the various forms of service whereby the Church is built up; all these ministries are distributed and empowered by the Holy Spirit and may be seen as corresponding to different gifts. By *the ministry* we could suggest the special or distinctive office of what we are accustomed to call 'holy orders' in the Church. It is not easy to assess precisely the relationship between office and spiritual gifts in the early

Church. What is clear however is that all ministries are 'gifted', for all are for the sake of the Church. All are given by the Spirit, but the 'spirits' must be tested to see whether they are of God: being filled with the Spirit is one of the criteria for the Seven, and the gift to Timothy as the prophets spoke and hands were laid upon him is also from the Spirit. A disinterested reading of the New Testament encourages neither a complete separation of office and charisma nor a merging of the two. From the call of the first disciples (or we might wish to say, from the baptism of Jesus) onwards we have to reckon on 'individual' gift and on 'public' commission where the former is always, for the sake of the whole body and the latter requires personal gifts. The distinction may in part be between the gifts which are freely given and concerning which the question is always, 'How may these be regulated?' and the choice of leaders for a community (whether by the apostle-founder or by the community itself), in which case the question is, 'What personal gifts are required for this office?'

A distinction may also, of course, be drawn between the gifts which are of individual or local significance, and those which are universal and concern not just the integrity of the local church but also its fellowship and unity with other churches. Not of course that this fellowship is unrelated to the local church and its internal integrity. This particular distinction is easily confused with that between charisma and office, but it is a mistake to do so; some difficulties have undoubtedly arisen as a result of assuming that office (above all episcopal office, but also presbyteral and diaconal in so far as these are 'universal' ministries) is the *only* ministry whereby the universal fellowship of the Church is maintained. We should perhaps recall, with nostalgia, the peripatetic ministry of prophets until Gnostic and even more so Montanist challenges to order led to a narrowing of perspective. We should also recognise with gratitude the wide variety of charismatic ministries represented by the religious orders, the burgeoning new ministries 'thrown up' by charismatic renewal and by 'private' charitable and missionary ventures of all sorts which have been such a feature of the life of the Christian community throughout the centuries and in our present time.

From this we may infer that both in the New Testament

period and in later history the Holy Spirit has enabled the Church both to receive and to exercise the ministry of Jesus Christ, its head, in a wide variety of forms. It is the indwelling power of the Holy Spirit which makes the whole Church in every age the living body of the reigning Christ. This shapes the distinctively Christian view of tradition. Despite the painful legacy of past controversies, we should now be able to recognise that the principle of *sola scriptura* is not compromised by an affirmation of dynamic tradition, and neither is the latter unhistorically fettered by slavish bibliolatry.

Such a view is in no way an attempt to resurrect a 'two sources' theory. Rather it seeks to explain the actual lordship of Christ over his Church by the Holy Spirit in a way that does justice both to the unique historical moment of the incarnation and to the reality of the present of the Church, in which the Church has a genuine, although always derivative, dependent and co-operative part to play in the work of reconciliation. Scripture testifies to the descent of the Spirit upon Jesus at his baptism, to its remaining with him, and to its permanent indwelling of the Church, the body of Christ, from the first Pentecost, and of the individual Christian. For this reason it is a mistake to play off the Church today against the Church as it is in the earthly flesh of Jesus. The Church is always 'in Christ', or it is not the Church at all; and the Church which is in Christ is always thus, corporately and in its individual members, by the work of the Holy Spirit.

The whole 'Christ-event', to which Scripture testifies, is the unique reference point for the whole course of human history. We mean by this that we are not talking about a particularly significant event in history but about *the* significant event in history. In some sense, one must suppose, all events are related to all other events; but it is our faith that *this* event sums up, draws into itself, all other events whatsoever, and that only so may the latter be redeemed. Some may wish to express this in terms of Jesus Christ's being our contemporary, others in terms of our being his contemporaries. Any such attempts to explain the mystery of Jesus Christ as the same yesterday, today and tomorrow are bound to be metaphorical and symbolic; they are in continual danger of mistaking philosophy for doctrine. For faith and for history what is most important is that Christ who is the present Lord is the same as Jesus of Nazareth, and therefore every 'now' is eternally significant to the extent that it is subject to him; certainly there should be no explanation of salvation which either ignores any element of the total reality of successive events (every historical 'now') or which fails to relate them to the unique moment of God's work in Christ, sealed and completed in his great Passover.

All the 'ministries' with which the Holy Spirit furnishes the Church have as their underlying objective precisely this relating of now to then – they are, we might say, 'sacramental'. Among the means of this relating are some which most particularly and permanently constitute the Church in its reality as the body of Christ. The proclamation of the gospel message, the dominical sacraments, the oversight of the Church correspond to the traditionally identified categories of the prophetic, priestly and royal aspects of the ministry of Christ. To these we should add the diaconal ministry of pastoral care. To recognise such functions as uniquely constitutive of the Church is neither to isolate them in some clericalised manner (as if they were what we meant by ministry), nor to restrict the exercise of the corresponding gifts necessarily to those more particularly charged with them.

In affirming, as we already have, the biblical and traditional nature of a view of ministry in which *all* have received gifts and ministries to exercise and in which there also exists a structured office and order, we do not attempt to justify each and every development in the history of the ministry. Nevertheless, in acknowledging all ministries whether 'charismatic' or 'official' as the work of the one and the same Holy Spirit, the way is open to explore further both the ministry of the whole Church (section 3) and the 'special ministry' (section 4). In both cases the Holy Spirit is enabling the Church to re-present Christ and to make his salvation known. This is another way of saying that the Holy Spirit is constituting the Church as the body of Christ, his members and members of one another. Seen thus, no ministry can be without implications for the personal life and qualities of the 'minister'.

If this is generally so, it is particularly true for those exercising special ministries of oversight and service; there is a widespread expectation on the part of church members and others that their leaders will 'practise what they preach'. It is indeed the practising as well as the preaching which is the work of the ministry, and this quality of integrity so clearly demanded in the Pastoral Epistles, not to mention the Anglican Ordinal, is also the work of the Holy Spirit. Nevertheless, given the frailty of our wills and our responses to grace, it is well that neither at the outset (the call of the Twelve) nor since has the representative function of office been seen as entirely dependent upon personal worthiness. There is a touch of healthy realism here, and also a much more important recognition that however weighty the demands on those who have received gifts or are called to ministries, it is no private attribute which they exercise, but the ministry of Jesus Christ through the indwelling and empowering Spirit.

3 THE MINISTRY OF THE CHURCH

The application of the effects of Christ's victory to successive ages of the continuing human story is a historical as well as an eschatological reality. Jesus Christ is Alpha as well as Omega, and as we live in the light of the end our hope is not only in the one who has gone to prepare a place for us but also in the one (the same) whose sacrifice won our salvation and who promised to stay with us to the end. The actual history of the world remains relevant and continues to be what is to us, at least, the most obvious arena of the conflict between Christ the victor and the forces which seek to prevent his being made known. It should not therefore be denied that, even if the remaining task is to proclaim the gospel of Christ, announcing his triumph over sin and death, what is envisaged in that proclamation/response is at all events something happening, and that something is relevant to salvation. This is somewhat coy language and understandably so in view of past controversies. All, however, will want to avoid any suggestion either that the work of Christ is somehow incomplete, or that earthly existence after Christ is simply irrelevant. If we wish to maintain the view both that the decisive victory over sin and death has been won and that there is still a real work to be done in bringing that victory to light in the lives of men and women, in the social structures and institutions of human existence, and indeed in all creation, then we shall have to find a way of speaking which avoids the polarised language which so often divides Christians. It cannot be stressed too much that this work of submitting and disclosing is itself divine in origin and execution; the Holy Spirit continually makes the work of Christ and its effects real as time proceeds.

The Church, which is always the body of which Christ is the head, is the principal sign in history of this truth. Precisely because it is a sign in history it is ambiguous. By this we mean not only that the Church can be misunderstood, but that its reality as a human institution, its social and historical existence as a community with sinful and fallible members, make its form fallible and peccable. It is, however, one and the same Church, *sancta simul et semper purificanda*, which is the chief symbol of the historicity of salvation. As such it is a symbol which is sign, instrument and foretaste of the realities which it serves.

This one Church subsists in various forms of which the most typical is the local church. It is not part of our present purpose to consider the difficulties created for such a view by denominational divisions, but Scripture and tradition alike testify to the reality of the local church as the concrete manifestation of the one body of Christ, in and through which the ministry of the head is exercised.

The ministry of Christ in and through his body is both like and unlike the ministry of Jesus during the years of his earthly life. The ministry of the church as the body of Christ is in union with the head to show forth the *ephapax* (the once-for-allness of Christ's ministry) and its fruit. This gives shape to the various ministries which build up and sustain the body, enabling it to fulfil its proper part in the mission of Jesus Christ. Within the Church and to the Church God gives charismata of different kinds for its life, mission and ministry. Through the work of the Holy Spirit the radical character of Christ's ministry shapes it for its task and through the same Spirit it is empowered for its ministry. So Schweizer accurately commented, 'the Church *is* ministry'; that is to say, the Church cannot be separated from its task, and ministry cannot be severed from what it is to be a Christian. This is at the heart of Paul's great picture of the local community in 1 Corinthians. The Spirit is given to all and therefore all have 'charisms' to offer. There is no such thing as the Spirit-less or gift-less Christian; each person is a 'minister' in his or her own right. Here then is the central nervous system of the New Testament doctrine of ministry. Ministry belongs to the people of God as a gift.

This concept of ministry belonging essentially to the 'laos' of God sharply divided the New Testament Church from its Jewish background or, indeed, pagan religions of its day. No room is found in it for a separate caste which alone is a channel of salvation for others or which alone has the right 'to minister'. On the contrary, the revolution of Christianity is centred in its understanding of the entire body as being a 'royal priesthood' with a variegated diversity and richness about the ministries given by the Holy Spirit which are offered to its Lord. Bishop Geoffrey Paul stated in one of his ordination charges:

> The Church of God is not divided into two groups, two unequal elements, clergy and laity, but the people of God is what it says it is. It is all and only laity, and it needs to be glad of it and remember it all the time. Clergy are laity, with a special calling, a special anointing, a special function and they are a special sign that God means redemption for all the world, but they remain laity, and woe betide them if they ever forget it.

This is not, of course, to deny the very real and Spirit-given ministries within the body such as 'apostles, prophets and teachers' which indeed stand out in the New Testament communities as separate and crucial ministries. Nevertheless, the point still stands that in spite of these being different functions within the body, each person is essential for the body's well-being and life. This important principle has not always been clearly seen in the Church and we are grateful for the Charismatic Movement for reminding us of the import-ance of 'every member ministry' for the life of the Christian community. The great richness of ministries which flow from the presence of the risen Christ in his Church include, however, not only the obviously demonstrable gifts of speaking, leading and witnessing, but more hidden gifts which no less 'show forth' the reality of Christ's victory over sin and death: charisms of prayer, whether intercessory or contemplative, of patient endurance under suffering, of sensitive listening, are examples of this.

It is true that we have all too often neglected the spiritual gifts adumbrated in the Pauline Epistles and we acknowledge that sometimes we have relied upon the 'one-man band' thus stripping the laity of their right to ministry. 'Turn up, pay up – and shut up' sums up tersely the traditional areas conferred upon the laity. Although these errors are being recognised it cannot be said that every Christian is aware of the God-given nature of his ministry, neither is every ordained Christian minister aware that, in part, he exists to serve the ministry of the whole 'laos'.

So then, all ministries and gifts are for the sake of the body, but never for its own sake but rather for its effectiveness in bringing in the kingdom. All charismata, therefore, relate to the disclosure of the triumph of Christ; hence the importance of proclamation and the ministries by which the Church is enabled to be a more effective and authentic sign of God's kingdom to those who do not yet believe. This dimension is often forgotten when Christians talk about ministry and as a result the average member of the average congregation thinks of ministry as a religious or liturgical act. It is something we do on Sundays or after work. But a fully orbed doctrine of ministry will include what a Christian does at work, how she or he sees the nature of being a Christian where he is or she is in the world. A progressive church will want its ministry to embrace the activity of the Holy Spirit in its locality; to recognise what God is doing in the world; and to take its part in witnessing to what it has seen and heard. Too quickly we forget the reality of the incarnation when ministry is discussed and planned. No church can claim to have a fully Christocentric ministry unless its members are living out their ministries where they live and work, representing the kingdom there.

Any talk, then, of ministries must always be firmly set within the context of and be understood as entirely dependent upon the ministry of Jesus Christ himself. Once again this raises the question of the relation between Christ's ministry now exercised in and through his body and his ministry in the days of his first appearing; in both cases philosophical problems concerning time and eternity are inescapable. The incarnation is however not least significantly the divine overcoming of the separation between time and eternity, and, to the extent that the Church is the place in which the Word of God is proclaimed and celebrated in word and sacrament, it is legitimate to describe the Church, as body of Christ, as the 'extension of the incarnation'.

The exercise in the Church of the ministries which are given for the sake of *the* ministry is not different from the ministry of Jesus Christ; rather it is his exercise now of the ministry which. *mutatis mutandis*, he exercised in various ways during his earthly life. His victory in time means that time is now different. Eschatologically the kingdom has already included all that is to be saved, and the union of the Church now with its head who is the one and the same Jesus of Nazareth and king of all creation means that the light, love and power of the end already illuminate and animate the Church in every age. When the Word of God is proclaimed, when it is heard and received, when the sacraments of the new covenant are celebrated, heaven and earth are indeed one, and as a result earth now, this bit of earth, is shown to be the place of God's rule. And not only then; based on the certainty of the victory celebrated in word and sacrament, every instance of the rule of love is also a bringing together of the two ages – or more correctly is a demonstration of their essential oneness. In this way the whole of human life can acquire a share in the ministry and priesthood of Jesus Christ. Through faith and baptism human beings are made members of Christ, who is both minister and priest; they therefore participate in his self-offering and in the benefits of it.

The ministry of the Church, therefore, is the one ministry of Jesus Christ now exercised in the power of the Spirit by means of gifts freely distributed to all the baptised so that corporately and individually they may play their full part as members of a priestly body.

4 THE SPECIAL MINISTRY

The difficulty of choosing an appropriate title for this section is a telling indication of the problem, not to say muddle, experienced by most of the churches today as they seek to find language in which to express their own essential convictions about the ministry in a way that is faithful to their particular past while being open to the insights of other traditions. However, with a few exceptions, all denominations have inherited and still maintain a set-apart ministry in one form or another. It is no less true that at the level of piety and practice, even if not at the level of official theology, to most such ministries some sense of 'apostolicity' is attributed. In other words, even when the special or distinctive ministry in a particular church is theoretically understood in relation not to the Twelve or the Seventy-two, but to the bishops/elders and deacons of some parts of the New Testament, it is nevertheless frequently seen also in terms of the Lord's own commission to those whom he chose to be with him, to go before him, to go and make disciples of all the nations.

Another feature of this paradox is the expectation that such ministers should have some sense of personal vocation, again, even in Christian communities which in principle deny any direct charge from Christ to an individual apart from the call and commission of the Church. In recent years, even churches with the most sacerdotal and/or clericalist views (these are *not* synonyms) have begun again to recognise and even to stress the interdependence between the common priesthood of the people of God and that of the ordained. On the other hand, the assertion that the 'special' ministry is not only a specially focused form of the common priesthood, but occupies its own place and has its own proper functions within the purposes of God for his Church, has been made clear not only by the Anglican-Roman Catholic International Commission (ARCIC) – where it might have been expected – but also by the much more broadly representative Faith and Order Commission of the World Council of Churches (WCC) in their report *Baptism Eucharist and Ministry*. The growing ecumenical consensus is significant, especially in the light of the earlier polarisations of view.

It is at all events clear that the Christian churches have not usually been without priests or ministers. The responsibilities of such people varied, but have usually included the duties of preaching and teaching, of presiding at, leading and animating public worship, of pastoral care and intercession, and of representing the Church. They have commonly in practice as well as in some churches in theory also had a particular role in the preservation of fellowship between local churches, and have therefore been a significant symbol of the unity of the Church.

Many consider that the distinctive function of the special ministry is leadership. Here, of course, we encounter the same danger met in every theory of detracting in some way from the uniqueness of Christ and his work. Equally, however, it is possible to understand the leadership of the clergy in an acceptable manner. Jesus made it clear to his first disciples (a word which inevitably suggests following a leader) that his own leadership was one of service, and that they had to copy what he did for them in washing their feet. Perhaps 'leadership' is a useful general term for holding together the areas of responsibility listed above and certainly demands a congruence between office and personal character. The leaders of any community both express and impress the characteristic values of those they serve. Within the Church these values are uniquely given by the head of the body and are the possession of the members through their communion with him. It is in part through the ordained ministry that the Holy Spirit preserves the Church in its essential character and in its absolute dependence on the Word of God.

There is, therefore, an inescapable sense in which those who exercise such a ministry have a representational role. We are aware that this is for some a difficult and historically controversial expression, but consider that it enshrines something of importance for the insights of many Christians which need not be unacceptable to others. Like all ministries the special ministry is a gift of God to the Church as well as in the Church. The leadership it exercises is a manifestation of the headship of Christ and of the absolute dependence of all upon him.

The appropriateness or at least the compatibility of the

existence of a special ministry with the gospel is established in the practice of Jesus himself and in the provision made by the apostles for the churches of their foundation or made by those churches for themselves. From an early date, to put it no more precisely, the involvement of those already exercising a ministry of oversight in the appointment of new ministers became first normal and then universal. We would affirm that in principle the special ministry is (a) dominical in origin and (b) one of the symbols of catholicity which unite the Church in time and space. No particular conclusions should be drawn from this respect of various issues controversial at the present day. In particular, the doctrine of the apostolic succession, which has been so much abused and so much misused, should be carefully distinguished from the narrowly defined and mechanical notions of its 'transmission' which have, all too often, been the basis upon which it has been both defended and attacked. At its heart is precisely the recognition that the special ministry is a gift of God to, in and through the Church, and that continuity in office and responsibility is one of the signs of the continuity of the whole Church in the faith and witness of the apostles.

Such a view does not claim too much for a clerical caste within the Church nor for any undemonstrable 'tactile' succession, nor does it pass any judgment upon ministries lacking what some might regard as necessary aspects of the 'pedigree'. It does, however, value highly the succession through the ages of those with the care of the churches as one of the symbols (i.e. both signs and instruments) of the universality of the Church in which the three moments of ephapax, eternity and linear time are brought together. In this way we believe that the historic and distinctive ministry is one of the constitutive elements of the Church of Jesus Christ; one, that is to say, of the means by which he himself exercises his own headship of his body, and by which the Holy Spirit reminds Christians now of what Jesus taught his first chosen disciples and leads them into all truth.

Within our own Communion the threefold order of ministry with monarchical episcopacy at its heart has been our inheritance from the primitive Church. We share this concept of ministry with other episcopal churches and it is our contention that our continuity anchors Anglicanism in the undivided Church. But we are not unaware of the problems as well as the privileges of this claim. Anglicans should probably now be prepared to admit the extent to which their devotion to a so-called principle, that of the 'historic' episcopate, has muddied the theological and ecumenical waters. We share faith, however, with other ecclesial communities in which episcopacy is expressed in different forms. They point out a fact which is all too well known to us all, that our threefold order with its insistence upon this form of episcopacy, and no other, may restrict other ministries which God wants to give to the Church. We need to heed this warning and to seek ways in which a revitalised threefold ministry can lead forward the mission of the people of God without denying such ministries which lie outside that structure. Nevertheless, this form of ministry we have inherited is not something to be ashamed of, or to apologise for. On the contrary, it is something we can offer with confidence to others because, for all its admitted inadequacies, it is for us a God-given pattern of ministry which we have received from the primitive Church and in which we have confidence.

But what form might such revitalising take? We have to acknowledge that our form of the diaconate is but a pale shadow of the form we see depicted in the post-New Testament Church where it was a ministry in its own right. We, however, have reduced it to being but a probationary year for the presbyterate. Questions could also be usefully put about the role of the bishop in the Church where confusion often reigns over the nature of his office. Is it mainly pastoral? If so, are not many of the dioceses too large for them to cope with such responsibility? What about his role as teacher, theologian and leader of the 'mission of the people of God'? This must inevitably lead also to a serious attempt to revive the reality of a truly collegial conception both of the presbyters in relation to their bishop and of bishops among themselves.

Both of these points are closely related to the growing recognition that 'communion' is an essential characteristic of the Church. This recognition also requires the giving of attention to the symbols of universal communion. In recent years Anglicans have been considerably exercised by this and several new instruments have been forged to implement its reality. The Lambeth Conference, the Anglican Consultative Council, the Primates' Meetings and the International Theological Commission have joined the Archbishop of Canterbury as examples of this. The role of the last has also developed considerably. We must acknowledge however that these all lack juridical authority and may tend to encourage a federal rather than a genuinely 'communion' conception of the Church. No doubt the direct, immediate and ordinary jurisdiction of a papacy or its equivalent will remain as unacceptable to some Anglicans as ever, but we cannot for ever avoid the challenge to express the universality of Christian communion in visible and credible forms. We should certainly ask what contribution our history and tradition might make to a renewal of the Petrine office for the whole Church.

The revitalising of the threefold ministry cannot be independent of wider issues. Clearly one of the most pressing is: 'What is it to be a communion of men and women in the Church?' Whatever answers are finally given to the question of the ordination of women to the presbyterate and episcopate, all must agree that the present situation is highly unsatisfactory and much gifted talent is being frustrated. Women, and for that matter men also, need to be affirmed in their right not only to exist in the Church but to express their very real God-given talents in the service of the kingdom. Underlying so many aspects of the problem, however, is our widespread failure to recognise that the ordained ministry needs a renewed laity. Only a Church in which every person is growing into the recognition, development and exercise of his or her gifts for ministry will ultimately be able to have the special ministry it needs.

While we acknowledge the insolubility of some of these issues we hope that they will be addressed and modifications made if necessary to ministries which are in danger of losing their coherence and identity.

It will easily be inferred from what we have just said that we regard the principle of the special ministry as a consideration prior to any questions concerning its structure (that is, the threefold ministry) or its theological character, that is to say, its priestliness. To suggest as we have that priestliness is a question secondary to distinctiveness is not to imply that it is irrelevant or unimportant. On the contrary, we wish to affirm, on the basis of the conviction repeatedly expressed that all Christian ministry is a form of the ministry of Christ, and that Christ's ministry is itself priestly in character, that priestly language is at the very least an appropriate way of speaking about the ordained ministry in the Church.

We must note, however, that the word 'priest' when used of the special ministry in the Anglican communion has been used cautiously and carefully. Our Articles make it plain that a cultic priesthood offering a propitiatory sacrifice on behalf of others is not what is meant by the word priest. Rather, they had in mind a ministerial priesthood who were set apart to do something which belongs to the whole people of God. 'Ministerial' priesthood expresses this concept of ministry because it is a ministry which is offered for the people, on their behalf and in their name.

It is certain that the Reformers knew of the misunderstanding that would arise from the use of the term, but it continued to be used within our Communion because of its antiquity as well as its connection with the word 'presbyter'. By broadening the concept of ministry to include the pastoral, leading and teaching roles as well as priestly task of presiding at the holy communion or Eucharist, Cranmer, Hooker and other Anglican divines saw no strong reason to break with the tradition of the early Church where, at least from the early third century on, this term came to be applied in the first instance to bishops, then to presbyters. (We should resist the restriction of the term to the second order of the ministry.) To those who feel anxious at the use of such language, we should say that to speak of ordained Christian ministers as 'priestly' need mean no more than that their only calling and office is to minister the priesthood of Christ, and that this priestly ministry is both commemorative and contemporary. In this the priesthood of the ordained ministry is no more dangerous than the priesthood of the whole Church.

Priesthood need not mean any more than that. But

Christian ministry must not mean any less than that. Undoubtedly many medieval Western Christians did understand by priesthood a view of ministry which verged on the magical, and lent itself to the superstition of propitiatory sacrifices all but independent of Calvary. To the extent that this was the case the Reformation protest was and remains necessary. It is, however, no less necessary to remember that it is through the sacrifice of Christ alone that our peace is made with God. Elsewhere we have attempted to clarify some of the problems of relating the historical death of Christ and his eternal intercession. In both we acknowledge his own priestly character and activity; Christians are priestly as they receive the benefits of the former and as through their incorporation into him participate in the latter. Their ministers are priestly as they 'lead' them in both.

In affirming that there is a 'priesthood' of the ordained ministry we wish also to maintain both the integral relationship between the common priesthood of the Church and that of the special ministry and also the distinctiveness of the latter. *Ex hypothesi* the special ministry is priestly; not, as we have emphasised, independently of the priestliness of Jesus Christ. It is a two-way relationship with the ministry of the Church as a whole; the ordained ministry is priestly because the whole people of God is priestly, but the Church is also enabled to exercise its own priesthood because within it God has set those specifically commissioned to represent in various ways the ministry of Christ as head, who are to show forth in function and in being the self-offering by which Jesus himself consecrated himself for our sake.

CONCLUSION

Throughout this essay our understanding of 'the ministry' has been shaped and conditioned by God's action of reconciliation in Christ. This unique and unrepeatable work has to be applied to every succeeding generation of human history, so that everyone may be drawn into the salvific activity of Christ that they may, responsively, learn how to offer themselves in union with his own offering. This is, we acknowledge, an inadequate way of expressing the matter. Christian faith declares that the atoning work (ministry) of Christ is full, perfect and sufficient, and that it is of a priestly character. Furthermore, it affirms that although nothing essential can usefully be added to this work, nevertheless there remains a real responsibility of every Christian age to bring the various aspects of its own life and environment into submission to Christ. This responsibility is more than a retrospective gratitude, but involves through thanksgiving an actual involvement of the present features of the life of the world in the victory of the kingdom of Christ.

As we stressed earlier, this ministry means above all the shared ministry of the people of God. Perhaps one of the most urgent tasks facing us today is how we may utilise the tremendous resources of the gifts latent in the congregations in our charge. In this essay we have seen that the theological understanding of ministry gives us no warrant to take ministry away from them. Rather it demands a radical revision of inherited assumptions to give ministry back to the people of God. Even if we cannot talk in the way the New Testament does of 'apostles, prophets and teachers', we cannot avoid the challenge of trying to interpret in our own day and culture the following demands which the gospel of reconciliation lays upon us. For example, we are bold to ask:

What is it to be an *Apostolic Church*? How may the Church of God be truly apostolic in its mission and life? What structures need to be erected to support and enable the ministries God gives for the fulfilment of that task?

What is it to be a *Prophetic Church*? How may the Church of God be truly prophetic in its secular witness and as a 'sign' and 'sacrament' of the gospel? Again, we ask, what challenges does this concept bring to our traditional understanding of ministry and how may we react positively to the demands facing the contemporary Church?

What is it to be a *Teaching Church*? How may the Church of God be one in which people are well grounded in their faith and grow into leadership? If this is not happening, why not? What structures might have to be changed or erected for the Anglican Communion to be a well-taught body?

Within this ministry of the entire people of God, however,

we recognise from the beginning a distinction between those who participate in virtue of their baptism in the priestliness of the whole Church and those who are specifically set apart for ministry and in the greater part of Christendom have been designated 'priests'. To the extent that this priesthood of the ordained ministry has been misunderstood as a priesthood analogous to that of Christ, we would reject it utterly. On the other hand, the all but universal 'priesthoods' of world religions we would regard as essentially not so much vain human attempts to attain to divinity as divine attempts to foreshadow the perfect mediation between God and humankind presented by the sacrificial life and death of Jesus Christ. This we regard as the only priesthood and ministry so called. The one, holy, catholic and apostolic Church which exists in every age and every place we consider as the concrete manifestation *now* of the reconciliation once achieved and to which we look as the fulfilment of Christ's earthly work.

Attention has already been drawn to related theological issues; no attempt has been made to discuss these or the particular matters of controversy at the present time. We do not claim either that fundamental questions of the ministry can be resolved without agreement on such matters as the ordination of women, the status of non-episcopal ministries, lay presidency of the Eucharist or, for that matter, issues connected with synodical government. What we do believe, however, is that in this essay we have managed to combine the distinctive thrusts of both Evangelical and Catholic concepts of ministry as expressing insights which have always been there in the Anglican understanding of the people of God. As theological college principals committed to the task of equipping people for the work of God in our own day, we are convinced that the Church falters in its ministry if it either denigrates the high calling of the ordained or despises the ministry of the entire 'laos'. What integrates these often polarised groups is Jesus Christ himself, the same yesterday, today and tomorrow, whose own eternal Priesthood calls the entire Church of God to celebrate him as our Prophet, Priest and King.

BIBLIOGRAPHY

C. K. Barrett, *Church, Ministry and Sacraments in the New Testament* (Exeter, 1980). *A perceptive and scholarly examination of eccesiology in the NT.*

Board for Mission and Unity, *The Priesthood of the Ordained Ministry* (London, 1986). *Presents a contemporary understanding of Anglican faith.*

J. Galot, *Theology of Priesthood* (Ignatius, 1985). *A reading of the Vatican II theology of ministry.*

L. Grollenberg (ed.), *Minister? Pastor? Prophet?* (London, 1980). *Chapter 4 will be of special interest.*

J. Laurance, '*Priest' as Type of Christ* (New York, 1984). *A study of Cyprian of Carthage.*

R. C. Moberly, *Ministerial Priesthood* (London, 1897).

Jürgen Moltmann, *The Church in the Power of the Spirit* (London, 1977). *Chapters 5 and 6 will be of special interest.*

E. Schillebeeckx, *Ministry: a case for change* (London, 1981). *A breathtaking revision of Roman Catholic ministerial theology.*

W. Werning, *Vision and Strategy for Church Growth* (Chicago, 1977). *A basic book about Church growth principles.*

DISCUSSION QUESTIONS

1 In what way are the renewal of the laity and revitalising of ministry connected?

2 From your experience, what are the *limitations* as well as the *advantages* of the ordained ministry as we have inherited it?

3 Do you agree with the authors' reflections on the revitalising of the episcopacy?

4 The authors challenge the Church to take seriously apostolic, prophetic and teaching ministries. What might be the practical consequences of this for our diocese?

4

IN SEARCH OF AN ANGLICAN IDENTITY

INTRODUCTION

In many and various ways Anglican writers have sought to account for the existence of their Church and to offer sound reasons for belonging to it. Much of this apologetic, even in recent years, has been done in exclusively English terms, and has depended for the cornerstone of its reasoning on the concept of the Church of England as the 'national' or 'established' Church. Such an approach to Anglicanism evidently ignores the Anglican Communion, or tries, awkwardly and unconvincingly, to accommodate it as 'the Church of England in those parts'. Thus one famous English reference book lists the Bishops of England (and, illogically, from this point of view, of Wales), followed by the Bishops Overseas (by which it means the British Commonwealth); whereas the bishops of Scotland and Ireland are listed separately, among the other Christian denominations; and the bishops outside the British Commonwealth are omitted altogether. Needless to say, such a point of view does violence to the self-understanding of most, if not all, of the provinces of the Communion. Furthermore, it is a point of view which was actually undermined by the summoning of the first Lambeth Conference in 1867, when the question of whether bishops who owed no allegiance to the British Crown belonged to the same 'communion and fellowship' as the Archbishop of Canterbury was answered decisively, if controversially, in the affirmative. Any account of Anglicanism which is not an account of the Anglican Communion as a whole, is self-condemned.

Other Anglican apologetic, not surprisingly, has swung to the opposite extreme, and sought to drain Anglicanism of its Englishness altogether. It has been proposed simply as 'the best type of Christianity' (as Michael Ramsey in a memorable passage once described this kind of apologetic). Typically, this approach has fastened upon Anglicanism as the middle way between the Scylla of Rome and the Charybdis of unbishoped Protestantism, a kind of moderate Christianity which rationally embraced the best of both sides and endeavoured to avoid the errors of either. The attraction of this point of view is that it appears to be independent of any specifically English origin of Anglicanism, and thus suitable for export anywhere in the world. But whatever value it may once have had, it cannot be said to have survived the advent of ecumenism, or the colossal developments which have taken place in recent years within both the Roman Catholic Church and the Churches of the Reformation. An account of Anglicanism which simply feeds for its existence upon the excesses of other Christian bodies, holds no attraction for us.

We do our best to explain why we are driven back to examine our historical roots – and as Anglicans those roots for better and for worse are mainly English. If a large part of this essay is devoted to English history, that is not because we are unaware of how alienating such an exercise at first glance is likely to be for the majority of our readers outside England. Nor is it because we are falling back into the typically English confusion of the Anglican Communion with the Church of England. We try to make clear that it is only through an examination of those roots that we can grasp the precise way in which the Anglican Communion can interpret its fragile and uncomfortable place within the universal but fractured fellowship of Christian Churches. As Michael Ramsey said in the passage already referred to:

While the Anglican Church is vindicated by its place in history, with a strikingly balanced witness to Gospel and Church and sound learning, its greater vindication lies in its pointing through its own history to something of which it is a fragment. Its credentials are its incompleteness, with the tension and the travail in its soul. It is clumsy and untidy, it baffles neatness and logic. For it is sent not to commend itself as 'the best type of Christianity', but by its very brokenness to point to the universal Church wherein all have died.[1]

If further apology for the historical material of this essay is needed, we would say that for too long Catholics and Evangelicals within the Anglican Communion have each claimed Anglican history for themselves; and have preferred the comfort of defending those claims polemically on the barricades to the pain of explaining them eirenically at the negotiating table. We can no doubt be faulted at many points of the story we tell; our only reply is that we have tried to tell one single story, and tell it together.

BACKGROUND TO ANGLICANISM

1 The Church's Unity and Faith

The Church of God on earth is, according to the New Testament, a single organic whole created by God through the redemption that is in Christ to further his purposes on this earth and to share his eternal glory. It is constantly identified by metaphors of unitariness – bride, body, temple. These images are not simply eschatological, not just describing how the corn currently on separate stalks on the mountain tops may one day be turned into flour and thus into a single loaf. No, the argument is that the parts need each other now – and the more unlike they are (1 Cor. 12), the more they need each other, and the more in turn they are to love each other (1 Cor. 13). Indeed a 'common' baptism (Eph. 4:5) witnesses not just to one Lord, but to one Lord who cannot be rightly served – and is not rightly declared or understood – when Christians divide from each other into separate enclaves or even clones (1 Cor. 1).

Although the specific treatment of the Church at the beginning of this essay is bound to relate to its organic unity (as that is a special problem arising in respect of 'Anglican Identity'), yet the unity question is also closely bound to the question of the Church's profession of faith. A true statement of the faith may be the initial instrument under God to draw newcomers to Christ – yet it is only as people are won for Christ and built into the fellowship that the living Church can not only express the faith, but continue refining its expression of it. And down Church history unity has been strained and sometimes broken by differing expressions of the faith, or by differing weight given to sources of authority from which those expressions come. A quest for what is distinctive in an Anglican identity constantly bumps against these factors of history.

We return to look at the Church and its unity in the New Testament, where theory is itself in tension with practice. But in the New Testament there is only one legitimate division between different groupings of God's people – and that is the geographical one. In any one place they meet at one table, share one bread, and exhibit in microcosm the organic unity of the Spirit which just as really, though slightly less obviously, bonds the whole worldwide Church. The Church Catholic is thus, in essence, a network of dispersed communities, and the only positive use of 'sectional' terminology in relation to it is when such terms describe the physical sundering which inevitably constitutes them 'the saints which are in Rome' or 'the church at Thyatira'. 'Anglican' is initially not a term for a distinctive ethos or constitution, but simply the Latin word of the twelfth-century Church to indicate 'the church which is in England'.[2] We now necessarily face a meaning less distinct, and perhaps less scripturally justifiable, as first the Reformation, and latterly and most pronouncedly the development of worldwide 'Anglicanism' have turned the term into one with connotations other than geographical.

Thus Anglicans describing their 'identity' are bound to do so against a background of doctrinal understanding which is condemnatory of the whole principle of denominationalism, and thus almost certainly puts the more obvious ways of expressing an 'Anglican identity' under judgment also. Anglicanism in today's world is bound to have a provisionality about it, is bound to be seeking a true catholicity, is bound to be in eschatological tension. Thus its own self-description is itself as on the way, and is bound to include putting a brave face upon what actually is, as well as setting out what desirably ought to be. There also has to be a brave face – not quite so bold, but still in essence brave – put upon Church history, and upon our own Anglican history. If the Roman Catholic and Eastern Churches are sealed somewhat too tightly into the prison of their own histories, yet Anglicans, sitting more loosely by their past, have nevertheless got to have an apologia which exhibits them in some kind of visible continuity with their spiritual forebears and with some integrity in their own persons in so acknowledging their ancestors.

2 The Undivided Church

We turn to the Church of the early centuries, not so much at this point to establish principles as to record characteristics. It was a Church which, being clearly already episcopal in the second century, slowly developed a provincial, patriarchal, and even ecumenical structuring during the succeeding centuries. It was a Church which, being clearly already committed to a scriptural faith in the second century, developed it into a credal and confessional faith in the succeeding ones. And it was a Church which, being clearly an unpopular minority cult in the second century, was to become the unchallenged master and virtual owner of Western Europe.

The ecumenical, credal, and imperial Church of the second half of the first millennium was not without internal tensions. In various ways these reflected differences of ethos and style as between different places, rather than differences of structure or creed (or, for instance, of intention to govern earthly kings). Arguments between East and West, which culminated in the so-called 'Great Schism' of 1054, were of this sort. Similar differences also existed for generations between different places in the West, but the Carolingian reforms of the ninth century imposed considerable centralisation, not least in the use of the Latin language, and in the *de facto* authority accorded to Rome itself.

It was into this kind of worldwide Church that the Anglo-Saxon converts of the sixth and seventh centuries were initiated.

3   The Origins of the English Church

There had been an ancient British Church, spread by the Roman occupation of the first four centuries, and with its own bishops at the Council of Arles in 314. But by the time of Pope Gregory (590–604) this had been virtually eliminated by the pagan Anglo-Saxons who invaded from 449 onwards and took over what is now England. Ancient Christianity remained in Wales, in the Isle of Man (the most ancient see of the modern Church of England), and in Ireland and Scotland as the Celtic mission spread. There were at intervals individuals in England who confessed Christ – the Queen of Kent was Christian before Augustine got there. But there was no organised English Church, and it was an organised, a recognisable and, by all except the most exacting criteria, a *new* English Church which grew from Augustine's mission and episcopate (597 onwards). And although it was acknowledged by Gregory that in ethos and ceremonial the new English Church could differ from the Gallican, yet it proved within England itself, for all that it was still several kingdoms, that a common style had to be established when the Northern mission through Scotland clashed in the mid-seventh century with the spreading Roman mission from Kent. In any case, Gregory had from the first envisaged a unified bi-provincial structure for the whole of England, the senior of the two archbishops taking precedence over the other.

It is appropriate to trace the continuity of today's English Church from 597 – but of an English Church which had its point of origin in a continuity with the worldwide Church which preceded the specific mission of Augustine, and indeed mounted it. Continuity itself is an important 'Catholic' insight – indeed one of the 'notes' of the Church concealed within 'one holy catholic and apostolic'. It derives not so much from any specific scriptural mention (such as Jesus's words about the gates of Hades not prevailing against his Church), as from a whole set of New Testament presuppositions. The very nature of the visible institution is bound up with its still being there tomorrow in some form of organic continuity with that which is today. It is similarly bound up with its scriptural opposition to schism or secession or even 'choice' of affiliations. The very identity of the Church of God – let alone of the Church of England – depends upon this organic continuity, as a prerequisite for its contemporaneous organic unity. Discard history, and the residual basis for unity is frail indeed.

However, such continuity, for all that it is built into the very being of the Church, does not necessarily entail a tight or over-rigid organisational framework. Our later discussions of doctrinal formulae, liturgy, and 'orders' may well exhibit this. Certainly the style of Church life required of a minority under persecution is very different from that required of a state Church (which may possibly even be in danger of becoming a persecutor). Linguistic, artistic, architectural and commercial factors affect the life of the church in one place and one time differently from the way they affect another in a different place at a different time. It might even be argued from the sixth century itself that, although the Pope had given his goodwill for a difference in ceremonies between Kent and the Continent, yet within the land of England some common patterns were needed – one notable point (which still is a problem for the world today) being the way of fixing the date of Easter. This was resolved by the giving way of the Celts and Northumbrians at the Synod of Whitby in 664. There would remain open here a question as to the appropriate size unit for such decision-taking, a question taking the following form: what changes can be implemented at the desire of a parish or congregation; what require the consent of a bishop and his whole diocese; what need a provincial or national process, and what need a worldwide one? It has often been due to differences about this 'What size unit for what size decisions?' that the worldwide Church has divided. Certainly it has been at the heart of the origins of distinctive Anglicanism.

The Cornish, Welsh, Irish, and Scottish Churches each followed their own separate course of development in the second half of the first millennium, but each in turn, while from the beginning attributing some primacy of honour to

Rome, and sustaining communion with her, also became in time subjected to Roman authority. They have a later part to play in the story of 'Anglicanism'.

4   The English Church in Latin Christendom

As with the Celtic Churches, so with the Church of England itself. Its relationship with Rome was originally part of a 'loose-knit' nexus of Western Christendom, as is illustrated by Bede's account of the Synod of Whitby. The protagonist of the 'Roman' position, Wilfred, acknowledges a role of honour for the Church of Rome, but urges conformity not only to her customs but to the customs of the 'universal Church'. If a specifically Roman authority is in view, it is that of a Church rather than of its bishop, and it is the precedent of customs rather than the force of rules which Wilfred invokes. No doubt these distinctions are both fine and latter-day, but they indicate points of departure for the changes of the succeeding centuries, and writers of the twelfth century easily fall into our alternative terminology (i.e. of 'rules' not 'customs') which it would never have occurred to Wilfred to employ. In particular, after the Norman Conquest the grip of the papacy tightened, sometimes through the agency of the Crown, sometimes despite it. Even so we need to recall that centralisation in the Middle Ages, in days of poor communications and no printing, was never of the sort that latter-day models would suggest. Perhaps its chief agent was a universal Canon Law, which was a strong unifying force in the Western Church. But at the same time regional variety (within broad limits) endured in the liturgy and other customs. Furthermore, as the papacy worked up its temporal claims (which in turn worked through the system to provide special privileges for the clergy, even to the point of putting them above the law of their own land), so at regular intervals the focus of ecclesiastical authority found itself in conflict with monarchs and civil authorities. The history of medieval England can even be written in terms of the chronic conflict between Crown and Popes over rights in respect of the English Church. But, heretics and the occasional interdict apart, the Western Church remained a cohesive unity, totally in communion with itself, and with little doubt that Rome was the centre of this unity and had both immediate and ultimate authority over the Church.

THE REFORMATION

1   The Reformation Process

Medieval western Christendom blew up in an explosion for which St Paul provided the fuel, the printing press the fuse, and Martin Luther the spark. Explosive outworkings in England were contained by the power of Henry VIII, and went largely underground, though all the ingredients – fuel, fuse and sparks – were to be found, often quite near each other, above ground also. Thus in the course of time explosions duly occurred, but it has been a commonplace to contrast them with the force of continental ones – there was a series of much smaller blasts, and, although they did damage, they left the landscape and buildings in a much more recognisable continuity with the past than on the continent.

Thus the Reformation was the ecclesiological crisis point in Anglican identity. Any rationale must have this factor at its centre. And the Reformation itself was, even on the most simplistic explanation, a two-stage process for the Church of England. There was first a separation from the authority of Rome, and an assertion of a national independence for the Church of this country. That was the change effected in Henry VIII's reign – and it led to excommunication of monarch, bishops and country. The Church of England generally chose to ignore this excommunication, and went its own way. There was then the second stage, the flexing of the muscles of independence in Edward VI's reign – and that in six short years ushered in a thoroughgoing doctrinal reforma- tion. The relationships of reigns to reformation, and of monarchs to churchmanship may be surprising to us, for changes are not now so causally related to the varying successors of Henry and Edward. We do not delay here to retell the whole story as it unfolded chronologically (for that has been done a thousand times), but rather to isolate certain features, and present different approaches to evaluation. It is inevitable that monarchs played a larger part in such events than they could ever do today.[3] It was the aegis of two differing monarchs which distinguished so sharply the two vastly differing stages in the Reformation.

2 A Traditional Roman Catholic View

From Rome's point of view, the first of these two stages was schism, and was only heretical in so far as schism is itself heresy. From Rome's point of view at the time, Henry's schism left the Church of England in the same attitude of doctrinally orthodox defiance as the Eastern Churches had adopted in the eleventh century. The Church of England was a Church in rebellion, but still part of the Church of God – conferring valid orders, and presumably celebrating valid (if not actually 'grace-ful') sacraments. The defiance was, however, very serious indeed – according to the Roman rule-books, a nation which from king downwards was excommunicated ought to have come to its senses, sought reconciliation, and swallowed whatever terms the Pope cared to impose. It had not done so.

From Rome's point of view the second stage in Edward's reign added thoroughgoing Protestant heresy to the sin of schism. Prayer Book, Ordinal, Articles, and Homilies alike, for all their orthodoxy in areas like Chalcedonian Christology, jumped the Protestant way at virtually every point in dispute between Rome and the continental reformers. It was at that stage, according to *Apostolicae Curae*, that the Church of England fell into such doctrinal error that it ceased to have the objective 'intention' of ordaining true priests to offer the true sacrifice of the Mass.

It is hardly surprising, once an evaluation of this sort was current, that Rome sought from 1570 onwards to re-establish its own claims over the people of England, and this was done both by public denunciation of Elizabeth, and by sending in an ideological fifth column to run a robust, and technically rebellious, underground Roman movement. And Roman Catholicism has not only persisted in England to the present day, but is arguably the largest single religious body on the contemporary English Church scene in terms of its regularly worshipping adherents. It is, of course, this existence of the Church of Rome alongside Anglicanism as an apparent competitor, in England itself as well as throughout the world, which points up the need for an apologia for Anglicanism which goes beyond saying simply, 'we are the catholic Church of Christ in this place' – which is, obviously, how we would prefer to identify ourselves.

3   The Living Church Continued

The Church of England itself has necessarily and consistently demurred from any such Roman Catholic interpretation as we have set out above, and has inevitably stressed the continuity of the Church through the Reformation – a continuity expressed most obviously in the sheer continued existence of parish churches with parish congregations, often with the same parish priest and certainly without any point at which the Church started anew from scratch. If the continuity consisted at root in this parish persistence, it also had other notable public symbols. Three are worthy of note here.

First, there was credal continuity. In one sense, this is only to say that the Scriptures were normative – indeed more normative than they had been before. But the actual Catholic Creeds, Apostles', Nicene and Athanasian, were retained as embodying the central articles of Christian belief, and each was to be used regularly in worship. A Church which threw over the Creeds would inevitably look different from one which retained them.[4]

Second, there was a continuity of the framework of ministerial order. The ordered sequence of bishops in the ancient sees, duly consecrated by existing bishops, matched the continuity of the clergy in their parishes – and the due episcopal ordination of deacons and priests went on providing for the parochial succession.[5] The significance of such continuity is discussed below. But the sheer fact of it added to the general sense that, despite ups and downs, the same Church was continuing steadfastly on its way.

Third, there was continuity of the liturgical principle and, up to a point, of liturgical texts. The character of the various liturgical texts can be seen from the contents of Cranmer's Prayer Books, in which his own Preface (called 'Concerning the Service of the Church' in the 1662 Book) describes a process of simplification, standardisation and purification of liturgical texts – but the process is based upon the acceptance of great underlying principles. Liturgy itself, with prescribed texts and detailed rubrics, is not only preserved, but becomes a corner-stone of the reformed Church of England. Calendar and lectionary; offices and creeds; psalter and canticles; provision of confessions, absolutions, collects, litanies, and blessings; the sacraments of baptism (yes, and the baptism of infants) and of the Lord's Supper; the rites of confirmation, matrimony, visitation of the sick, burial, and ordination – all these point to a deep continuity of principle, whatever reforms were made in particular rites or their ceremonial or other emphases, and whatever other lesser rites were eliminated in the process. There was, of course, an enormous cultural jump for the average rural parishioner as the liturgy went from mysterious Latin to reasonably transparent English, but even so, once it was accepted that the vernacular was appropriate at all (and this followed from the use of the English Bible), then the liturgical principle itself was well demonstrated in the reformed rites. In this area, as in the preceding ones, it was entirely plausible to claim that the one Church of England, without damaging her anatomy, had nevertheless 'washed her face'.[6]

4   'The Washing of the Face'

It would be absurd to suggest that the Reformation was solely about words or superficialities. The leaders of it were perfectly content to be called 'Protestants'.[7] The widespread sense throughout Europe of being embattled against a dangerous common foe in the papacy held the leaders in the various countries together in a tense network of communications – but, however great that tension, it was clear throughout that they stood on the same side of a divide, and viewed the unreformed Church of Rome as standing on the other. The Church of England bishops, in Edward's, Mary's, and Elizabeth's reigns alike, are found sharing this same stance.

If they were washing the begrimed face of the part of the Catholic Church which subsisted in England, what powerful cleansing agents did they use, and were those both successful as cleansers and yet also without harm to the life of the body?

Over against inherited Roman Catholicism, the reformers were insisting on three doctrinal points, upon which in turn hung virtually every other point of difference from the old religion. These three points were:

1. The supremacy of Scripture over every tradition of the Church.
2. The full and sufficient character of the cross of Christ for atoning for sin, thus making us dependent upon God's grace alone for salvation and for his justifying of us through faith.
3. The consequent doctrine that the sacraments necessarily convey what they signify only to the worthy.[8]

Each of these points can be easily exhibited several times over in the Reformation formularies of the Church of England, and countless times in the writings of the leading reformers.[9] Where such discontinuity with the past character of faith was openly acknowledged (as it then certainly was), then at those points the opinion of Rome was irrelevant, and an attempt at ecclesial self-justification on Roman Catholic terms would be in direct contradiction to the points at issue. This would have been true whether the exercise were deemed successful or not.

Yet, when in Elizabeth's reign the apologists for the English Reformation set out their rationale of their separation from Rome, it was clear that although there was an appeal to the ultimate authority of Scripture, yet a bare appeal to Scripture would not suffice. The actual lines of reformation in Edward's reign had been dominated by Cranmer's understanding of Scripture, tempered by his general understanding of continental Protestant thinking; by his declared policy of reforming step by step; and by his willingness to accommodate those whose minds took time to change. He himself, in his controversies over the Lord's Supper, cited the Fathers on every page – though it would perhaps be true to say that he was for the Fathers when they were for him. Now in Elizabeth's reign more thoroughgoing use of precedent was necessary – the Church of England had to be shown as not only generally scriptural in its patterns of worship and ministry, but also as specifically entitled to act separately from other parts of the historic Church in making reforms.

Jewel, the great apologist, claims that the Church of England is but a part of the Church Catholic, but a part that properly has provincial powers to take the reforming steps it has taken – comparable indeed to independent steps taken by the English Church at intervals in various preceding centuries. Part of the argument is to show that the papacy has not always exercised those dictatorial powers now claimed for it: part is to show how provinces and other subdivisions have taken reforming steps independently.

The Church of England, on this analysis, has not only the power but also the duty to conform itself to the best primitive models. 'Primitive' may often have meant 'as revealed in the New Testament', and at other times meant 'in accordance with a romantic view of the perfection of the English Church of the seventh century' – and we do not stop now to examine these undeclared shifts of meaning. The point is simply that the 'historical' argument is acknowledged – that the Elizabethan churchmen were not simply trying to create a latter-day church *de novo* (by disruption, schism, or spontaneous generation), but had a concern to recognise the credentials of their own past, and, subject only to the higher authority of Scripture, to act in conformity with that recognition.

There was undoubtedly a tension here. In their sense of obedience to Scripture the Reformers claimed the right to act independently of the rest of Western Europe, and indeed produced (among other things) a distinctive liturgical pattern of their own. Yet, at the same time, to them the nation was the unit, and they denied to sectarian or fissiparous groups the right to make reforms on a local basis over or against their national patterns, even while they claimed for themselves a national independence from the patterns of Europe generally. The tension lay in their sense that there is a worldwide Church, that it does have the right and power to co-ordinate, though not to coerce, patterns of Church life, and thus in a modified way they respected General Councils of the past.[10] They would even look to them for the future (provided the parties came freely and not under papal coercion). But they could not accord the same liberty to differences of opinion within the one nation as they claimed for themselves within the fraternity of nations.[11]

One has also to recognise that under the pressures of their own times (and certainly of the priorities they inevitably had to observe) the reformers generally regarded the three cardinal points listed earlier in this section as far more important than the point about 'continuing' an episcopal framework. But that is the subject of a separate treatment below.

5   Bishops and Orders: Face, Cleanser, or Grime?

'To the intent that these orders may be continued . . .' says the Preface to the Ordinal. Does that not then simply fix episcopal ordination among the Catholic continuities, and preclude further discussion? Hardly so. For the reformers not only failed to write the doctrinal necessity of episcopal ordination into the Thirty-Nine Articles (or the Ordinal itself) – they showed clearly by the Christian company they kept, and the writings they published, that they viewed the form of orders and ordination as in principle negotiable and open. The very Ordinal from which this one phrase in the Preface has often been asked to carry such weight is itself, throughout its liturgical contents, radically rewritten compared with the Sarum rites, and exhibits a highly reformed understanding of the nature of ministry, with a prime emphasis upon 'the Word' and with the sacraments seen as underlining and reinforcing that prime ministry. No, a blanket citation of 'continuity' does not settle the issue.

A deeper probing is needed. The continuity of ministerial orders may or may not be as important as other matters already cited, but, because of the ink (and sometimes blood) which has been spilled over the issue, it requires more space to discuss.

In part the continuity was to be seen in the retention of the actual bishops (though at the accession of Elizabeth this was more to be seen in the parallel Church of Ireland than in the Church of England), and of cathedrals, deans, convocations, and many many other features of institutional church life built around the notion of 'orders'. This we have seen above. But now we have to look at not just that retention but also the continuing 'succession' of bishops. The Preface to the Ordinal (in 1550 and 1552, just as much as in 1662) declared that the purpose of the ordination rites was that 'these orders' should be 'continued', and thus indicated that such an episcopal framework to a threefold order of ministry was still to be integral to the character of the Church of England, however much both Church and episcopate might be reformed. The existence of this firm framework of episcopal ordination, which was actually strengthened in 1662, has particularly seemed the guarantee to Anglican Catholics that the Church of England continued as the Catholic Church of this land – with true bishops, true priests, true sacraments, and at least an adequate doctrinal basis.

This retention by the Church of England of episcopacy raises several further questions. While the Reformers did not unchurch continental Protestants who lacked what later Anglicans have come to call the 'historic episcopate', they obviously not only defended the propriety of episcopal succession and episcopal consecration and ordination, but also took considerable care over the matter – as is well known in the case of the consecration of Matthew Parker. They did not think in wholly mechanical terms about this, nor in the terms to which the twentieth century has become more accustomed; for on the one hand Jewel (as noted earlier) claims to be in the episcopal succession because he is the lawful Bishop of Salisbury in true sequence (rather than because he names the pedigree of the bishops who laid hands on him), and on the other hand the claim of Elizabethan bishops to be true bishops sprang as much from the decree of the monarch as it did from episcopal consecration. Indeed, if we were to ask how Parker could ever be viewed as organically in sequence to Pole, the answer would have to take the tortuous legal form that the Crown had nominated him, the Dean and Chapter of Canterbury had elected him in accordance with the fearsome provisions of the 1533 Act, and the four bishops mandated by the monarch had duly laid hands on him. The monarch spoke for the Church of England (all that was also included in the Royal Supremacy); therefore the Church of England had chosen and appointed its chief pastor – it was by this very fact a truly churchly act! Any criticism lying against this 'Crown = supreme-authority = supreme-authority-over-the-Church' equation (which might be shortened to 'Crown's actions = Church's actions'!) would certainly undercut the Act of Supremacy of 1534 just as much as it would undercut the actions of Elizabeth. Anglican critics must therefore watch lest they cut the ground from under their own feet – and Roman Catholic critics must realise both that at times their own Church has equally swayed unresistingly to imperial winds and also that Anglicans, while acknowledging the defensibility of such a stance in Tudor times (as the Pope himself would have had to acknowledge it in earlier times), do not erect this particular principle into divine revelation, and are free both to criticise it as a principle and also to live in total independence of it today, as most Anglicans on the world's surface in fact do. We return to this consideration later.

Nevertheless, there was great care taken not just to have legally respectable occupants of posts appointed by the Crown, but also to provide due episcopal consecration or ordination, and, although it was argued by Cranmer that in an emergency a godly prince could create bishops *ex nihilo* (so to speak), it appears that there was no intention or expectation of ever following out such a bizarre debating point with action.

Two other factors bear upon this. First, we recall that the Reformation was implemented in England by power politics, led in large part by bishops and archbishops, and thus, even had they willed it (which we do not suppose), they could not, by definition, impugn their own ordination – or their very power to act would have disappeared with it. As opportunists (and they were certainly that) they were inhibited by this very givenness of their own office and orders from an over-radical critique of inherited patterns. They could not begin by cutting off the branch on which they were sitting and still then be able to cut anything else.

Second, it must be recalled that by Elizabeth's reign five bishops had paid for the Reformation with their lives – and were being immortalised in Foxe's *Book of Martyrs*. While there were those who wanted a further root-and-branch reformation, there was also a reverence for actual bishops, the romance of whose death now helped to conserve the office they had held.

None of this means that the Tudor reformed bishops, or even the Elizabethan formularies, taught as necessary to the Christian faith or as of the essence of the Church of Christ, the exclusive claims for the 'historic episcopate' which marked, say, the teaching of the *Tracts for the Times* in the 1830s, or the opposition to the Church of South India in the 1940s. These exclusive claims were simply not there.[12] But there *was* conserved a structure of orders which was held the more rigidly in the seventeenth century because of shrill opposition to it on the one hand, and the apparent necessity of it on the other hand, not to the being of the Church directly, but as the foundation of the *monarchy*, without which the Church, as Anglicans then knew it, was unimaginable. Indeed Charles I died for episcopacy, not so much out of theological conviction about orders as from a certainty that the divine right of kings and the actual powers of the monarchy could not be sustained on any other ecclesiastical/political basis. And the conserving of the structure meant that, when 'higher' theological claims were being made in later centuries, the framework to contain them existed and they fitted into it easily. A close study of the 1662 Ordinal, both in what it says and in what it does not say, is instructive about this.

It is at least arguable that Anglicans have made much of the 'historicity' element, and have justified their orders on so-called 'Augustinian' grounds, partly because they have understood those to be the grounds on which any justification towards Rome had to be made. But it is probable that in the safeguarding of the actual consecration of bishops on the one hand, and the working up of the doctrinal significance of this on the other, Anglicans have failed to make sufficient use of a practice which has developed so generally (with only infrequent and tiny exceptions) as to have become virtually a basic principle. Bishops are only consecrated for a specific ministry in a specified diocese. The Anglican Communion conceives of the episcopate not just in corporate terms, nor just in sacramental or symbolic terms, but in a highly functional and actively pastoral role fulfilled by individual bishops towards identifiable flocks. The 'flocks', following the scriptural and Catholic principle we noted at the outset of this essay, are defined in purely geographical terms; a particular church within the whole Catholic Church is only a church of a particular *place*. And, we may note, the original 'place' of a particular church is a 'city'. This is visible (even without discernible latter-day bishops) in the role of the church in cities in the New Testament, and it is developed in conjunction with early monepiscopacy in immediately post-apostolic literature. Anglicanism has preserved this pattern, with the cities serving the flocks of the surrounding countryside.

The only variant on this worth noting has been the occasional (and very 'apostolic') consecration of a 'missionary' bishop, where his area of operation is carefully specified, and he is expected to minister the gospel there, while there are, at the time of his consecration, few or no Christians to be his 'flock'. If today there exist retired bishops, or, occasionally, bishops called to tasks other than oversight in a diocese, it is certain that they began their episcopal ministry in a diocesan role, and could not have been consecrated on any other basis.[13]

THE DEVELOPING IDENTITY

1   Further Entails of the Reformation Period

It is axiomatic that any distinctive features of Anglicanism are likely to have their roots in the changes of the Reformation period – though, of course, tremendous adaptations, alterations and innovations upon the Elizabethan Settlement have led to the Anglicanism we know today. No account of identity can ignore these 'distinctive' features, and all attempts to live with our own history, such as we recommend above, involve making *something* of the following such matters.

(a) Self-government   If the crucial point in separation

from Rome was the assertion that a 'particular or national' Church (see Article XXXIV) had the right and power to make its own decisions, so this point has continued within first of all the Church of England, and more latterly in worldwide Anglicanism. We doubt whether anyone can demonstrate from Scripture that the appropriate unit for legislative decision-taking is an autonomous 'national' church (though the Reformers certainly acted and wrote as though they had so demonstrated it). But, once the concept of a diocese is conceded, groupings of dioceses into provinces (or even patriarchates) are at least sensible, and have some correspondence with patristic precedent and Eastern Orthodox practice.[14] On the other hand, the famous 'Tulsa affair' (corresponding in odd ways with the Colenso affair which sparked off the first Lambeth Conference in 1867) has demonstrated the weakness of a fabric of undefined 'family' co-operation for worldwide Anglicanism, without organs of intervention or international decision-taking.

For the sake of clear discussion and etching the matter by contrast, we note that the Roman Catholic Church has in post-Vatican II days been groping towards a greater 'national' independence in its Bishops' Conferences, especially with regard to the kind of considerations listed in Article XXXIV. But we do not anticipate the reduction of the papacy to be simply a federal office, or the guardian of solely a primacy of honour. We recognise that ARCIC, for all its reductions in the role of the universal primate, would still leave him in a position to 'intervene' in any diocese in the world – and we are unsure whether this is not too high a price to pay to avoid a further Tulsa, as well as being unsure whether it would in fact avoid it![15]

(b) *Doctrine*   There were doctrinal changes at the Reformation, and considerable shifts of emphasis. In earlier paragraphs we have discussed different ways in which these may be seen. It may be helpful here to consider the *status* of the Reformation formularies, as it is this which has often been in debate between Anglican Catholics and Evangelicals – certainly as much as has the *meaning* of them.

Evangelicals have been accustomed (at least until very recently) to view the Thirty-Nine Articles as a confessional *basis* to the Church of England – and indeed to lamenting the disappearance, or downgrading, of that basis in other Anglican Churches. Other Anglicans have often seen the Creeds alone (and often only two Creeds) as that basis. Creeds, however, have been agreed: and Articles sometimes have not. Latterly, in the Church of England itself, the new Declaration of Assent treats the Articles as a sixteenth-century (and thus historically conditioned) confessional 'witness'. This, we judge, is acceptable as providing a formula by which we in the late twentieth century can both affirm the formative role that the Elizabethan formularies have played in Anglicanism, and yet leave ourselves some freedom in relation to the jots and tittles of the formulation. But this is probably inadequate, as a matter of history, as a key, for instance, to understanding the role which the Articles originally fulfilled.

'Basis' will not quite do, because such a concept suggests that a new Church, or at least a drastically altered Church, came into being when the basis was adopted. But this was not the case. The Elizabethan Church went its reformed way for many years before the Articles were adopted or subscription imposed. The continuity of the *people* who confess the faith is logically prior to their confession and this logical sequence was clearly worked through in the Anglican Reformation. Similarly, if we follow through the building metaphor, a 'basis' cannot be changed without the destruction of that which is built on it – and so Evangelicals have tended in the past to view the role of the Articles. But if 'basis' will not do, will 'witness'? We read the sixteenth century as indicating that if 'basis' is too strong and rigid a word, 'witness' is too weak. The formularies had a role which was that of a *stabiliser* or *corrective*.

If we may continue the imagery of a building, then, it looks as though the role of the Elizabethan formularies was to act as a buttress to support that which was solidly built on Scripture, Creeds, etc, but gained in stability by the additional support. A buttress might, if we pursue the imagery to the limit, be more needed at one time than at another, according to pressures upon the building; and thus we may say that, provided the Anglican Churches understand the relationship between Scripture and tradition aright, formularies over and above the Creeds may be deployed, changed or withdrawn as particular Churches see fit. If any other Church takes the view that such formularies breach the common faith (as happened over Quarto-Decimanism in the second century, and has now happened among Anglicans over the ordination of women in the twentieth), then there is no big stick which can be waved, no given formulary over and above Scripture which can decide the matter or even determine whether the matter is large or small – and conferencing, mutual love and prayer are the only clear procedures open for resolving the issue.

It should perhaps be noted that the developed ethos of Anglicanism has included an element of cool intellectualism. The lack of imposed limits to speculation has encouraged a spirit of enquiry, study and sometimes of academic frontiers-manship. There has been an atmosphere of inductive approach to issues. There has been a shrinking from heresy trials or too close an enquiry into how individuals framed the Christian faith for their own personal spirituality. There have never been anathemas. And thus it is not surprising that there has existed a 'liberal' ethos in Church life. This, however, should not lightly be erected into a formal principle, let alone a prescriptive one. Even less should the necessity of open debate and unafraid mutual encounter be erected into a charter for Christian teachers and pastors publicly to deny the very essentials of the faith. The 'liberalism' of Anglicanism consists, as we see it, not in encouraging deviations from historic Christianity to flourish, but in a *style* which hesitates long before bringing punitive rigour to bear upon deviations when they do arise. While this can look very close to conniving at error, we judge that it is formally distinguishable from it, and is far preferable to regular recourse to heresy trials or the banning of particular persons from teaching.

In general, at the present time, the Anglican Churches can reckon the future lies with orthodoxy and can thus encourage themselves to cling tightly to revealed truth on the one hand, and yet give very long ropes to individuals who want to stray from the centre on the other. 'Liberalism' should be viewed not as a doctrinal position, but as a reasonably patient and even pastoral ethos. It is the doctrinal outworking of

'Let both grow together till harvest' – a text in which the spokesman of the maxim was far from indifferentist, or unclear as to what was true and what was false.

(c) Liturgy The Church of England may have split formally from Rome in Henry's reign, but the Latin Mass and other rites continued in the parish churches at that stage with only infinitesimal alteration. The changes the layman would have noticed came at the second stage in Edward's reign: the use of the vernacular, the restoration of the cup, the prohibition of a Eucharist unless there were communicants (usually there were not), the reordering of church interiors, the restriction of music, and the sweeping simplification of ceremonial. The wording of the English Prayer Books was both a translation from earlier sources (and therefore in some formal continuity, as we noted above, with the tradition of liturgy), and also brilliantly innovatory as Cranmer forged a whole liturgical language, virtually single-handed and in a matter of months, and poured into its mould an understanding of Scripture which related closely to the work of the Swiss Reformers. It is of purely historical interest whether Cranmer's liturgy should be dubbed 'popish' (as the Puritans tended to call it), or 'Zwinglian' (as Gregory Dix lampooned it). As with the Articles, the character of living Anglicanism has moved on, and the 1662 book, which was thought (perhaps by wishful thinking) to be a common bond of the Anglican Communion as late as the 1948 Lambeth Conference, is now to be found among the museum pieces in many parts of the Communion. Revision has occurred, often on a one-province-only basis, through pressures of Catholic churchmanship (Evangelicals were usually happy with 1662, even for the middle of Africa), through the fascination of modern liturgical scholarship, through changes elsewhere (notably Rome), through a modernisation of liturgical English, through a provision of greater choice and flexibility, and for other doctrinal, pastoral and occasionally constitutional reasons.

It has to be confessed (or perhaps boasted) that there remains very little that is *distinctively* Anglican about the resultant liturgical materials. Alongside the apparently centrifugal forces encouraging each province to produce its own forms, there has been an ecumenical convergence on the one hand, and a worldwide Anglican conservatism on the other, which has meant that Anglican liturgical texts look much like each other and not far distant from those of, say, Roman Catholicism or Lutheranism or Presbyterianism. There are, of course, some remaining *doctrinal* differences. But these, though important, usually occupy only a tiny proportion of the total liturgical material, and they do not affect the question of general similarity mentioned above.

The provincial independence which might in theory have led to *very* distinctive rites – that is, by liturgical indigenisation – has never in fact worked that way. The Anglo-Saxon parts of the Communion have had both the scholarship, the resources and the will to provide new texts – and have produced Anglo-Saxon ones, which the rest of the Communion has then tended to follow. Yet provincial autonomy *is* autonomy, and much scope for creative liturgical work in the 'Two-Thirds World' clearly exists. (One problem built into this is that, because the Church of England engineered its Reformation partly by imposing liturgical changes, there is a strong idea around that liturgical forms must be 'authorised' from the top downwards, rather than grow from ground-level as truly indigenous liturgy would more usually do – a point which can be illustrated in the Anglo-Saxon world by comparing the enormous current diversity of songs and music with the relative uniformity of eucharistic prayers, etc.) While there may be risks to Anglican cohesiveness if different provinces, dioceses and parishes go their own way liturgically, yet we must shout from the housetops that the Anglican Communion is currently facing other far greater dangers of disintegration than this move could possibly entail, that each Province is genuinely free to obey God as it sees fit, and that pastorally enculturation of the liturgy is health-giving for the building up of the faithful, as well as for removing stumbling-blocks in the path of enquirers and seekers. At least we offer our shout here.

How do Catholics and Evangelicals stand in relation to this? Once it is accepted that neither party is going to use liturgical texts to 'un-church' the other, then the quest is on for forms of worship which are unitive, which promote their worshipping together, which foster theological debate and clarify (and narrow) true issues dividing them. At intervals such texts have to be restrained in what they officially authorise, but this procedure chimes in very well with the 'open' structure of much modern liturgy and is neither forced nor artificial. It is, however, important that the theological dialogue does go on behind the formulation of texts, and our predecessor, *Growing into Union*, and the ARCIC Statement on the Eucharist, as well as other essays in the present volume, are good examples of these. Such debate should, if possible, be closely related to actual liturgical texts and their revision – an activity which is natural on a Liturgical Commission, but less natural in an ecumenical dialogue.

At one point where it looked in Cranmer's lifetime as though he had failed, the passage of centuries has led to his triumph. We refer to the whole pattern of sacramental life that revolves around a weekly communion at which the faithful receive. Indeed, in parts of the Anglican Communion where young children receive communion, Cranmer has obtained more than he bargained for! For centuries the Church of England was simultaneously clericalist and largely non-sacramentalist. In the nineteenth century there was a revival of sacramentalism – all too much of a revival in the eyes of some. This has so far permeated the structures of worship and the spirituality of lay people that it is no great stretching of the truth to say that Anglicanism is now everywhere in principle sacramentalist, though in many places the sacrament can only be celebrated once a month or even less often.[16]

(d) Comprehensiveness   In one sense, so-called 'comprehensiveness' is not so much another category in sequence with those set out above, but is simply the product of them. Where the Church genuinely sees people as logically prior to their confession, where it disavows punitive steps against frontiersmanship, where it is characterised by a somewhat imprecise liturgical style (albeit in association with a robust confession of a scriptural faith) – in such a Church different expressions of Christianity may flourish alongside each other (which other things being equal, we view as gain), and yet – for it is sadly true – they may also fail to engage in serious encounter with each other's theology and spirituality (and that detracts

immediately from any gain). Thus there appears to be something slightly more to our ecclesiology than a *de facto* comprehensiveness, though even of that many would make a virtue.

The case for it rests in part upon the undesirability of the alternatives available – usually a church life-style with an element of coerciveness or judgmentality built in. We ourselves would judge that a case which simply tries to make respectable the inevitable (without assessing it on its merits) is almost certainly inadequate; rather, the case can only be conscientiously sustained if the existing liberty of interpretation is conjoined with an eschatological quest for a purer statement of the faith, and a convergence of differing ecclesial life styles into that which will distinctively characterise the church of the end-time. 'Positive' comprehensiveness is nothing like ecclesiastical *laissez-faire*: rather it is a charter for dynamic interaction with all the participants ready to go where the arguments take them. And, while it admits faults and inadequacies on every side, it is wholly compatible with deep conviction and with refusal to acknowledge that all points of view are equally valid. And the role given to Scripture in the Anglican understanding provides the basis for the interaction, the agenda for the argument, and the promise of the power of God for actually 'going where it takes them'.

(e) Church and State The English nation was the English Church long before the Reformation, and 'Ecclesia Anglicana' occurs as a phrase both before and in Magna Carta. Both before and after the Reformation there was no question but that all English people 'belonged' to the parish church, and were all supposed to be there (and nowhere else) on Sundays. The only point of difference about the role of the state related not to numbers, but to powers. Whereas before the Reformation the state (usually embodied in the monarch) was in theory autonomous in most respects, in the ecclesiastical sphere (and particularly in the role of clergy and monks) appeals could be made to Rome, and ultimate loyalty lay there. After the Reformation, no doubt on this issue could be allowed to remain – the supremacy of the national government was as supreme in matters ecclesiastical as in any other matters. In theory the new consistency of powers in government made for homogeneity and unity in the nation – in fact

the religious divisiveness of the rising Puritan movement in Elizabeth's reign meant that the theory was never realised.

And yet the 'establishment' of the Church of England lasts to the present day in England. It is much reduced, much disinfected, somewhat crippled and certainly without prospect of survival – but, like an iceberg which has drifted into warm seas, though it is slowly disappearing it is still *there* – and there in great strength. What are we to make of it?

Clearly it cannot now be defended as the people of England governing their religious life through their elected Parliamentary representatives, that is (on the Tudor theory) through those laity best qualified to speak and legislate for them in religious matters as in everything else – indeed in religious matters as *part* of everything else. Some other more latter-day rationale now has to be invented, perhaps in the form of a specific trusteeship the nation is deemed to hold by divine providence for keeping the light of the gospel alive in society. But a secular, and religiously pluriform, state is inherently unlikely to sense that trusteeship, and it is no matter for surprise that the state organs at intervals view the Church of England as a form of punchball rather than as an opportunity for parliamentary trusteeship for Christianity.

The matter is brought into proportion by a world view. 'Anglicanism' worldwide can in no sense involve a state connection as part of its basic ecclesiology or doctrinal self-definition. Where the English state once helped to export the Church of England to the rest of the world, that sending agency has long since ceased to operate in that way, and Anglicanism has had to learn to live in the constitutional form of a voluntary society set in the midst of secular or religiously pluriform states. The message is slowly touching England itself also. Establishment as it remains is now an accident of history from which most parts of the Anglican Communion are free, and in England itself it is not an entrenched doctrinal necessity, but rather among the doctrinally negotiable.

(f) A Theology of the Kingdom While the constitutional embedding of the Anglican Churches in the machinery of state has finished its course in virtually all the world, save in England where it is on its last lap, yet a very significant run-on from the past of the Church of England is to be found in

Anglicanism almost everywhere. This is a true concern for society, for the health of society, for society as created to reflect the image of God, and for the permeation of this world with the prophetic Word of God's righteousness. Sometimes this sounds as though it has lapsed into a moralistic message; sometimes it sounds as though it is mere bleating into hostile winds; sometimes it is an excuse for condemning ills in other countries while ignoring what is under the noses of the condemners; and sometimes it sounds as though it has been twisted into a thisworldly political or even revolutionary bias. But, these aberrations apart, underneath is that godly concern which stems from the time when Church and society were one people, and the trusteeship of the Church was to yield the whole of society (and its public life as well as its private) into the hands of God, and to work out his will in that society. There is an eschatological touch here also – whether enunciated or not, it is the kingdom of God, greater in every way than the visible Church of each age, which is being heralded and even partially experienced as the Church fulfils its calling. There are no formularies of Anglicanism to give expression or authority to this stance – it is simply a general characteristic of a form of Christianity which has traditionally been both firm in doctrine yet inclusivist in policy.

2   Toleration in England

In England the inherited 'Christendom' concept survived the Reformation virtually unscathed. Anglican confrontations with at one time Romanism and at another Puritanism were all about which one colour English Christian society should wear – and not about whether it could be multicoloured, or even uncoloured. Thus when the Restoration saw the triumphal (and vengeful) re-establishment of Anglicanism as the religious face of the nation, nothing in the formularies gave any positive place to other forms of Christianity, and the assumption of the 1662 Act of Uniformity was that the nation would be reduced to conformity. When this proved not to be the case, then penal laws were enacted against nonconformists. And the Christendom concept finally collapsed when the excesses of James II's Romanism led to Anglicans and nonconformists making common cause on a broad constitutional platform of tolerance.

The change of theory was accompanied (whether coincidentally or not) by a parallel change of practice. A nation which had been largely church-going in Charles II's reign fell into Arianism, apathy and apostasy by George II's. Nonconforming Puritanism, which had generated Baxter and Bunyan in its time, lapsed as badly as the established Church. The subsequent Evangelical Revival and the birth of Methodism led to a different pattern of nonconformity, and the Church of England, while still basking in its riches and its privileges, had to acknowledge lively dissenting-houses set alongside it and in active competition with it for the soul of England. It must be recalled that it was not episcopacy that the average Free Churchman was rejecting – it was the actual parish church of his village or hamlet – whether its incumbent, its snobbery, its pew rents, its deadness, or its mores.

This was the collapse of the underlying theory of the Anglican parish church – that it provided within clear boundaries a uniting of all Christian people into one Church fellowship. There was an end now of a vicar's task to reconcile warring partners. There was an end now of any discipline through excommunication. There was an end now to the monopoly of the parish church. And there arose a need of justification for the complex multiplicity of assemblies and conventicles which occupied the ground. They themselves operated on a wholly voluntarist principle, and in the last analysis had either to denounce all previously organised forms of Christianity (as did the Brethren Movement), or alternatively to make some kind of a virtue of the opportunity of choice (as Methodism tended to do). Anglicanism never came to terms with this, and nonconformity was regularly cold-shouldered by the Church of England.

The point is made not to emphasise the superiority of any Anglican practice, nor to vaunt the desirability of being established (on which we have grave doubts), nor to blame those who struggled to make sense of the religious scene two hundred or one hundred years ago. No, the point is solely that, if the unity of the people of God is to be taken seriously as needing expression on earth, then everywhere (as far as

England is concerned) the Church of England must strive to find ways which do not necessarily justify our pasts, but in healthy ways unite our futures. Our doctrine of the Church commits us to the eschatological quest, and we live uneasily with the present sundering, while seeking both local and supra-local ways of transcending the divisions. This is basic to the argument of the next paragraph.

3 Spread of Worldwide Anglicanism

'Anglicanism' as an ethos, rather than as a geographically distinguishing title, must trace its origins to 1689 also. In that year a semi-underground Episcopal Church took its beginning in Scotland, as a community evicted from the parish churches by force, by covenanters, by opportunists, by Presbyterians, and by non-juring scruple. What had for a hundred years been a struggle for possession of the parish churches (with virtually no weapons barred) was finally settled through the unanimous refusal of the Bench of Scottish bishops to swear allegiance to William and Mary. This thus became old-fashioned episcopacy – closely allied (as in England at the time of the Civil War) to the divine right of kings, though in this case to kings whom others dubbed 'Pretenders'. Naturally such an Episcopal Church was not only not established, it was virtually a rebellion! And thus in due time it was the natural source of episcopal consecration when another rebellion – the American – equally rejecting of Hanoverian monarchs, needed Samuel Seabury to receive such consecration to the episcopate ninety-five years later. But, although the line came from Scotland, this was new episcopacy – Seabury was being elected by a young and war-torn Church to be actual chief pastor of disestablished, but wholly above-ground, congregations in Puritan Connecticut. A new pattern of Anglicanism was being born.

From Seabury's time to today, Anglicanism has spread across the earth's surface, with plenty of hot gospel, plenty of pioneer spirit, plenty of actual success – but perhaps a slight dearth of ecclesiological rationale. The national Church of the land of England turned itself into a worldwide Communion without internal debate, self-conscious reflection, or change of admitted goals. Thus the apologist for Anglicanism is set a puzzle. We may note the developed Communion's thirty independent Provinces, its participation in schemes for united episcopal churches in the Indian subcontinent, its more recent creation of a federal body, the Anglican Consultative Council, and the existence since 1867 of a tradition of Lambeth Conferences (of no constitutional force whatsoever, and yet of considerable weight). Our concern here is not so much for description as for ecclesiological analysis – and our view of *that* task is to recognise it as uniquely difficult!

In the early days of the Oxford Movement, William Palmer put forward the so-called 'branch' theory of the Christian Church. On this theory only episcopal Churches were to be viewed as Churches at all, and those had split into three 'branches': the Eastern, the Roman Catholic, and the Anglican. The theory naturally assigned the earth's territory to the various branches, and each in its own territory could properly claim to be *the* Catholic Church – the Eastern Orthodox in Eastern Europe, the Roman in Western Europe, and perhaps in South America, and the Anglican in the Anglo-Saxon world. This theory (which in time led to Newman's stumbling at the proposal to create a quasi-Anglican bishopric in Jerusalem) preserved both episcopalianism *and* the geographical basis for naming parts of the Church of Christ, but at what cost! The Catholic Church in Calais became the Italian Schism in Dover, and the anomalies ran on from there.

Notably, neither of the other two 'branches' was ready to function on the basis suggested in England (and probably unknown to them, and certainly quite contrary to their own principles). For, after all, there was also a primitive concept of the whole Church being in communion with itself, which the branch theory abandoned. Nevertheless, many Anglicans have held on to the principle behind it, so that South America was viewed for a century as an illegitimate field for Anglican endeavours, and the continent of Europe is still viewed somewhat in that light. Furthermore, there has been a slightly absurd (or perhaps merely paradoxical) quest to find anywhere on the earth's surface episcopalians separate from Rome with whom, and with whom alone, Anglicans could enter full Communion. Thus the Spanish Reformed Episcopal

Church and its sister in Portugal, the Lusitanian Church, the Old Catholics, the Mar Thoma Church in India, the Philippine Independent Church, the Swedish Lutheran Church, and a sprinkling of others have come up for 'full communion' at various stages in recent history. The branch theory is forgotten, and the quest for episcopalians has been pursued virtually without reference to the specific question as to whether or not any particular exponents of historic episcopacy might be viewed as in schism from Rome, or as occupying territory which ought in principle to be viewed as Roman Catholic! Principles of recognition have rather overtaken each other. The proposal to create 'parallel episcopates' in England in the unity schemes of the 60s, 70s, and early 80s, became another variant on this.

Worldwide Anglicanism has thus far evinced evangelistic, missionary and even fraternal instincts, unbounded by any doctrinnaire approach to the meaning of 'Catholicity' in a sundered world Church. And yet this family of Churches has never been prepared to yield to mere individualistic choice, or to allow that any number of denominations could cheerfully and acceptably occupy the same ground and all be recognised as full and complete Churches or congregations in happy competition with each other. Somewhere at the heart of Anglicanism has remained this much-clouded but no less present principle of Catholic action – that in essence, in a divided Church, we hold a specific trusteeship for finding our way back to a territorial description of the Christians in each place, holding responsibility for their area and for the proclamation of the gospel and the serving of the community in the name of Christ in that area. If it is incompletely exhibited, or not fully understood, yet the principle exists (behind its cloud) and we long to see it better manifested. An Anglicanism which has no concern for this has little attraction for us, and little consistency with itself.

4 Discovery of the Layperson

The Reformers were profoundly aware of the need to recover the idea of the *whole* Church, uniting laity and clergy on an equal spiritual footing within one fellowship, though without confusing the particular functions of the ordained minister. They disliked a sacerdotal concept of priesthood (for all that they retained the ambiguous word 'priest', and even, occasionally, *sacerdos*). If they had not directly instigated the Dissolution of the Monasteries, then at least that chimed in well with their conviction that there was but one 'religious' life, and that the religious life of the whole people of God. They disallowed celebrations of the Lord's Supper unless there was a communicating congregation. They cast the liturgy into the vernacular. They removed all constraints upon the free access of the literate laity to the Scriptures. They did their best to rescue the daily office from its monastic influence, and restore it to the parson and the parishioner together. All this bore witness to their determination to retrieve the Church for the *plebs sancta dei* – the 'holy common people of God'.

In the view of the Church's Puritan critics, this laudable programme was fatally hampered by the equal determination of both Crown and bishops to impose limits upon the freedom of Christian people to meet for Christian purposes outside the formal worship of the parish church; to ban preaching or celebrating in private houses; and to exclude from the liturgy any words other than those closely prescribed by the rubrics. The English Reformation, as we have seen, was imposed from above; and the state deemed that the expression of religion required tight control. The laity of England partly rebelled; mostly acquiesced; but they had not initiated the Reformation and the results were predictable. They were as reluctant as they had ever been before the Reformation to receive the holy communion with any frequency; and the result of the Reformation was that frequent non-communicating celebrations simply gave way to infrequent communicating ones, and the liturgy of word and prayers became the unlooked-for staple diet of Anglican worship for generations. While individual laymen or women might be given to great piety, just as before the Reformation, the bulk of the laity conformed, attended and were devout or otherwise just so far as they felt moved. All of which is to say that the parochial system which gave certain rights and responsibilities to certain laymen (patrons, wardens, sidesmen, clerks, vergers, sextons and schoolmasters), but which left the spiritual cure of souls exclusively in the hands of the solitary parson – survived the Reformation unscathed.

None of this prevented the laity of England from exercising a greater or less degree of Christian influence in the secular sphere. The glittering example of a group of lay churchmen altering the course of history by the strength of their Christian convictions must be the so-called 'Clapham Sect'. Their inspiration was Evangelical. The towering example of a solitary statesman impressing the stamp of his Christian conscience upon the policy of government must be that of Gladstone. His inspiration was Tractarian. But there had been village Gladstones and mute inglorious Wilberforces for generations, moved by their Christian faith to do justly and to love mercy and to walk humbly with their God.

The recognition, however, that the Christian layperson could be called of God not only to exercise a Christian ministry within the world, but also to exercise a Christian ministry within the Church, has dawned far more slowly. It might be argued that parishes of both Catholic and Evangelical tradition have afforded more opportunity, and taught more thoroughly the need for lay participation in the Church's ministry and worship. But it must be true that it is the younger Provinces of the Anglican Communion, relatively bereft of ordained ministers, which have developed the ministry of laypeople – of missionaries and evangelists, of readers and catechists – far more thoroughly and effectively than the older and inevitably more clerically dominated Churches.

A similar slow dawning of the role of the laypeople in church government has also occurred. Apart from the ancient office of churchwardens (and the extraordinary and random role of lay patrons, the relics of which still survive in England), the layperson had no place in the government of the Anglican parish or diocese till long after the Reformation. The first reforms came with the constituting of the American General Convention and its diocesan and parish counterparts in the late eighteenth century – with many formal parallels to the creation of the American Constitution itself. The slow development of autonomous Provinces in other parts of the world, with synodical structures for self-government, led in turn in the nineteenth century to the formal entrenching in many places of the duties and powers of laypeople to share with bishops and clergy in decision-taking for the Church. The Church of Ireland, in its post-disestablishment steps of 1870–1, set a good precedent in this respect, and virtually all other parts of the Communion have followed America and Ireland since – with the Church of England bringing up the rear in 1970, and the Anglican Consultative Council, first formed in 1971, putting the capstone on a principle which is now universal in Anglicanism.

We write of this not to labour the bureaucratic side of the Church's institutional life today, but rather to draw attention to a different implication. The organs of Church government are *representative*. That is, they relate to the whole worshipping people whom they represent. If the mission of the Church is to be pursued and sustained by the whole people of God, which we earnestly advocate, then the policy-making and direction-setting must stem from true representation of that *whole* people of God. Only the constitutional affirmation of the layperson in the decision-taking will truly lead to liberating and equipping of the layperson for that mission in the world, on behalf of Christ and his Church, to which the man and woman of God are called. The point has been dimly discerned by Anglicans, however imperfectly expressed so far. We believe it to be now fundamental to our 'identity'.

5 Spirituality

Connected with both doctrine and liturgy, and nourished by both, is what may conveniently be called spirituality, by which we mean the living prayer-life of Anglicanism, over and above the texts of official liturgy. The influence of liturgy upon spirituality has been both negative and positive. Given the powerful and cohesive effect of the Book of Common Prayer upon the Anglican Communion for so long, it was inevitable that all other expressions of piety or devotion would be formed and judged by that. The Prayer Book set a standard of Catholic prayer, deeply rooted in tradition yet freely reformed and clothed in exquisite English. The principal offshoot of this has undoubtedly been hymnody. Given the absence of virtually any metrical hymns in the Prayer Book, due mainly to Cranmer's confessed inability to write verse, hymnody offered unlimited possibilities to enrich the liturgy and remedy the excessive rigidity and monotony of the Prayer Book. Hymns could mark the feasts and seasons; they could express more exultant thanksgiving and adoration; and they could voice a more personal and reflective piety. For the Tractarians, the translation of ancient hymns provided a further valuable link with the Church of the early centuries. Names that would be great in the history of the Anglican Church, even if they had written no hymns at all, such as Herbert and Ken, Heber and Keble, must be chiefly familiar to most Anglicans because their hymns are still sung.

Many of our great hymns, however, were written by those whose main poetic works were meant for reading rather than singing. George Herbert's hymns are but a tiny part of his whole poetic corpus. Others, like William Cowper, were not principally writers of *religious* poetry at all; and other writers of religious poetry, such as John Donne and T. S. Eliot, wrote no hymns. The point here is not that there is such a thing as 'Anglican poetry', or even that Anglicans have made a significant contribution to English religious poetry; but that there is in Anglican spirituality a poetic sensibility, that Anglican hymnody is a small part of a wider poetic English tradition; and that poetry is both characteristic of and congruous with Anglican spirituality.

A further way in which the Prayer Book has been supplemented has been in the writing of prayers, and the recovery of other ancient prayers of Christian tradition. Here we think of Lancelot Andrewes, William Laud, Jeremy Taylor, and others of the seventeenth century; among the Nonjurors especially we find an increasing fascination for the liturgy and piety of Eastern Churches. As well as books of prayers, there have been great books *about* prayer. The classics in this field are, to use a convenient distinction, more ascetical than mystical. Prayer and practice go together; duty is never far from devotion. We think of Taylor's *Holy Living* and *Holy Dying*; Traherne's *Centuries*; Law's *Serious Call*; and the uncertainly attributed *Whole Duty of Man*.

Finally, we note the practice of great men and women of

prayer down the centuries, though they may have left little or nothing in writing; perhaps most honourably of all, the family of Nicholas Ferrar with their lonely and extraordinary witness to all that was best in what had been swept away a century before in the Dissolution of the Monasteries; and precursor of the remarkable revival of religious orders within the Anglican Communion during the last century and this.

Pope Paul VI referred on a famous occasion to 'the worthy patrimony of piety and usage proper to the Anglican Church' which ought to be preserved in any future united Church. From an ecclesiological point of view, there can be no 'patrimony of piety' or 'usage', however worthy, which in itself justifies the separate existence of a particular Church or denomination; nor have we sought to justify the existence of Anglicanism on these grounds. Given, however, the justifiable existence of the Anglican Communion, it is then legitimate and indeed important to draw attention to valuable features of the Anglican inheritance. Its tradition of spirituality is a part of the 'identity of Anglicanism', and without it, the existence of the Anglican Communion would be the less worthy of serious defence.

On the other hand, we must guard against any suggestion that Anglicans should be restricted by the limits of their classical inheritance. If the classical tradition of prayer was more ascetic than mystical, that constitutes no everlasting ban on mystical theology for Anglicans. If the Charismatic Movement is a phenomenon practically without parallel in seventeenth-century Anglicanism, it is not thereby un-Anglican. But just as one expects the Benedictines to be the guardians of Benedictine spirituality for the whole Church, whatever other influences they are properly open to; and the Methodists to preserve the piety and discipline of the Wesleys, whatever new directions Methodism is called to follow; so it behoves the Anglican Communion, however many injections from other spiritual traditions it welcomes into its bloodstream, at least to cherish and be moulded by that tradition of prayer to which it has itself given birth. And by and large the Anglican record for bothering about Anglicanism is a poor one!

6 Ecumenical Movement

Our description of Anglicanism gives evidence that the Communion is simultaneously stating that it has *no* distinctive characteristics other than being part of the 'One Holy Catholic and Apostolic Church', and also that it has, almost by mistake, exhibited certain historical distinctiveness, doctrinal emphases and lifestyle ethos which characterise it over against the rest of worldwide Christianity. But its principle of a single eucharistic fellowship uniting 'all in one place', and giving expression to the New Testament teaching on variety in unity, means that it is a norm of Anglican thinking to seek organic unity with other Christian bodies. It is more than arguable that the eschatological orientation which we have endeavoured to portray through this essay is the key to actual progress. However, it has to be admitted that the Anglican Communion has proved better at asserting ecumenical principles than at following them, and better at self-defence than at self-liquidation in the actual maelstrom of ecumenical encounter. The concern for 'all in each place' has often sounded more like a concern for episcopal ordination (even where providing parallel episcopates), and the eschatological dimension has too often been exchanged for a more static covert judgment against other people's forms of Church life, even when couched in ecumenical politeness.

The paradox is the keener when it is asserted that the Anglican Communion fulfils a 'bridge' role – able to talk sensibly and credibly to both the Roman Catholics who are on one wing of us, and to the Protestant churches which occupy the other. But we should not kid ourselves – there is much straight talk now between, say Roman Catholics and Methodists, and they can properly take the view, as Ian Henderson once did, that Anglicans are insisting on sticking themselves in at points where they have no necessary role, and no street credibility.[17] However, the Lima document, *Baptism, Eucharist and Ministry*, does seem to go close to Anglican patterns of both sacramental life and 'threefold orders', and to pose questions to the world Church which, if it is ultimately answered positively by the denominations, would suggest there is scope for fruitful ecumenical dialogue initiated by Anglicans thereafter.

What is true is that Anglicanism can, in most parts of the world, take actual decisions on a national basis to unite with other autonomous Churches of the same territorial scope. Anglicans have actually done so in India, Pakistan, and Bangladesh, and have at intervals come very near to so doing in Nigeria, Sri Lanka and New Zealand. The 'Lambeth Quadrilateral' (first enunciated at a Lambeth Conference in 1888) was specifically oriented towards reunion, and was intended to provide minimum terms for opening discussions. And the ecclesiology we have set out summons true Anglicans not just to wrap a self-defensive cloak of denominational identity around themselves, but rather to expose themselves to the painful quest for ecumenical church life which is coming to be. And even if the hopes of success look small – as so often they do – that should not still deter us from a quest which is right in itself, and which should be pursued even if no fruitful ending can be envisaged.

7   Catholics and Evangelicals Together

We are not just a surprised pair of authors who were raked into partnership with each other by persuasive friends, but rather are ourselves convinced that hard dialogue is the key to discovering God's truth. That which we desire for Anglicanism in its public organs, we long for Anglicans in their informal relationships. Unless believers in Christ will keep company with those from whom they differ, put their formulations, yes, and their spirituality too, upon the table, and engage, listen, adapt, reform and renew themselves by conflict in the Spirit, then all our vaunted virtue of 'comprehensiveness' is claptrap, and all our ecumenical and missionary zeal is so much self-deceit.

NOTES

1 A. M. Ramsey, *The Gospel and the Catholic Church* (London, 1936), p. 220.
2 This is perhaps well brought out by the subtle change of history which

led to the term 'Anglican'. Until the mid-twelfth century, as far as we can see, the term used was *Ecclesia Anglorum* – 'the Church of the English people'. This well expressed the geographical concept. The change to '*Ecclesia Anglicana*' traced first to Pope Alexander III in 1165, was not meant to imply anything different, but followed the (much older) use of '*Gallicana*'. If anything, the change implied a stronger recognition of the 'national' rather than the provincial level of ecclesiastical organisation (though it coincided with a certain tightening of papal authority over each). For an English use of it, see Hubert Walter (Archbishop of Canterbury 1193–1205) who described *Ecclesia Anglicana* as *hanc occidentalis ecclesiae portionem quam in Anglia plantavit Altissimus* ('that portion of the Western Church which the Most High has planted in England'). The Reformers kept the same usage – cf. *Apologia Ecclesiae Anglicanae*, by John Jewel.

3 Monarchs, polity, and religion were closely interlocked in this period. Consequently the Royal Supremacy must be seen as a typical not an exceptional contemporary issue. On a contemporary understanding it should never have led to a permanent sundering, and indeed in Elizabeth's reign the papal excommunication was delayed for over a decade after 'the supreme governorship' had been declared.

4 Article VIII (*Of The Three Creeds*) lays down that the Creeds are to be believed because 'they may be proved by most certain warrants of holy Scripture' – which is marginally different from adherence either on the grounds of conciliar infallibility, or on the grounds of *quod ab omnibus, semper et ubique*. But this shift, important though it might be in the Reformation process, could hardly be viewed as adversely affecting the credal position of the Church of England.

5 It is worth noticing that Jewel relies more upon being lawfully installed in the bishopric of Salisbury than he does upon episcopal consecration – in other words, he has a somewhat Irenaean approach to the matter! (Jewel, *Works*, Parker Society, vol. iii, p. 339). On the other hand, the importance of Parker's consecration, and indeed the details of it, became a *cause célèbre*.

6 A Roman Catholic heckler asked an Anglican apologist at Speakers' Corner; 'Where was your Church before the Reformation?' and he answered, 'Where was your face before you washed it?'

7 The word 'protestant' had originally the neutral meaning of 'attestation'. In England it distinguished established churchmen from Papists and Puritans alike. The leaders of the Oxford Movement used it negatively and pejoratively of the continental reformers who were thus distinguished from English 'Catholic' reformers.

8 N.B. The *Growing Into Union* team went some way to an accord on the issue in 1970 (op.cit. pp. 69–70), and the ARCIC Statement on the Eucharist also works at an accord. But in the Reformation era Articles XXV–XXIX were drafted to make a confrontational and Protestant statement on the matter.

9 These original reformers might well be called 'Evangelicals' according to later definition, and even at the time sometimes were.

10 Particular credal formulations are viewed with hindsight by the Church of England as scriptural, and consequently orthodox. E.g. 'And when they [General Councils] be gathered together . . . they may err, and sometimes have erred, even in things pertaining to God.' (Article XXI, *Of the Authority of General Councils*.)

'The Church of England receives the four first Generals [i.e. General Councils] as of highest regard, not that they are infallible, but that they have determined wisely and holily', (Jeremy Taylor, *A Dissuasive from Popery*, Part II, Book 1, para, 1, quoted in P. E. More and F. L. Cross, *Anglicanism*, London, 1957, p. 162).

11 It is thus not surprising that Elizabeth's reign saw the burgeoning of a group (the origins of which lie further back) of Puritans who in the first instance wanted more thoroughgoing reform, for they thought that the shreds of popery had been retained too long, and in the second instance were prepared to call for 'reformation without tarrying for any' – i.e. an instant change *where it could be made*, which might well sunder the unity of the Church of England. Such men were not willing for peace and unity 'at any price', but counted principle and conscience above any duty to unity. It could be argued they were simply and logically applying the 'national' Anglican argument to the more localised scene. Here was the seedbed of the Civil War.

12 There were some ambiguous actions by English bishops exporting episcopacy to Scotland in 1610 and 1661. In 1610, presbyters, ordained by presbyters, who came to London to be consecrated bishops were accepted as the members of the 'second order' of the ministry, and consecrated accordingly. In 1661 two of the four were in Episcopalian orders already, two in Presbyterian. This was no time in England for recognising them as in any way 'equal', and the latter two were thus ordained deacon and priest before being consecrated. However, bishops returning to Scotland after both these starting-points, found themselves presiding over dioceses served by presbyters, partly ordained presbyterally, partly episcopally. Indeed, in theory, there could have been found among the living ministers of 1662 *four* contrasting layers of the archeological dig into holy orders – those ordained (a) pre-1610, (b) 1610–38, (c) 1638–61, and (d) since 1661!

13 The suffragan bishop is often viewed as anomalous in terms of classic Anglican rationales for episcopacy. Yet there are some possible rationales which establish episcopacy without thereby identifying it with *mon*episcopacy. And all rationales must include an element of the *descriptive*, for if we seek divinely revealed first principles to canonise some particular expression of episcopacy we shall seek in vain.

14 Development of a worldwide 'Communion' from the former island Church of England is only coincidentally parallel with the development of a worldwide Commonwealth from a former Imperial Britain! But Bishop Hugh Montefiore views the Commonwealth as a positive model from which to argue for patterns of worldwide ecclesiastical reunion – see H. Montefiore, *So Near and Yet So Far* (London 1986).

15 All this is without reference to the widely-felt Anglican unease at the

ARCIC discussion of 'Authority' – that is, that the relative powers of a reformed papacy and a collegial episcopate are discussed without any role apparently being assigned to 'inferior' clergy or the whole body of the laity.

16 It may well be that our changed context – one of mission to an unbelieving world such as Cranmer never knew – while it makes it all the more certain and natural that when the Church meets, it meets for the Eucharist, may leave the Church an insufficient starting-point for the world to encounter the people of God as a community at all.

17 Ian Henderson, *Power without Glory* (London, 1967).

DISCUSSION QUESTIONS

1 What do you think is the essence of Anglicanism now?

2 Do you find the 'branch theory' of the Church helpful? Can you think of a better picture?

3 What signs are there in your part of the Anglican Communion of 'the rediscovery of the laity'?

4 What parts of Anglican spirituality have been most helpful to you?

5 What experience have you had of talking or working with Anglicans of different persuasions from your own?

6 What contribution do you think Anglicans can make to ecumenism?

5

THE CHURCH

'Today there are many and contradictory reasons for no longer remaining in the Church.' These words begin the text of a lecture delivered some fifteen years ago by a man who is seen by many as the most influential conservative Roman Catholic theologian, Joseph Ratzinger. The lecture was entitled, 'Why I am still in the Church', and it was perhaps the first of the now popular apologetic genre which allows prominent figures, lay and clerical, to say why they are still Catholic, Anglican, Christian, or whatever, in the face of critics who envisage a future for Christianity which will lack doctrinal and institutional structures, and will be neither ecclesial nor ecclesiastical.[1] Cardinal Ratzinger drew attention to an urge to leave, to abandon the Church felt both by those who are alienated from its faith, finding it all out-of-date, medieval, at odds with the contemporary world, and by those whose perception is the reverse, who love the historical form of the Church, its worship, agelessness, and embodiment of eternal truth, and see those very values being lost, being deliberately abandoned in modern and unbeautiful worship and in doctrinal liberalism.

He also pointed to quite contradictory reasons for staying in the Church. There are those who stay because they have immovable faith in the Church as the community founded by Christ and endowed with his grace (as well as those who continue a tenuous membership out of habit) and there are those whose liberalism is such that they disavow the Church's whole historical form and yet remain in order to make of the Church what they think it is intended to become. Ratzinger wrote at a time when many felt, as he did and still does, that the 'new Pentecost' (heralded by Vatican II) had become instead a Babylonian captivity.

We need to be alert to the fact that the Anglican situation does not immediately parallel that of Roman Catholicism, and yet the same hopes and the same misgivings have also been felt. And there is the same uncertainty and the same urge to change. One feature of this is that the Church of England, or Anglicanism, or Catholics or Evangelicals, or priesthood or parish life, are constantly described as 'being in crisis'. And whether this is true or not – and constant repetition does not make it true, though it may make it easier to believe – a significant number of clergy and laity have deserted Anglicanism for Rome or the Orthodox, for fundamentalist or liberal bodies, while accusing Anglicans of being peripheral, hypocritical, excessively liberal or rigidly conservative. No wonder then that there are contradictory reasons both for staying in and for leaving the Church.

THE THEOLOGICAL FOUNDATIONS

This attempt at a theology of the Church is written against such a background and can neither ignore it nor refuse to be influenced by it. To do either is to fall into the ecclesiological trap of opting for an ideal or idealised picture. It is not a new trap. The teaching of St Augustine of Hippo (354–430) on the nature of the Church, ministry and sacraments, is one of the foundation stones of ecclesiology in any age.[2] His thought developed in the context of the Donatist heresy, which had begun with a dispute about whether those who had surrendered the Scriptures to the Roman authorities, when their possession was forbidden by Diocletian the persecuting emperor, should subsequently be allowed to be priests or bishops or to administer the sacraments.

The Donatists, named from one of their leading bishops, Donatus, were rigorists who held that the Church of the saints must be holy and that any who had betrayed the Church, even under persecution, could not validly confer the sacraments. They went on further and asserted that since the Church is one and holy, they alone were the true Church. In the face of this idea, Augustine identified the visible Church, with its combination of saints and sinners, as the true Catholic Church and the sole ark of salvation. In the context of his writings on grace and salvation, by contrast, Augustine felt able to define the Church, not in that more inclusive way, but as the invisible body of the elect, foreknown to God alone. Yet we should not presume to do now what God himself will not undertake to do until the Last Judgement, that is, to separate the wheat from the chaff, the saints from the sinners.

Archbishop Michael Ramsey expressed this insight quite briefly in his book, *Introducing the Christian Faith*, in 1961[3] The chapter on the Church carried the subtitle, 'Its Scandal and Glory'. He acknowledged 'that the Church repels' because it is defective in very many ways, and echoed William Temple who spoke of 'the vast chaos which for us represents the Church, with its hateful cleavages, its slow-moving machinery, its pedantic antiquarianism, its indifference to much that is fundamental, its age-long ineffectiveness, its abundant capacity for taking the wrong side in moral issues'.[4] And, he said, that is the scandal. But he also pointed to its glory, to the unshaken purpose of God in using the Church to show himself to the world, despite the obstacles we put in his way: 'Do not shut your eyes to scandal, or your ears to hissing. But have them open to the glory, and it is the glory of Christ in his saints. If you want to be a Christian, you have your duty to the scandal and to the glory, both.'[5]

One frequent response to the scandal has been the idea of purging the Church, 'turning out . . . those who do not conform to a certain standard, and so getting a "real Church" of the godly'. But what standard do we apply? It is all too possible, as Michael Ramsey has said, 'to turn out fornicators and persons otherwise visibly scandalous, and yet to keep in the respectable, the proud, the smug'.[6] Yet many who leave the Church to go to house churches or 'holiness' churches do so because they want to belong to such a body of 'saints'; in so doing, no matter how well-intentioned their motives, they fall into the Donatist trap. The Church they leave has many faults, but until it starts actually expelling people for faithfulness to the gospel (which can happen, even today), to leave it is premature.

If we are to avoid such pitfalls, then a contemporary ecclesiology must be deeply rooted in Scripture, in the teaching of the Fathers and of the Reformers, in liturgy, and in the tradition and concrete life of the Church, expressed in her spirituality, mission, and engagement with the world.[7] This is the key to all our thinking about the Church, and it involves a more serious engagement than has perhaps taken place hitherto with the resources of the Christian tradition. Both the present writers believe that the Christian future is an ecclesial one, and that the Church, in her concrete reality, is not an optional extra whose disappearance would offer us greater freedom in the service of the gospel. But we are also aware that this belief does not immediately commend itself to everyone and that it is necessary to show, though we can only do so most inadequately, that behind *our church* is Christ's Church, and that where reform and renewal are necessary, it is because his Church must be allowed to shine more clearly through our forms and structures. That we Christians are the temporal and concrete manifestation of the Church between the resurrection and the *parousia*, the glorious return of the victorious Christ, inevitably creates a tension, making the Church both definitive for the faith today and provisional when judged against eternity. Yet it does not mean that the Church, whose norm is the gospel and the experience of life in Christ, exists primarily or at all as an institution or community to be constantly restructured and reorganised according to the latest sociological and psychological insights.

RENEWAL – CATHOLIC AND EVANGELICAL

Part of the context within which we write is the recent experience of Anglican Evangelicals and Catholics as they have sought to renew their traditions. So, we might say, the Keele Conference of 1967 was a turning-point for many English Evangelicals. Some would now describe themselves as 'post-Keele' (and even 'post-Buchanan'!), meaning that they have turned from the anti-sacramentalism of earlier days with its ambivalence towards the visible Church and now hold a 'high' doctrine of both Church and sacraments, though of a Reformation rather than Tractarian sort. Some, at least, of the thinking at Keele had come from an awareness of questions of ecclesiology and sacramental theology involved in the Anglican-Methodist Unity Scheme. Two further landmarks are the publication of *Growing Into Union*[8] in 1970, in the wake of the Scheme's anticipated failure, and of *Evangelical Essays on Church and Sacraments*[9] in 1972.

Growing Into Union was the product of some fairly intensive theological reflection by two Catholics and, originally, three Evangelicals (Eric Mascall, Graham Leonard (now the Bishop of London), Colin Buchanan (now the Bishop of Aston), James Packer, and Michael Green (who was not able to continue as a full member of the group)). In it they wrote that

> as long as Catholics see Evangelicals as bogged down in a biblicism which refuses to contemplate theological justification for formulations and institutions not exemplified in the Scriptures, or to entertain exegetical hypotheses which posit as the background of biblical statements factors which only later worked their way into explicit historical expression, and as long as Evangelicals see Catholics as trapped in a traditionalism which refuses to face requests for scriptural justification of elements in tradition, or to allow that what cannot be so justified may not be put forward as a universal norm, little can be done together in dealing with matters of conventional dispute.

The situation has not changed and any theology which expects to find approbation from both Catholics and Evangelicals must 'take with full seriousness any theological justification of traditional positions and institutions that may be offered on the basis of biblical witness to the living Christ and his Church' and must 'take with equal seriousness any plea for such justification, or complaint of lack of it.'[10]

In the Introduction to the volume of *Evangelical Essays*, Colin Buchanan raised another issue: even among 'post-Keele' Evangelicals there will not be, nor can we expect, complete identity of views. Evangelicals are engaged in a theological dialogue 'in the attempt to recreate a theological tradition which has seemed to have run down', but, more seriously, this engagement is in the context of a reformation of Evangelical parochial practice. The burning issues, therefore, continue to be practical ones – the centrality of the Eucharist, infant baptism, communion before confirmation, lay celebration or presidency at the Eucharist, ministry of non-episcopally ordained ministers, vesture of the minister, together with questions raised by the reception of *The Final Report* of the first Anglican-Roman Catholic International Commission – and their very practicality has raised difficult questions for Catholics. It is one thing to disagree on a doctrine; it is another to disagree, and that very deeply, about the theology of a practice prescribed in prayer-book and rubric, and to want to change it.

Uniformity of basic practice, e.g. episcopally ordained eucharistic presidents for all Anglican celebrations, allows a diversity of interpretation within a basic agreement. Diversity of fundamental practice, e.g. both ordained and lay presidents, strikes at the whole doctrinal and practical consensus. Liturgical revision, in prescribing practice, has inevitably brought many of these issues to a head and made it more difficult to write this essay on the Church and its structures in a way that expresses positive affirmations rather than sketching out areas of conflict and dissent. Evangelicals today often seem to be intent on creating, through a further and more systematic reformation, what they consider to be a thoroughly biblical ecclesial structure and ministry. Yet the experience of synodical debate on certain issues suggests that the bibilical model or models is not immediately convincing to those who take seriously the Church's engagement with her tradition and with the world, and acknowledge the inevitability of certain changes and developments in the face both of cultural and social pressures and of practical necessity. Conversely, in liturgical revision and on the questions raised by ARCIC, it is Catholics who have been seen as promoting change and, in so doing, creating problems for many Evangelicals.

Catholics, more often aware of historical development, also cherish order and continuity, and value dogma, law and structure, and yet lack the rigorous theology that gives substance to vision. So, for example, Catholics believe in the necessity and desirability of authority, but find it impossible, it seems, to express that belief adequately in the creation or retrieval of structures of authority that make sense in a divided and non-papal Church. Catholics do not operate with a clear set of affirmations to be implemented or defended in liturgical or pastoral reconstruction, and there is not a 'post-Loughborough' Catholic in England, named from the two Catholic Renewal conferences, in the way that there are 'post-Keele' Evangelicals. There is no Catholic monolith today, if there ever was one, and Anglican theologians who stand in the Catholic tradition are themselves in dialogue with one another, especially over these vexed questions of authority, lay ministry, and the ordination of women, where prominent Catholics are quite likely to take up opposing positions. The Second Vatican Council has also had a significant effect on the worship and practice of Anglican Catholics.

But much that has happened, including much of the experience of synodical government and of developments in the Anglican Communion, has been seen as threatening the Catholic tradition. Liberals and Evangelicals have argued that Catholics do not have a sound foundation for their positions; they do not know what is meant by 'priesthood', even though they value it so much, and they have no coherent theology of ordination; there is no foundation to their claim that episcopacy is of the essence of the Church (a claim disputed by some who might otherwise have been counted as Catholics, including Hugh Montefiore, Kenneth Woolcombe, and W. H. Vanstone.[11] Some Roman Catholic theologians, such as Tillard, Küng and Schillebeeckx,[12] have undermined traditional dogmatic positions and have often been quoted in debate against the arguments of Anglican Catholics. It is probably true to say that the last twenty years have been less productive theologically for Anglican Catholics than any other period this century, and that they are more disunited, though the signs are that Catholics also are attempting 'to recreate a theological tradition which has seemed to have run down' and to regain a unity of purpose, even if it is too early to say what the nature and fruits of this renewal will be.

WHAT IS THE CHURCH?

Christians of every tradition have lately had to turn their attention to this question. They have done so in the face of internal denominational issues and of the exigencies of bilateral and multilateral dialogues. Unity schemes that involve Anglican churches and provinces, as well as issues that affect the whole Anglican Communion, have brought Anglicans to ask the question in the context of their faith and life. Answers abound and do not always dovetail neatly together. Some new answers cause doubts to be expressed about old ones, and new words, indeed a whole new terminology has emerged that expresses and describes the relations between different churches, traditions, and communions. Perhaps for the first time there has been a frank acknowledgment of being a divided Church with all the problems that emerge from such an admission.

Michael Ramsey described the ecumenical venture of ecclesiology as having three phases: the first saw the recovery of the doctrine of the Church as theologians of all traditions concentrated on ecclesiology (he dates this as 1948–54); the second began to appear during the first and involved a shift away from the attempt to understand the Church as such towards an affirmation of the Church's mission and praxis; the third phase has turned to the renewal of the Church as the basis of unity. This phase began in the 1960s and it posed the question, 'How may our churches be renewed and reformed so as to be more obedient to Christ in their form, their behaviour, their mission?'[13]

This has proved to be a most fruitful line of advance, though the diversity of thought about the Church which it has generated and the enthusiasm with which different lines have been pursued makes it impossible to talk anymore about clearly defined phases. There are significant new emphases. So, the two main descriptions of the Church, already identified by Augustine, have been found to be unsatisfactory in the situation of disunity: that is, the true Church as the Body of Christ, consisting of all men and women so far as they are truly incorporated into that Body, or that of the Church as the divinely ordered and visible community of God's people, whose offices and structures belong to the divine law, to whom is entrusted the apostolic faith preserved by the apostolic succession of bishops. The contrast is between the Church seen primarily as a spiritual society which, though at present outwardly divided into different branches which embody different traditions and ways of ordering the common life, is essentially one, and a Church whose parts are validated by their faith and their ministry (not now everywhere episcopal) and whose relations to the whole depend upon the preservation of both faith and structure.

Yet this contrast and the assertion of the Church's essential unity cannot be allowed to stand alone. They illuminate the mystery of the Church's unity as one full of tension. The precise nature of the links between the Christian churches and communities cannot be systematically determined. Some of them are external, as indicated by the Lambeth Quadrilateral. Others are internal, concerned with the direction and quality of spirituality. Many combine both. The recognition of this variety and the desire for unity leaves us with the necessity of explaining how in concrete reality a Church whose only legitimate division is said to be geographical can maintain within itself those strands which are naturally divided on the basis of ethos and emphasis. In the simplest terms, what is the explanation of the real rather than theoretical unity between the congregations in one parish who prefer old rite or new, Matins or Eucharist, morning or evening, congregational or choral? In more complex terms, what is the explanation of the existence and relation of culturally and linguistically divided churches in one building or parish, a problem well known in Wales? And such explanations will lead on to one that affirms the value and integrity of a radically pluriform Church whose fundamental identity is more complex than that indicated by our fellow contributors' 'In Search of an Anglican Identity'.[14]

The various dialogues have chosen to avoid this primary question of the right of parts of the divided whole to be called 'church' and have turned instead either to a deeper fundamental concept, such as ARCIC's use of *koinonia*, or to a studied and respectful attitude to another Church and its tradition seeking understanding and the means to an affirmation of a common faith. At the same time we have seen the truth of the statement that Harvey Cox made in 1966: 'The real ecumenical crisis today is not between Catholics and Protestants, but between traditional and experimental forms of Church life.'[15] The areas of experiment range widely, from those modifications of existing structures found in the renewed diaconate, the rapid growth of non-stipendiary ministry, the existence of 'base-communities', to radical and revolutionary change inspired by the struggle of Christians for justice and peace. Much of the inspiration for more radical experiment has come from the experience of the Church in Latin America and from theological reflection upon it and especially from an ecclesiology that combines the three essential elements: Kingdom-World-Church.[16] Both Catholics and Evangelicals must wrestle with these insights as they challenge traditional thinking.

At a less abstract level, we might turn for our answer to the question 'What is the Church?' to what the 'organised human communities or assemblies' which call themselves 'church' actually do: we might look at liturgies as characteristic of common action. In them, these assemblies

> read and expound sacred books; they offer prayer and praise; they initiate members by ritual washing; they solemnly celebrate a sacred meal. Further, in each of these actions they refer their shared life to a transcendent source which is named 'God' and 'Christ' and 'Spirit'; and they testify that this transcendent reality to which their actions point is experienced as redemptive – as at once liberating and fulfilling.[17]

Or perhaps, and finally, we should seek a short almost credal answer, such as that which Michael Ramsey gave:

> What does the Church exist to do? It lives towards God, and towards the world. Towards God, it worships: towards the world, it preaches the gospel, it brings people into fellowship with God, it infects the world with righteousness, it speaks of divine principles on which the life of humanity is ordered.[18]

The diversity of possible answers, and we have only touched on a very small number drawn from recent writing, creates a dilemma for us. Should our essay address the general question and explore those facets of the Church which we affirm together as a part of our life and inheritance, seeking in them the basis of our unity? Or should it grapple with those questions and issues which divide Catholic and Evangelical and which are no less pressing? The experience of recent ecumenical dialogue, both in the national and international bilateral talks and in the work of the Faith and Order Commission of the World Council suggests that we should begin from our mutual affirmation of the Church and explore its structure and its relation to other fundamental doctrines with the assurance that substantial agreement on essential matters will allow a diversity of interpretation and practice in those less central areas where this may be admitted.

CHURCH – BIBLICAL IMAGES AND THEOLOGICAL MODELS

We need to begin with a fuller answer to our basic question. The mystery of Christ, Scripture affirms, is extended to the Church, through his presence within it, though the word 'church' does not always bear a consistent meaning. It sometimes means the congregation of Israel wandering in the wilderness (Acts 7:38). Again, it refers to a Christian society, a household (Rom. 16:4,5) or in a city (Acts 8:1) or in a district (Acts 9:31; 1 Cor. 16:19). Or else it refers to that society which comprises all the sons of God, redeemed by Jesus Christ and built upon the foundation of the apostles (Acts 20:28; 1 Cor. 12:28). In addition, and significantly for ecclesiology, Scripture uses many metaphors in referring to the Church. She is called the Body of Christ, the bride of Christ, the Temple, the new Jerusalem, the household and the people of God, a holy nation, the new Israel. Each image is a partial expression of the Church's experience, as communion and fellowship, of partaking in the saving work of Christ. Each one, as is the nature of metaphors, stresses one particular feature of the true Church.

Ecclesiology, the systematic theology of the Church, endeavours to combine these diverse elements and images which go to make up the mystery of the Church so that we may perceive that living and unified reality which stems from the revealed and active presence of the Triune God. Inevitably, therefore, ecclesiology will overlap other theological disciplines, especially Christology and the theology of grace and salvation. It also presupposes the Church's proclamation, the preaching of the gospel and the celebration of the sacraments and sacramental ministries which embody God's self-communication in Christ and which create a lasting community, built on faith and the experience of the bond of faith, in which Christ is himself present and which is both a sign and instrument of his saving activity.

The Church is a concrete and tangible reality which, as Christians, we encounter. It is the locus of faith. As we learned from Augustine, we cannot take refuge in the idea of an invisible, spiritual Church that is different from and barely connected to the Church we encounter. The Church is a reality, and we experience it and live with and within it even before we have a clear idea of what it is and before we have begun to understand, by faith, something of its mystery. And that understanding, albeit partial, when it does come, comes first from that multiplicity of concepts and images found in Scripture. Theologians have elaborated ecclesiologies based on most of these. Recent theology has spoken of the Church as the community that confesses and proclaims Christ, as the mystery of salvation, as sacrament, as pneumatic, charismatic, and eucharistic, in addition to the credal epithets, one, holy, catholic, and apostolic. Of course, theologies that take one or another image or metaphor as primary overlap, when developed, theologies based on others and so we can reduce them to a smaller number of more complex theologies, or, as Avery Dulles calls them, models, of the Church.[19]

In the characteristically Pauline letter to the Ephesians, the Church is seen as the 'mystery of Christ', because the eternal plan of the Father, the economy of salvation, by which all mankind is united through the cross, is continued in the reconciling work of the Church. The Church is acknowledged as a wonderful and saving mystery, too great for final definition and full description. In fact, we may say that she is the meeting place of all mysteries, imbued with the hidden and invisible presence of God. The word 'mystery', with its roots in Jewish apocalyptic, here means the act whereby God manifests his love in Jesus Christ, to bring mankind to glory. The Church can only be called 'mystery' because it is an image of the incomprehensible God, whose life and love sustain it, who is the innermost reality of the Church. God's plan involves his self-communication, his revelation of the 'secret' hidden for ages, and the Church, through the preaching of the Word and the celebration of the sacraments is the continuance of this revelation and the means by which mankind is drawn into the glory of heaven.

The Church is, therefore, both sign and instrument: the sign of that intimate union with God in Christ and of the unity of the whole human race, and the instrument by which men and women are drawn into that unity and glory. In all its life, the Church is to be subordinated to the mystery of Christ. The visible, social and institutional structures of the Church are only the sign and means of the action of Jesus Christ in the Spirit.

We have spoken of the unity of the Church and of a unified ecclesiology, and, at the same time, of a tension between different metaphors, between theological expressions and expositions of those metaphors, and between the diversity of cultural appropriations of the mystery of the Church that express themselves in its life by what has been clumsily called 'inculturation'. This inculturation will show itself in language, ritual, art and even manner of thinking. Donald Allchin has pointed to the different approach of the Eastern Christian tradition and the way in which it 'has managed to maintain a reciprocity and a balance between different elements in the Church, which have too often become separated in the West',[20] especially after the Reformation, when Catholics (and especially Cardinal Bellarmine) had stressed the visibility of the Church in contrast to the Reformers' view of the 'Hidden Church'.

In his study of Orthodox doctrine, Vladimir Lossky insists that there are two aspects of the Church that are particularly important. It is certainly the Body of Christ, 'the historically founded institution with its continuous sacramental life and ministry representing the givenness of the divine revelation', but it is also 'the communion of the Holy Spirit', the

Spirit-filled community marked 'by personal freedom and initiative, by the ever new and constantly unexpected activity of the Spirit'. Since it is through the Spirit that the Church becomes the Body of Christ (1 Cor. 12:13), these two aspects must not be divorced. The Church involves a clear, if not easily explained, link between the institutional and the personal, between faith and order, doctrine and discipline, and personal insight and holiness expressed in charisms and in the life and example of the saints.

A basic grasp of these tensions is vital for our ecclesiology. A theology of the Church cannot be a neat package precisely because we are not dealing with the ideal, even if we knew what the ideal should be, but with the real and concrete. There is a danger of pursuing an ideology whose limits and method define everything brought under its scrutiny. As we see a variety of metaphors and related ecclesiologies in the New Testament, so we must expect concrete variety now, and not be afraid of it. It does not mean that we abandon order and method.

Western theology is no longer so rigidly imprisoned in the categories of polemic, and in recent Catholic theological reflection on and about the Church, as evidenced by the Second Vatican Council, two images stand out as normative: the Church as the Body of Christ and the Church as the people of God. The image of the body expresses both unity and diversity. It refers to the organic unity of members with different forms and functions. This unity comes only from being the 'Body of Christ', a unity from above that comes through Christ and in Christ, who is the head of the body, and which is realised by the indwelling power of the Holy Spirit. The diversity is maintained both by the natural personal difference of the members, and by the multiplicity which is a divine gift and which is seen in the variety of spiritual gifts and ministries, and in the difference between charism and office. Commenting on the Council's Constitution on the Church, *Lumen Gentium*, Alois Grillmeier expressed the tension between these two elements:

> Hence the true life of the Church demands that both the unity and diversity of the Body of Christ should be personally realised and

lived. This is true of each individual, as it is also true of local and regional churches, especially in the missions, where variety can flourish most richly in social, cultural and religious matters. The authentic life of the body is only guaranteed where the acceptance of unity in obedience and love goes hand in hand with personal responsibility and right use of freedom in the Church.[21]

The image of the body is complemented by that of the Church as the new people of God. This image expresses the continuity of the Church with Israel and so invites us to see it as a part of God's economy and plan of salvation. Briefly, it combines ideas of election and call, of consecration to God, of covenant, and of eschatological fulfilment, relating 'Church' more clearly to 'Kingdom'. It also lends itself to the idea of pilgrimage, of a servant and witness, of a people advancing toward the complete fulfilment of its destiny.

These two major images have come to the forefront of thinking about the Church. Catholic theology has built on them (and quarrelled over them) to achieve a more dynamic picture of the Church. In a very different tradition, the late David Watson found in them clear teaching about God's call to corporate life, about growth into unity and maturity, and about right use of the gifts of the Spirit.[22] Their significance lies in the combination they offer of the vertical (i.e. Godward) and horizontal (i.e. community) aspects of the Church's life, together with a proper valuation of unity and diversity, continuity and renewal.

BAPTISM AND MEMBERSHIP
OF THE CHURCH

It is generally agreed that entry into the faith and life of the new people of God is effected by the proclamation of the gospel and the sacrament of baptism. Baptism is the rite which indicates a person's initiation into the Christian way;[23] it is once-for-all initiation into Christ, consecration to membership of the new, messianic people of God. Where the image of the 'body' is applied to the Church, we may speak of incorporation. With the image of the Church as the new

temple, we may speak of living stones being built into it.
When we think of the Church as the Spirit-filled community,
we acknowledge with John Meyendorff that

> the Spirit simultaneously guarantees the continuity and
> authenticity of the Church's sacramental institutions and bestows
> upon each human person a possibility of free divine experi-
> ence, and therefore, a full responsibility for both personal
> salvation and corporate continuity of the Church in the divine
> truth.[24]

The Anglican baptismal liturgies hold together the personal and the corporate, and stress that the 'Christian way' is an
ecclesial way. The Church is a *sine qua non* of faith, a
necessary, if not sufficient, condition, and faith and baptism
are inseparable in the gospel. But the two approaches to
baptism and baptismal faith are often divided in practice. So,
those who place the stress on the individual, ask what baptism
achieves and what personal faith and commitment are
required. Those who stress the corporate and point primarily
to the ecclesial dimension of baptism ask what initiation does
to or for the Church and about the corporate implications of
faith. Discussion of both approaches has been enlivened by
the work of the Faith and Order Commission of the World
Council of Churches and especially by the process of reception of the *Baptism, Eucharist and Ministry* document.

In particular, renewed thinking about baptism has led to
questions and proposals about baptismal discipline and
admission to communion. A variety of positions have been
adopted and it is obvious that support for each is not all
Evangelical or all Catholic. There has been a shift of emphasis
from individual (cleansing from sin, participation in the death
of Christ) to the corporate (incorporation into Christ and into
the eschatological community), together with a new (or
renewed) stress on the unity of the rite of initiation – baptism,
confirmation and first communion. Incorporation and justification are perceived as going together: as Colin Buchanan
puts it, baptism is the sacrament of justification; justification
is experimentally inextricable from incorporation; incorporation establishes a visible Church. It follows from this that

baptism is generally efficacious, such that 'as many of you as were baptised into Christ have put on Christ' (Gal. 3:27). Christ was received in baptism. A child of a Christian home should be baptised at the beginning of life, but with a fairly rigorous baptismal discipline, and gradually the proportion of adult baptisms to infant baptisms will inevitably increase. Equally, if we mean by baptism what we say we mean, we must, on this view, admit children to communion.

The Lima text affirmed both the 'necessity of faith for the reception of the salvation embodied and set forth in baptism' and that 'personal commitment is necessary for responsible membership in the Body of Christ'.[25] However, in its Commentary, the text posed the question about 'how a further and separate rite can be interposed between baptism and admission to communion' and whether denial of communion until after confirmation involved a full appreciation and acceptance of the consequences of baptism. But some Evangelicals and some Catholics, perhaps a majority of the latter, would affirm that baptism is a necessary but not sufficient condition both of membership of the Church and of salvation, stressing that the invisible and spiritual nature of the person must conform to what is signified by their outward baptism before participation in communion. Some Evangelicals would want to stress faith as the outcome of the preaching of the gospel, together with a mature confession of faith and commitment to Christ after due instruction. Some Catholics would want to say that the baptism-eucharistic communion lobby have oversimplified the whole question. Christian initiation has been through a 'Christendom' phase, which involved many in a socially correct but superficial profession of Christianity, and has come to a post-Christendom situation. Here it is less clear who is to be counted as Christian and the so-called anomaly of non-communicating yet baptised persons is the product of this diverse understanding. The early Christian equation, baptised=Christian, and its counterpart, unbaptised=non-Christian, is not immediately applicable.

A Catholic position would involve an affirmation (with the Council of Florence, 1439) that by baptism 'we are made members of Christ and belong to his Body, the Church'. But 'belonging' involves something more: the Christian is one who has been baptised, professes the true faith, and has neither cut himself off from the Church nor been cut off by lawful authority because of grave fault. Full membership involves personal implementation of that conformity to Christ which is indelibly imparted by the sacrament of baptism. Conformity involves incorporation into the visible community, by one's profession of faith, reception of the sacraments, and communion with the bishop and other Christians, but these must be outward expressions of the inner faith. Baptism and faith form a unity. In adults, baptism is itself the fundamental profession of faith. Yet, though baptism is fully effective for grace, when it is properly conferred and received with appropriate dispositions, and so incorporates into Christ and gives rebirth, it is not just an action of the Church received by an individual as an isolated person. It is a fundamental act of the Church as community and belongs to the essential nature of the Church.

In the celebration of new life in Christ, an individual is accepted by the Church into the visible sacramental communion of faith. As such, baptism is a beginning, a point of departure. It is about an inner dynamic leading to eschatological completion. As the Faith and Order Commission put it: 'my little life is taken up into God's plan of salvation, the mighty movement of salvation-history, whereby it is carried along towards its eschatological fulfilment at the *parousia* of Christ.'[26] But full incorporation into the visible communion of the Church exists only where there is complete profession of faith, recognition of the institutional elements of the Church as sign and instrument of God's grace, and eucharistic communion. Karl Rahner expresses the Catholic position in this way: the baptised Catholic

> who believes and obeys the Church and lives in a state of justifying grace is a full member of the Church. His membership really effects what it signifies. Here grace has achieved its maximum historical embodiment and membership of the Church is bound up with what it is meant to signify: with faith and grace.[27]

This signification includes spiritual conformity to Christ, something which must be evident in the life of the visible

Church. Donald Allchin has pointed to a similarity of approach between Methodism and at least one strand in the Orthodox tradition, that represented by Symeon the New Theologian (949–1022). Methodism and other renewal movements have been characterised by 'a whole-hearted acceptance of traditional Christian doctrine coupled with the conviction that such doctrine is useless unless verified in life and experience'. By contrast, the Catholic and Anglican traditions tend to think of the sacraments as being effective without our having any specific feeling of what they are doing, so that grace acts at a level below that of consciousness and feeling. Canon Allchin says that this view is dangerous 'when it reaches the point of saying that we ought never to expect this consciousness and feeling of God's action within us and when it thus discourages people from expecting any direct awareness of God.' Symeon says that it is not enough that we have received the Holy Spirit; we must also be consciously aware of it. This is a point that needs to be taken on board in our theology of grace and the sacraments.[28]

The point does not seem to be taken seriously where confirmation before communion is abandoned, as the traditional sequence affirms that baptism is not a full and complete rite of initiation when it lacks an affirmation of faith and its reception by the whole Church, signified by the presence of the bishop. Rather initiation is a process which may be spread over a period of time. Not a series of hoops to jump through, but the ritual and symbolic expression of what is happening to the individual and to the Church.

A number of theological problems in this field arise from our failure to grasp the fact that baptism and confirmation are essentially acts of the Church and not primarily acts done to an individual. The sacraments and sacramental ministries are both the celebrations of the Christian community and the means by which God addresses his definitive Word of grace to individual men and women at moments critical for their salvation. As celebrations, they draw the people of God together, realising ritually its intrinsic unity in the confession and celebration of a common faith. The initiation sequence reveals the nature of the Church, as those who are baptised enter into the Spirit-filled community of faith, acknowledge that faith as their own, are publicly recognised and affirmed by the bishop, and participate in the eucharistic action. At the same time, this sequence constitutes the Church, making it what it is. Baptism admits to the Church. The Eucharist celebrates the salvific nature of Christ's saving death for his Body. Confirmation celebrates the new life in Christ, as an acknowledgment by the whole eucharistic community of what has been brought about by the indwelling of the Spirit which was bestowed in baptism, and it makes clear, through its minister, the universal nature and (normally) episcopal ordering of the Church.[29]

Of course, there will also (and always) be those who stand on the edge, the fringes of the Church, possibly baptised, possibly confirmed, possibly communicant, possibly aware of the sort of experience of God's grace of which Symeon spoke, and committed to some form of Christian belief, but not committed to the institutional structures of the Church as represented by any denomination or its full teaching as found in Creed or Catechism, and for whom the visible and invisible aspects of membership may not be as closely linked as they might be. This group requires its own terminology: some will say that they are 'not fully Christian', others will talk of 'membership' and 'full membership', and others of a relationship to the Church created by faith and/or baptism or a desire for baptism, a relationship which is not the same as membership. Visible conformity to the Church and its institutional structures is easily observed, but the degree to which this conformity expresses real faith and commitment cannot be determined. This is a theological as well as a practical problem.

THE FAITH OF THE CHURCH

When an infant is baptised it is because he or she is a human being, in need of redemption, who has a place in the order of salvation, by virtue of God's creative and redemptive acts, and upon whom God is pleased to bestow salvation in Christ through the intermediary of the Church, thereby giving the Church, the parents and the godparents the duty of bringing the child to the point where he or she can freely affirm the saving grace he or she has been vouchsafed and thenceforward seek to respond to it. The child is placed in a covenant relationship to the Church, and so to God.

The baptismal faith is expressed by the candidates, or by their parents and godparents, in two ways. First, by the affirmation that the candidate 'renounces the devil' or 'turns to Christ' and second by an expression of belief involving assent to the Apostles' Creed or by a statement of 'belief and trust' in God, Father, Son, and Holy Spirit. In the English *Alternative Service Book 1980* this expression of belief is echoed by the minister and congregation – 'This is the faith of the Church.' 'This is our faith.' Christian faith involves both belief, including intellectual assent to propositions, and trust, in the sense of commitment to God and to the Lordship of Jesus Christ. As the Faith and Order Commission so aptly expressed it, faith is directed through the sacrament of baptism to the Lord, and involves invocation for the fulfilment of the promise of grace, confession of trust, submission in obedience to Christ.[30] This faith is the faith of the Church and it is expressed in the context of the Church's life and witness.

The gospel – the fundamental message of salvation, with its call to repentance and to faith in Jesus Christ as Lord – which is not simply identical with Scripture, has always worked in the Church as a means of breaking through all kinds of institutionalisation and dogmatism. But already in the biblical witness the message of the living gospel is tied up with incipient confessional formulae, as in 1 Corinthians 15:3–5, with its basic credal form; Romans 10:9 'Jesus is Lord'; the song of Christ's glory, in Philippians 2:6ff.; the doctrine of Christ as the firstborn of all creation, Colossians 1:15ff.; and the 'mystery of our religion' in 1 Timothy 3:16; etc., where we have formulae which go some way towards an expression of some part of the gospel. Yet the gospel is, necessarily, always wider and more comprehensive than these individual formulae of faith.

Truth can never be adequately contained in sentences. No verbal proposition is ever adequate to express the majesty and mystery of God, as the Archbishop of Canterbury pointed out in the debate on English House of Bishops' Report, *The Nature of Christian Belief*.[31] He quoted St Hilary, a supporter of Athanasius, who wrote: 'We are compelled to attempt what is unattainable, to climb where we cannot reach, to speak what we cannot utter. Instead of the bare adoration of faith we are compelled to entrust the deep things of religion to the perils of human expression.' The Archbishop continued by saying that 'words are fashioned to provide a springboard to propel us into personal response to the truth and love of God. We believe that words are signposts that we can trust, words through which we can receive the very Word of God.' The truth of the formulae of faith is, therefore, always at the same time decisive and provisional. As St Paul says (1 Cor. 13:9,12), it is now imperfect because it will only become manifest in the end, eschatologically.

The first place among the formulae that embody and express the Christian faith goes to the Catholic Creeds, that is, to the Apostles' Creed and those which go under the names of the Nicene Creed and the Athanasian Creed. We acknowledge that, in formulating these Creeds, which state and define certain central beliefs 'which are found, explicitly or implicitly, in Scripture, and had always been part of the living "rule of faith" in the Church', the Church was led to 'conclusions on the true implications of Scripture which are not self-evidently the only possible ones', though they are the most consistent and defensible ones.[32] We see in this the guidance of the Spirit in the establishment of certain normative teachings, agreeable to Scripture and authorised by the Church, which point beyond themselves towards the greater mystery of God himself and the economy of salvation. The implication, therefore, of the use of the baptismal Creeds as the normative confessions of faith is that heresy or heterodoxy consists in unfaithfulness in relation to that faith into which one was baptised.

After the Creeds and clustered around them, there grew up, from prayerful reflection upon them, a further body of doctrine and catechesis through which the Church guarded against misbelief. Sometimes this was expressed, as at Chalcedon, in a doctrinal definition, though not one that came to find liturgical use. There came also, particularly during the Reformation, a number of confessions that had authority only in the particular Christian body from which they came. The Church's doctrine becomes the *correct* interpretation of the confession of faith, the *regula fidei*, and this interpretation is embodied in the life and liturgy of the Christian community, a faithful echo, exposition and application of the gospel.[33]

This process and witness are parts of the essential function of the Church. She reflects on the message which Christ has given and which the primitive Church received and transmitted, and she does so in the context of her historically changing situation in the world. She reflects on the faith 'uniquely revealed in the Holy Scriptures and set forth in the Catholic Creeds' and proclaims it afresh. This proclamation is always grounded in and retains its reference to the message of the first witnesses to Christ and the faith of the primitive Church embodied in the normative and concrete form in which it is found in Holy Scripture, but it is also the here and now valid form of the Word in which God has addressed us and called us to himself.

Catholics and Evangelicals have often been at odds over the relative weight to be placed on Scripture and on Tradition. The role of Scripture in the Church is a major issue today, though one that is nowadays often concealed with an art that seems natural to Anglican liturgists behind a form of words that is amenable to a variety of possible and even permitted interpretations. This variation is found in the questions put at ordination in different Anglican ordinals. Some maintain a form of question closely following the *Book of Common Prayer*, 1662, asking not only whether the candidate believes the Holy Scriptures as containing or revealing 'all things necessary for salvation through faith in Jesus Christ' (a question common to all ordinals), but also whether they will 'teach nothing (as required of necessity to eternal salvation) except what you are convinced may be proved by the Scriptures'. This is usually followed by a question about believing and upholding 'the doctrines of the Christian Faith' as the Church in that place 'has received them'.

Here we have a balance that is vital for Anglican theology, for the English Reformers were at one with their continental contemporaries in affirming the supreme authority of Scripture in establishing the faith. As Canon Allchin has said, this principle of the primacy of the Scriptures can be interpreted in many different ways. Looking to the writings of Richard Hooker (1554–1600) and Lancelot Andrewes (1555–1626), he shows that they

> came more and more to rely on the concordant testimony of the teachers of the undivided Church, and in particular on the dogmatic decisions of the first four General Councils, as providing the way of approach to the understanding of Scriptures. The authority of Scripture was received in and through the witness of tradition.[34]

This understanding is found in the monuments of the Anglican tradition, in Prayer Book, Articles, Ordinal and Homilies. Catholics and Evangelicals would disagree about the relative importance of these monuments, but would affirm together their importance both historically and in the contemporary Church. The Prayer Book, in particular, has, by its constant and daily use, created an ethos – liturgical, doctrinal and spiritual – which enshrines and maintains the essentials of the faith of the Church, the fundamental teachings of a Catholic and reformed Christianity.

Questions about the relation of faith and Church, of Scripture and tradition, and about authority in the Church, have been raised in acute fashion by ARCIC and the responses, Anglican and Roman Catholic, to the *Final Report*. In particular, Cardinal Ratzinger raised several points about the use of the word *tradition* as a substitute for *confession* when we speak of *our two traditions*.[35] In the Catholic Church, he says, the principle of tradition refers, not only and not even in the first place, to the permanency of ancient doctrines or texts which have been handed down, but to a certain way of co-ordinating the living word of the Church and the decisive written word of Scripture. 'Here "tradition" means above all that the Church, living in the form of the apostolic succession with the Petrine office at its centre, is the place in which the Bible is lived and interpreted in a way that binds.' The Cardinal sees in Anglicanism a fundamental recognition of tradition in that the Creed and dogmas are taken over from the pre-Reformation Church, but he identifies a tendency to regard tradition as no more than a recognised heritage of texts from the past, and the living voice of the Church, in the Petrine office, is minimised in theology by the demand that it be tested against Scripture. There is much here that needs discussion, but essentially the question is one about how Anglicanism develops and how the well-known Anglican principle of dispersed authority can find a voice to 'proclaim afresh in each generation' the Christian faith and to interpret it in a way that binds.[36]

Many of these issues were considered in *Growing into Union*, where the integral relationship of Scripture and Tradition (considered both as the handing-on process and as that which is handed on), under Christ, was emphasised:

Tradition, however venerable, is not infallible as a mode of transmission, and needs constantly to be tested by the Scriptures whose witness to Christ it seeks to convey. Scripture, however inspired, was not meant to be self-sufficient as a means of instruction and life, but to operate within the common life of the Christian community by way of preaching, sacrament, fellowship, and prayers. Reformation Protestantism, arguing against the idea of an ecclesiastical *magisterium* acting as a second source of doctrine and an infallible interpreter of Scripture, rightly maintained that Scripture was *clear* in its meaning and *sufficient* in its content for the purposes of salvation, and that the *magisterium* affirmed by Rome was superfluous . . .[37]

A significant number of Anglican Catholics would no longer subscribe to that Reformation principle, but would ask how the Church is to express its mind on those matters on which Scripture is silent and how, in the absence of such a teaching authority, a *magisterium*, the faith and order of the Anglican Communion are to be maintained in the face of the many pressures for change and the sort of theological teaching, given even by bishops, that seems, in the public mind, to challenge traditional teaching. Evangelicals, for their part, would want to supplement that Reformation principle with another principle of the English Reformation found in Article 20, that 'the Church hath. . . . authority in Controversies of Faith'; which is not an independent or infallible authority, but rather an authority to state faithfully the teaching of Scripture. Evangelicals and Catholics alike see a constant erosion of Catholic and Reformed principles and this is a most serious common concern. Little advance on the question of authority appears to have been made since the 1981 Primates' Meeting and both the unity of the Church and its faithfulness to the gospel are thereby put at risk.

FAITH AND MINISTRY

Unity and faithfulness are central concerns because, as we have seen, it is possible to say that the Church is both a people on pilgrimage towards the fullness of the mystery of Christ, with all that that implies about the provisional nature of what we now have, and the appointed guardian and trustee of the apostolic faith, with a constant duty to confess and hold fast 'the faith once for all delivered to the saints' (Jude 3). To ensure that this people is guided and maintained in truth, Christ calls some to fill offices that promote the good of the whole people, that all Christians may be enabled to grow in faith, obedience, and spiritual maturity, and to fulfil their calling. Within the Catholic and Anglican tradition the orderly succession of bishops, and the ministers they ordain, is seen to serve, symbolise and guard the continuity of the Church in the apostolic faith. Apostolicity expresses the Church's fidelity together with her continuity and identity through the ages. She is maintained in the faith that the apostles, as witnesses to the saving work of Christ, first handed on, by the presence of Christ with his people, as he promised, and by the presence and action of the Holy Spirit, building up the Church day by day.

The apostolic office has been held by Catholics to have lasting significance for the life of the Church, a significance rooted not only in the exercise of the office, as it is recorded in the New Testament, but in the intention that Jesus had with regard to it. In a sense it is not a singular 'office' but a multiplicity of offices and ministries, dovetailed and overlapped, which may be properly termed 'apostolic'. Various qualities or qualifications have been proposed for the apostles: they have received a charge directly from the risen Lord (though in 1 Thessalonians 2:6 Paul refers to Silvanus and Timothy as apostles), they have met with the risen Lord (though more than this is required to be an apostle, cf. 1 Corinthians 15:6–9) and are therefore witnesses of the resurrection. Paul shows that an apostle is one who, delegated by Christ, proclaims the gospel, so that the apostles are responsible to God alone. The apostles are the instruments of Christ's proclamation, the 'aroma of Christ', the means by which he is present in the community, and on the acceptance of their message depends salvation or damnation (2 Cor. 2:15f.). Jesus at least occasionally charged his disciples to proclaim the kingdom of God in word and signs (Matt. 9:37–8; 10:1,5–7, 20; Luke 9:1f.; 10:9). This temporary ministry became an office, after the resurrection, through the gift of the Spirit (Matt. 28:18ff.), and the apostles share in Christ's own authority for he says to them, 'He who hears you hears me' (Luke 10:16).

Very early on in her life the Church saw in the apostolic office one of her essential marks (Eph. 2:20; Rev. 21:14). This apostolicity is seen as the guarantee of truth, especially when faced by the first Christian gnostic heresies, and this idea is most clearly shown in the Johannine teaching concerning the union of Christ with his disciples as they receive both authority and mission. Eric Mascall has stressed the necessity of taking the apostolate seriously as an enduring office and not one that was purely temporary and transient but one which continues in its new form, the episcopate, which functions as

the perpetual apostolate, to manifest and preserve the unity of the Church throughout space and time, a unity which is . . . organic, dynamic and expansive, because it is the unity of a living body and because its vital principle is nothing less than the life of the Holy Trinity communicated to men.[38]

Again, Catholic theologians have stressed that the transmission of power, from Christ to the apostles, was a real one

> so that the saving activity of Christ should have a visible continuation, and at the same time it represents a vicarious [i.e. representative] exercise of authority so that the unity of the mission might not be endangered, the mission which was reserved solely to the one mediator between God and man.[39]

Antonio Javierre describes the lasting confrontation of the Church with the apostles and their teaching as being guaranteed by the episcopate as 'the ultimate logic of the Incarnation'.[40] As 1 Clement expresses it: 'The Father sent his Son, the Son lives on in his apostles, and the apostles bestowed the teaching office upon their successors the bishops.'[41] But Evangelicals would not feel able to go along with this without sounding an important warning note. For their part, they would find it necessary to emphasise Clement's distinction between the 'apostles' and their 'successors'. It is one thing, in this view, to say that bishops are successors to the apostles entrusted with the apostolic gospel, another to say that they are themselves apostles, with all that this seems to imply about their authority and uniqueness.

As we have said several times in this essay, though the New Testament does not describe a single pattern of ministry as a continuing norm, the normal method of ordering the Church is episcopacy as part of the threefold ministry. We recognise that it is all too easy to think of the apostolic succession primarily in terms of the historic episcopate and so to 'unchurch' those who lack it. The orderly succession of bishops in sees is a powerful sign of the Church's fidelity to the apostolic faith, but it is not sufficient for such fidelity. Rather, as the Lima text says, 'the primary manifestation of apostolic succession is to be found in the apostolic tradition of the Church as a whole',[42] a tradition which manifests itself in faithfulness to the apostles' teaching, attested in Scripture and, under Scripture, in the Catholic Creeds, to their prayers, as expressed in the devotional, liturgical and sacramental life of the Church, and to their fellowship expressed in the common life of the people of God. And, of course, it includes faithfulness in mission and ministry, in being sent into the world to share the gospel of Christ and to proclaim the kingdom to all near and far, and in giving service to the poor, the outcast and all those in need.

Anglicans have adopted a number of theological positions to describe the importance for apostolicity of the historic episcopate. Catholics, standing in the Tractarian tradition, have argued – and most Catholics would still hold – that the historic episcopate is of the essence (*esse*) of the Church and that episcopal ordination is necessary for ministry in other orders. Among Evangelicals and others it has been argued that episcopacy is an order of ministry developed under the guidance of the Spirit for the well-being (*bene esse*) of the Church or as an aspect of the fullness of the Church (*plene esse*), in an attempt not to diminish its importance while not unchurching those who lack it. In the face of a number of unity schemes and covenants Catholics feel bound in conscience to say that they can only accept union based on recognition of episcopacy as normative and universal episcopal ordination, though the means by which existing ministers of other denominations are to be included in and affirmed as being in the apostolic succession of ministry may vary.

THE CHURCH AND THE KINGDOM

As we conclude this all too brief essay, we need to affirm two important points of Christian teaching that come from a proper understanding of the Kingdom-World-Church relation. The first is that the corporate life of the Church, as it is expressed in assembly for worship or in parochial, diocesan, or provincial structures and ministries, is not its fullness. This is well expressed in the first Report of the Inter-Anglican Theological and Doctrinal Commission, *For the Sake of the Kingdom: God's Church and the New Creation*, a document that is immediately relevant to our theme and which will repay careful study. The Commission speaks of the Church as 'a body of disciples' and says:

these disciples are usually to be found dispersed in their communities as . . . 'aliens and exiles' (1 Pet. 2:11) and it is in their various vocations and in the business of their ordinary lives and in their engagement with their neighbours that the world is made aware of its destiny as God's kingdom . . . the effective witness of God's people to the presence and coming of the kingdom of God resides more in the meaning and quality of their lives than it does in the decisions and acts of church councils.[43]

Second, and following directly from that point, we have to take up the consequences of the teaching of St Augustine against the Donatists. Archbishop William Temple wrote that 'the ideal Church does not exist and never has existed; some day, here or elsewhere, it will exist'.[44] The fulfilment of Christ's plan for the Church and for Christians 'some day' is part of the hope and expectation of every age. This hope provides the context into which all our thinking about the Church is to be placed. Ahead of his time (in 1954) Bishop John Robinson put it like this: 'Just as the New Testament bids us have as high a doctrine of the ministry as we like, as long as our doctrine of the Church is higher, so it commands us have as high a doctrine of the Church as we may, provided our doctrine of the kingdom is higher.'[45] This message, which enables us to make sense of so much of the Church's life and so not to take some parts of it too seriously, has nevertheless not always been received and understood and we must welcome its exposition in *For the Sake of the Kingdom*.

Our doctrine of the kingdom is to stand highest because what Jesus the Christ proclaimed was, not the Church, but the 'reign' or 'kingship' or 'kingdom' of God. In the same way, as the community that has Christ as its foundation and that lives 'in Christ' and is both sign and instrument of his saving work the Church proclaims the kingdom of God. This is the calling that we have as a body of disciples.

The church . . . is engaged in the same business as its Lord: that of opening the world to its horizon, to its destiny as God's kingdom. Not only by proclamation but also by deed, the church is called to let God's kingdom show in the world and for the world – to give the world a taste, an inkling, of 'the glory which shall be revealed'.[46]

And here too we find that double facet of which Michael Ramsey wrote, glory and scandal:

> Finally – and again as a body of disciples – the church follows the way of repentance, because that is the way along which God's kingdom is found . . . To be 'church' is always to be turning to God, always to be in transition to a better mind, always to be answering afresh the call of God in Christ as events and circumstances make that call concrete.[47]

At the end we might well ask, 'Why stay in the Church?' The background to this essay is the struggle to be the Church, to be truly the people of God and the body of Christ, to make concrete in the world the divine call to repentance and forgiveness, to proclaim effectively the kingdom. It is a struggle marked by both success and failure, by glory and scandal. In it we find women and men who have been alert to the prompting of the Spirit, who have loved the Church, and have been ready to suffer for it and its purposes. And this is why we stay and why we believe in a present and future Church. Joseph Ratzinger answered in the same way:

> To remain in the Church because it is itself worthy to remain; to remain in it because it is worthy of our love, and will constantly, through love, be transformed above itself into its truer self – this is the way in which, as always, the response of faith is made today.[48]

NOTES

1 'Why I am Still in the Church', in Hans Urs von Balthasar and Joseph Ratzinger, *Two Say Why* (London, 1973).
2 A helpful evaluation of Augustine's anti-Donatist teaching set in the context of late medieval and Reformation theology is to be found in Francis Oakley, *The Western Church in the Later Middle Ages* (London, 1979).
3 Michael Ramsey, *Introducing the Christian Faith* (Revised edition, London, 1970), pp. 67–76.
4 William Temple, in A. E. Baker, *William Temple and his Message* (London, 1946), p. 158f.
5 M. Ramsey, op. cit., p. 69.
6 op. cit., p. 70.

7 For the roots of Anglican doctrine, with special reference to the Reformation, see Thomas Wright, 'Where Shall Doctrine Be Found?' in the Doctrine Commission of the Church of England, *Believing in the Church: The Corporate Nature of Faith* (London, 1981), pp. 109–41.

8 *Growing into Union* (London, 1970).

9 Colin Buchanan (editor), *Evangelical Essays on Church and Sacraments* (London, 1972).

10 *Growing into Union*, p. 38.

11 See Kenneth M. Carey (editor), *The Historic Episcopate in the Fullness of the Church* (London, 1954).

12 The particular reason for Tillard's inclusion here is his paper, 'What Priesthood has the Ministry?', commissioned by ARCIC I and published as Grove Booklet on Ministry and Worship No. 13 in 1973.

13 Michael Ramsey, Robert E. Terwilliger, and A. M. Allchin, *The Charismatic Christ* (London, 1974), pp. 37–8.

14 See Chapter 4.

15 Harvey Cox, *The Secular City* (London, 1966), p. 160.

16 Leonardo Boff, *Church: Charism and Power* (London, 1985), pp. 1–11.

17 Inter-Anglican Theological and Doctrinal Commission, *For the Sake of the Kingdom – God's Church and the New Creation* (London, 1986), p. 19.

18 Ramsey, *Introducing the Christian Faith*, p. 72.

19 Avery Dulles, *Models of the Church* (Dublin, 1976).

20 A. M. Allchin, *The Kingdom of Love and Knowledge* (London, 1979), p. 48.

21 In Herbert Vorgrimler (editor), *Commentary on the Documents of Vatican II* (London, 1967), vol. I, p. 144.

22 David Watson, *I Believe in the Church* (London, 1982), chapters 6 and 7.

23 *Evangelical Essays*, p. 9.

24 Quoted in Allchin, op. cit., p. 49.

25 World Council of Churches, *Baptism, Eucharist and Ministry*, Faith and Order Paper No. 111 (Geneva, 1982), p. 3, par. 8.

26 World Council of Churches Commission on Faith and Order, *One Lord, One Baptism* (Minneapolis, 1960), p. 57.

27 Karl Rahner and Herbert Vorgrimler, *Concise Theological Dictionary*, 2nd edition (London, 1983), p. 303.

28 Allchin, op. cit., pp. 40–1.

29 See R. T. Beckwith, *Priesthood and Sacraments* (Abingdon, 1964); R. T. Beckwith, 'Church and Sacraments in Christian History', in *Evangelical Essays* (op. cit); Martin Dudley, 'Communion and Confirmation', in *Living Stones*, vol. 1, No. 1 (1987).

30 *One Lord, One Baptism*, p. 61.

31 General Synod of the Church of England, *Report of Proceedings* (London, 1986), vol. 17, No. 2 (July 16, 1986), p. 452.

32 House of Bishops of the General Synod of the Church of England, *The Nature of Christian Belief* (London, 1986), p. 6, par. 4.

33 J. I. Packer and R. T. Beckwith, *The Thirty-Nine Articles: Their Place and Use Today* (Oxford, 1984), pp. 48ff.; for a contrary view of the

doctrinal significance of the Articles in the context of sacramental theology, see Martin Dudley, 'Is Ordination a Sacrament?' in *Heythrop Journal*, XXIV (April, 1983), pp. 149–58.

34 Allchin, op. cit., p. 95.

35 Joseph Ratzinger, 'Anglican-Roman Catholic Dialogue: Its Problems and Hopes', in *Insight*, vol. 1, No. 3 (March, 1983), pp. 2–11.

36 This is explored more fully in Martin Dudley, 'Waiting on the Common Mind: Authority in Anglicanism', in *One in Christ*, vol. 20, No. 1 (1984–1), pp. 62–77; and in the same writer's tract, *Authority in Today's Church*, Additional Curates' Society (Birmingham, 1987).

37 *Growing into Union*, p. 38.

38 E. L. Mascall, *Corpus Christi*, 2nd ed. (London, 1965), p. 15.

39 Antonio Javierre, 'Apostle', in *Sacramentum Mundi* (London, 1966), vol. 1, pp. 78b–79a.

40 ibid.

41 World Council of Churches, *Baptism, Eucharist and Ministry*, Faith and Order Paper No 111 (Geneva, 1982), p. 29, commentary on par. 36.

42 *Baptism, Eucharist and Ministry*, p. 28, par. 35.

43 *For the Sake of the Kingdom*, pp. 24–5.

44 William Temple, *Christus Veritas* (London, 1924), p. 167. Two recent and valuable additions to writing on the kingdom are: J. H. L. Rowlands (editor), *Essays on the Kingdom of God*, Saint Michael's College (Llandaff, 1986), and H. P. Owen, *Church: Kingdom: World: The Church as Mystery and Prophetic Sign*, edited by Gennadios Limouris, World Council of Churches, Faith and Order Paper No. 130 (Geneva, 1986). The latter book only came to hand as this essay was being completed, but clearly follows a similar path, at least in part, as well as extending the Orthodox ecclesiology evidenced in the writing of Canon A. M. Allchin.

45 *The Historic Episcopate*, p. 17.

46 *For the Sake of the Kingdom*, p. 23.

47 op. cit., p. 24.

48 *Two Say Why*, p. 90.

BIBLIOGRAPHY

A. M. Allchin, *The Kingdom of Love and Knowledge* (London, 1979).

P. D. L. Avis, *The Church in the Theology of the Reformers* (London, 1981). *Perceptive study, including all schools of Reformers, especially Anglican.*

E. Best, *One Body in Christ* (London, 1955). *Important study of Pauline theology of the Church.*

Leonardo Boff, *Church – Charism and Power* (London, 1985).

Doctrine Commission of the Church of England, *Believing in the Church* (London, 1981).

C. Eastwood, *The Royal Priesthood of the Faithful* (London, 1963). *On the priesthood of the whole Church.*

R. Field, *Of the Church* (Cambridge, 1847). *A comprehensive Anglican classic, first published 1606–10.*

R. Hooker, *Of the Laws of Ecclesiastical Polity* (Oxford, 1845). *The standard Anglican treatment, first published 1594–7.*

Michael Schmaus, *Dogma 4 – The Church* (London, 1972).

J. R. W. Stott, *One People* (London, 1969). *This discusses the relation of the clergy to the laity.*

DISCUSSION QUESTIONS

1 Why do you stay in the Church? What answer would you give to those who ask Anglicans this question?

2 What is meant by the kingdom of God? How is it related to the Church?

3 The faith of the Church is what makes it a Church. Do you agree?

4 Do Anglican Catholics and Evangelicals have a common theology of the Church?

5 'Catholic and Reformed': is this how you think of the Anglican Church?

6 For what reasons do you value the office of bishop?

6

THE FUTURE OF THE FAMILY

1   THREATS TO THE FAMILY

A common conviction, at least in the USA and the UK, is that 'the family' is under threat. There is less agreement, however, when it is asked why this is so, what external or internal factors may pose a threat to the family, and especially whether the predicament which the family is thought to exhibit is a good or bad thing.

In his Reith Lectures of 1968 Sir Edmund Leach spoke disparagingly of 'the family with its narrow privacy and tawdry secrets'. Radical psychiatrists like R. D. Laing and David Cooper have written about 'the death of the family', arguing that the whole concept of family militates against the independence and therefore the emotional and mental well-being of the individual. Some writers in the tradition of Marx and Engels see the family as a barometer of the class struggle, and their prescription for a classless future requires the eventual demise of the family. Some radical feminists such as Shulamith Firestone have argued that the family destructively perpetuates what Betty Frieden in *The Feminine Mystique* called 'the cult of domesticity'. For such writers the threat to the family is seen as a positive good, an affirmation of the autonomy of the individual, a step towards the essential restructuring of society to allow more satisfactory social patterns to develop.

By contrast, *Family Portraits*, published by the Social Affairs Unit, in 1986 (edited by Digby Anderson and Graham Dawson), outlined threats to the 'normal' family, described as the family of husband, wife and their children, the parents intending to stay together, the husband being the principal if not the only breadwinner. These authors argue that there are increasingly pressures (from feminist ideology, from some legislative changes, from patterns of sex education, and so on) which undermine the stability of family life. This viewpoint, most strongly advocated by the conservative right, came to prominence on the political scene in the 1970s, primarily as a reaction against the 'wild detours' of the 1960s. It takes its stand on the positive values of the 'traditional family'. The family is in danger because of decadence. The positive stress on the family is usually coupled with a negative stress against pornography, abortion, homosexuality, feminism.

The ideological debate about the family came to a focus in the USA in 1980 in the White House Conference on Families. The purpose of the Conference was to clarify national policy on family-related issues; the result was a growing scepticism as to whether a unified policy was possible.

Alongside the ideological war over the family between the radicals and the traditionalists, there is a third interest group: 'the professionals'. In *War over the Family*, Brigitte and Peter Berger write of a built-in tension between belief in the sacrosanct nature of the family, and the claims of professional expertise. The increase in helping professions, such as social work, and the increasing incompetence of families to deal with some of the needs of dependent members leads, according to the Bergers, to 'the disenfranchisement of families by professionals in alliance with government bureaucrats'.[1]

These three diverse groups with interest in the future of the family agree in one respect: the family is under threat.

Concern for the future of the family is by no means a Western phenomenon, however. In Western industrialised societies, the change from extended family patterns to nuclear families has taken place over time. The relocating of certain economic, educational and problem-solving functions away from extended kinship groups and on to the wider political and social community has not all happened at once. In some other parts of the world (parts of Africa, for example, and in the Far East) the change from rural living, with a subsistence economy, to urbanisation and a cash economy, has been extremely rapid. Coupled with a massive population growth, the move into the towns, especially by husbands, has left rural populations of women, children and elderly people without adequate supports. Western-style nuclear families, based on privacy and materialism, are being established in towns – with very high expectations and consequently high disappointments. Sometimes a husband will take a 'town wife' and start a new family as well as having a 'rural wife' in the country. The divide between rich and poor, especially in a country such as Kenya, is growing fast. The breakdown of extended family life is causing social and economic problems on a scale in places too large to be coped with. The loss of the social and emotional resources provided by a context in which marriage was not a private matter of individual choice and romantic attachment, but was a link between not only individuals but also their wider kinship groups, has in some places yet to find adequate compensation.

In many parts of the world, therefore, there is concern for the future of the family. But what *is* the family?

2   WHAT IS 'FAMILY'?

In many of the debates between differing ideologies and professional groups, the assumption is made that 'family' means what has become known as the 'nuclear family' – the 'normal family' of *Family Portraits* – comprising working husband, wife at home and two children. However, the proportion of the population who actually live in such families is and always has been astonishingly low. In *The Third Wave*, Alvin Toffler suggests that only seven per cent of the population of the USA still live in this type of family. He goes on:

> Even if we broaden our definition to include families in which both spouses work, or in which there are fewer or more than two children, we find the vast majority – as many as two-thirds to three-quarters of the population – living *outside* the nuclear situation.[2]

In fact the concept of the 'family' is used in a very wide-ranging and fluid way. This can be illustrated by selecting the three commonly assumed features of family life: marriage, parenthood and residence, and noting the wide range of possible combinations. Only where all three are together do we have the complete nuclear family. Where two of the three are present, we may have families dispersed through children leaving home, or through separation of spouses (marriage + parenthood); childless couples (marriage + residence); a couple living together with a child, or an unmarried parent with a child (parenthood + residence). Where only one of the three is present, we may have a separated childless couple ('marriage' in name only); an illegitimate child adopted, or otherwise separated from its biological parents (parenthood only); or a couple 'living together' but unmarried (residence only).

There is debate about the meaning of 'marriage', particularly with the increasing number of homosexual liaisons; there is debate about the nature of parenthood, particularly with the recent work on *in vitro* fertilisation, embryo transfer and surrogacy; there is no clarity about the meaning of family residence – lodgers, friends, older relations may share the family home, while children may be far away.

Clearly there is ambiguity in the use of the concept 'family'. Clearly also, other family forms are developing and anti-family patterns of living are increasingly canvassed.

A rapidly growing proportion of the adult population of the Western world chooses to live alone. Many do so while they are 'in between' marriages. A quarter of all first marriage partners in the UK live together before marriage. More couples are choosing to be 'child free' for the sake of their personal independence and career needs. There are more than one million one-parent families in Britain – a proportion which has grown considerably with the rise in the divorce rate in the past decade or so. The proportion of remarriages has increased over the last twenty years from fourteen to thirty-five per cent of all marriages. Over thirty per cent of all British babies are born outside marriage. In some areas in the USA one in four children is brought up by a single parent.

The social, ethical and legal questions raised by these shifting patterns are complex. Some, for example the legal questions of kinship and inheritance being posed by some of the possibilities of reproductive medicine – AID (Artificial Insemination by Donor), embryo transfer, surrogacy – are only now being asked; What will the future bring?

The sociologist Jessie Bernard wrote in 1972:

> Not only does marriage have a future, it has many futures. There will be, for example, options that permit different kinds of relationships over time for different stages in life, and options that permit different life styles or living arrangements according to the nature of the relationships. There may be, up to about age twenty-five, options for childless liaisons; for years of maturity, stable or at least 'temporarily permanent' marriages involving child-rearing; for middle age and beyond, new forms of relationship, perhaps even polygynous ones. People will be able to tailor their relationships to their circumstances and preferences. The most characteristic aspect of marriage in the future will be precisely the array of options available to different people who want different things from their relationships with one another.[3]

Given this diversity, we need to come back again to the question, 'What is a family?' It is clear that the assumption that 'family' means 'nuclear family' is not well founded. Furthermore, the nuclear family pattern is a long way from the family patterns in other cultures and in other generations. Indeed, prior to the seventeenth century, it appears that *none* of the meanings attached to the word 'family' had the connotations so common today, of a small group of immediate kin sharing a dwelling.

The Roman *familia* was a household, the members of which were the servants (*familus* – servant) of the head of the household, the *paterfamilias*. It was not a kinship group. This was a common usage of 'family' in pre-nineteenth century England. Alternative uses indicated a widely dispersed group of relatives, loosely linked by blood kinship, but not necessarily part of one household. As Edmund Leach notes in *Social Anthropology*, most English people now use the word in several different senses. 'With all this variety it becomes almost a truism to say that families exist in all kinds of human society. But it is a statement that is quite devoid of interest.'[4] As many sociologists argue, it is difficult to avoid having some sort of family structure as the basis of child-rearing and the regulation of sexual relationships even if we wanted to.[5]

The issue for Christian moral theology is not whether the family will continue, but what sort of families *should* exist, and what assumptions, values and resources are needed to sustain them. These are the basic theological questions to which we must shortly give our attention.

3   A CHRISTIAN THEOLOGY OF FAMILY

The modern Christian Church has responded to the changing patterns of family life in a variety of ways. There has, for example, been a flood of popular literature calling the Church not to give way to current permissiveness and calling Christian homes 'back' to the pattern of white middle-class American traditional nuclear family life. Other Christian writings have been more careful. The Vatican II Document, *Gaudium et Spes*, said that 'the well-being of the individual person and of both human and Christian society is closely bound up with the healthy state of conjugal and family life.' It agreed that 'the family is, in a sense, a school for human enrichment' and said that 'Christians . . . should actively strive to promote the values of marriage and the family.' It gives some discussion of the meaning of marriage, but comparatively little on what is meant by 'the value of the family'. The Church of England Report to the Archbishop of Canterbury before the 1958 Lambeth Conference, published as *The Family in Contemporary Society*, and G. R. Dunstan's book, *The Family is Not Broken* (1962), were both serious theological discussions. It is striking, however, that the majority of Christian ethical texts which discuss family issues concentrate on marriage and divorce, and do not develop a very full theology of family at all.

What, therefore, we shall seek to do in what follows is produce some suitable theological models for discussing the family. For it is only when our understanding of that is securely based that the Christian Church will then be able to speak meaningfully and helpfully on the escalating departures from the norm that are now occurring.

First, however, what we say about the family must be placed in the wider context of what we are prepared to say about the Church as a whole.

(a) The Wider Context

This can perhaps best be introduced by noting the way in which biblical allusions to the family more often than not refer to the extended family.

In the Old Testament, for example, we find a very broad conception of 'family'. Hebrew has no word for the small social unit we call family. The concept covered by *mishpachah* is a fluid one, stretching from the smallest kinship group to the clan, tribal unit, and even the nation. *Bayit* carries the meaning both of 'dwelling-place' and of 'household'. The family concept refers sometimes to the communal lot of those who dwell under one roof, and sometimes also the biological link between generations: the heirs and descendants who are under obligation to one another for mutual support and protection. Noah's family includes his wife and sons and sons' wives (Gen. 7:1,7); Jacob's family runs to three generations (Gen. 46.8f.). The family in ancient Israel included the servants, resident aliens, widows, orphans and all who lived under the protection of the head of the family who was male. The members of the family had an obligation to help and to protect each other, seen most vividly in the *go'el* obligations in the desert communities to engage in blood vengeance to protect vulnerable members against unjust oppression. These early families were self-sufficient economically. By the eighth century, however, some things had changed. The transition to a more settled life, and the rise in material welfare meant that the family was no longer self-sufficient. There was more division of labour. Some judicial functions passed from the fathers to the elders of the town. The duty of mutual help was too often ignored: the prophets had to plead on behalf of the widows and orphans. Blood vengeance was severely curtailed by law. Family solidarity grew weaker.

It remains true, though, that by and large throughout the Old Testament, the family is never an isolated institution. To be part of a family is to be part of the covenant community with a share of the land inheritance and with a commitment to pass on to the next generation the knowledge and worship of God. The usual family pattern is the extended family of three generations. Although the narrator of Genesis 2:24 mentions that a man *leaves* father and mother to cleave to his wife, the new family unit was geographically close at hand. The Old Testament family is part of a religious, moral, social and economic context which gives it its point, its values and its resources. As with the extended families in pre-industrial Britain and in much more recent Kenya, family strength derived from mutual obligation, family honour and mutual protection.

As in the Old Testament, so in the New, the family concept is a broad and fluid one. *Oikos* meaning house, including 'dwelling together' and *patria* meaning 'lineage' are both used. They come together as synonyms in Luke 2:4: 'the house and lineage of David'.

As we glance through the New Testament, we find references to households with masters and servants (e.g. in some of the parables). We find Simon and Andrew living together with Simon's mother-in-law. We read of the household of Mary, Martha and Lazarus, but no mention of children. We find whole households coming to faith together in the book of Acts (the centurion and *his* household in 10:2; Lydia and *her* household in 16:15) In the Pastoral Epistles we read both of those men who aspire to be bishops and of younger widowed women who marry that they must 'rule' their households. The household codes of Ephesians 5 and Colossians 3 seem to focus attention on the nuclear family of husband and wife, parents and children, but obligation to wider kinship groups are stressed in Jesus's discussion with the Pharisees in Mark 7:9ff. and in 1 Timothy 5:8,16. There seems to be a variety of patterns of family life, and of authority structures within households.

There are three inferences to be drawn from this. The first is that we need to be careful not to draw specific structures of family life from selected parts of the Bible. Some Christians have sought, for example, to find social and economic norms for today's society from the social patterns of ancient Israel. This seems not to take seriously enough the discontinuities between the Old Testament and the New (particularly the fact that the people of God are no longer defined in national terms, and that the significance of the land as the setting for social cohesion has been superseded by the 'fellowship'), nor the extent to which some of the institutional aspects of the Old Testament life are fulfilled and made obsolete in Christ.

The second is that biblical allusions to extended family life explain how family language could come to be used for the Church as a whole, without thereby implying either that the modern Western nuclear family is an absolute commitment or that it is the only way of fulfilling one's vocation under God.

Thus Jesus's treatment of his family in Mark 3: 31–5 and his remark about hating father and mother (Luke 14:26) leave one in no doubt that he always required family commitments to be properly subordinate to a higher commitment. As these passages are sometimes read as an attack on the family, it is important to note that Jesus continues to use family language for this more fundamental commitment: 'Whoever does the will of God is my brother and sister and mother.' In speaking of 'hating' father and mother, Jesus in fact merely illustrates the common Hebrew resort to contrast where we might more naturally speak of priorities; cf. e.g. Genesis 29:30–1 and Deuteronomy 21:15–17. Again, the Marcan passage should not be taken as an attack on his mother, but simply as a reminder that there are times when natural ties are to be transcended. Indeed, when all this is combined with his central use of abba, it cannot be sustained that Jesus was in any sense attacking the family. Rather he at once endorses its imagery and at the same time insists that the implications of that imagery be extended by his disciples to all fellow-members of his kingdom and ultimately to all people. In so doing he continues a process which had already begun in the Old Testament. There one finds numerous references to fellow-nationals as 'brothers' (e.g. Exod. 2:11; Lev. 10:6; Deut. 15:3; Jer. 34:14), and indeed it is to this notion that Paul appeals in Ephesians 3:14f. with his pun on *Pater* (father) and *patria* (tribe or family). What Jesus does is simply take it one stage further. All human beings are now part of the one family under God the Father, and it is this fact which legitimates modern talk of the Church as the family of God, not simply endorsement of the nuclear family as the norm.

Third, Old and New Testament usage means that those who do not conform to the nuclear norm, such as widows, single adults or the divorced, can none the less just as easily be seen as part of such an extended family. So in using family language of the Church, what is being stressed is the intimate social bonds of interdependence which exist between us in the Body of Christ under God our one Father, not any suggestion that those who fail to conform to the nuclear norm are somehow inappropriately regarded as part of the family of the Church. Indeed, the New Testament insists that marriage and family life are something to be chosen as a call or vocation, not the only path, since both in the teaching of Jesus (Matt. 19: 10–12) and in Paul (1 Cor. 7, especially v.32) celibacy is placed alongside marriage as an equally legitimate option. However, three qualifications need to be added. First, if for much of the Church's past, the danger has been that celibacy was exalted too highly, and marriage sometimes seen only at best as an inferior good; a present danger is that we may fail to take celibacy seriously as an option at all, and so also distort our view of marriage as a vocation in the process. But second, the New Testament never recognises a vocation to individualism and singleness *per se*. Both Jesus and Paul mention some further objective. Social outreach and interdependence thus continue to be stressed, which is one reason why family language continues to be equally apposite for those whose vocation is celibacy. Third, there is one clear and obvious sense in which the family must remain the primary category to which other conceptions of our relation to the social will remain subordinate. This is because our growth and development as children, whatever our present status, will have come through a family model, or something closely analogous to it.

To the consideration of that norm we therefore now turn.

(b) Getting our Models Right

J. D. Zizioulas opens his book, *Being as Communion*, by saying that the Church is not simply an institution. She is a 'way of being'.[6] The same should be said of the family. The family, we argue, is a way of being which derives its meaning from the being of God. Our approach to the meaning of family begins by exploring our understanding of the nature of

God 'the Father, from whom every family in heaven and on earth is named' (Eph. 3:14f.). While we necessarily bring our own understanding of 'fatherhood' to the biblical text we also – and more importantly – need to allow the text to tell us what it means by the Fatherhood, or Parenthood of God, and then ask what that implies for our understanding of the nature of human family life.

Fatherhood and Intimacy The most common mode of reference to God used by Jesus Christ in the Gospels is 'Father'. This description of God has few Old Testament antecedents. There are some comparisons between God and earthly fathers (e.g. Ps. 103:13; Prov. 3:12; cf. Deut. 1:31; 8:5). But other references are few. When they occur, they refer primarily to the relationship of God to the whole people of Israel (cf. Deut. 32:6; Isa. 63:16; Jer. 31:9).

In Palestinian Judaism the description of God as Father is rare.

In the New Testament, by contrast, the concept takes on a new importance and a new intimacy. Here primarily and supremely the Fatherhood of God is seen in the relationship between God and one man Jesus Christ. He is the 'only begotten of the Father'. It is in relationship to him that Christian believers are 'adopted as sons' (Gal. 4:5; cf. Rom. 8:15) into the family of God. The epistles constantly refer to members of Christian communities as 'brothers' and 'sisters'.

In the patriarchal societies of the ancient world, the father figure is endowed with two primary characteristics: authority and the responsibility of protecting other members of the family. While these characteristics are true of God, the most significant characteristic of the 'family' of Father and Son is personal intimacy in relationship. This intimacy is seen clearly in the prayer recorded in John 17. It is seen, too, in the invocation 'abba' by which Jesus addresses God (cf. Mark 14.36; cf. also the use that is made of it in Rom. 8:15 and Gal. 4:6). Such fatherly love and personal intimacy can also be experienced within the Christian community: those who 'with all the saints' comprehend something of the length and height and depth of the love of God made known in Christ (Eph. 3:17f.).

It is this relationship within the Godhead which lies behind one traditional Christian interpretation of the Genesis text:

'Let us make man in our image, after our likeness . . . So God created man in his own image, in the image of God he created him; male and female he created them' (Gen. 1:26f.). The relationship between the sexes derives from and is intended to reflect something of the nature of 'being as communion' in the nature of God.

Here is our starting-point for a theology of family. Family is not merely a social arrangement, a conventional institution for the sake of exercising certain functions. Family is a 'way of being' in this world: a way of being which is essentially communal and personal because that is the way God is. The central focus of the Bible's view of family is not on the institution, but on the personal relationships within it of child to parent, of wife to husband, of all to God.

In *Marriage and Permanence* O'Donovan writes that 'the only answer to the question "Why marriage?" is that God has made it so'.[7] He acknowledges the controversial nature of this answer, but puts it in that form to express the Christian conviction that marriage is a 'natural institution' in the sense that no one invented it, and no one can abolish it: it is simply part of the way things are in the created world as Christians claim to discern them in the light of divine revelation. This claim would certainly seem consistent with the Genesis affirmation made by the narrator in 2:24: 'For this reason a man shall leave father and mother and cleave to his wife, and the two shall become one flesh.' This text forms the basis of Jesus's reply to the Pharisees concerning the permissibility of divorce, and it is linked there with the text from Genesis 1: 'From the beginning . . . God made them male and female.' The same text underlies Paul's caution to the Corinthian church about their supposition that they could separate out their sexual behaviour from their spiritual commitment. Even consorting with a prostitute, he argues, is engaging in an activity whereby the two 'become one' (1 Cor. 6:16). Further, the Genesis text is the basis for the exposition of the mystery of Christ's relationship with his Church discussed in Ephesians 5. There is, in other words, something primary about male/female diversity and complementarity which requires us to see that (in the mind of the Genesis author and his New Testament expositors) the marriage of a man and wife corresponds to the 'way we are' as human beings in the image of God.

The committed personal communion of man and wife, symbolised by and deepened through sexual union, is described by the biblical authors in the phrase 'one flesh'. This is not primarily a physical concept, though it includes the physical. It is a pointer to the depth of intimacy within the complementarity of male and female diversity which reflects something of the image of God. This is why an exclusive, committed permanent heterosexual love relationship is so seriously taken as normative. The seventh Commandment ('Thou shalt not break the one flesh'), like all the Commandments, reflects something of the character of God, and underlines the seriousness with which marriage is regarded. It is to uphold the 'one flesh' of marriage that the Christian Church has always taken a negative attitude towards divorce, polygamy, serial marriage and any sexual relationship outside marriage.

There are good psychological reasons undergirding such a view. As J. Dominian argues, marriage can provide a context for personal healing, sustenance and growth, but only if it is a context of reliability and consistency.[8] To make and keep a commitment to another person 'for better or worse' is not only to offer the other a means of grace by which they may grow, but also reflects something of the character of God's love (cf. Eph. 5:21 ff.).

As we noted earlier, however, the vocation to singleness affirmed in the New Testament requires us to see marriage as also a vocation rather than an obligation. And this means that, important and 'natural' as marriage is, we need also to affirm that there are other ways of 'being as communion' (singles households, for example, and a range of same sex and opposite sex friendships) which can also provide contexts of intimacy which express something of the divine image.

If the husband/wife relationship is one sphere of intimacy, the relation of parents to children can be another. Undoubtedly the family can also be the learning-ground of selfishness, hatred and discord, but – for all its difficulties – it can also, given the right resources, be a 'facilitating environment' for learning how to love. The removal of many of the economic and social functions of extended families has, it has often been pointed out, deprived the family of much of its cohesion, but conversely it has also opened up the way for family members to give more attention to their relationship with one another in the shared tasks of living.

Motherly Fatherhood   Although the concept 'Father' predominates the New Testament disclosure of the personal nature of God, it is by no means an exclusively 'male' picture. No doubt in the patriarchal context of the times this was the most appropriate language to use. Yet the motherly side to God is not hidden. Just as God-likeness is seen in the cohumanity of male and female (Gen. 1:27), so in the nature of God there are motherly as well as fatherly attributes. Moltmann uses the phrase 'Motherly Fatherhood', and we can give substance to this by recalling the Psalmist's pictures of God as a mother bird (Ps. 17:8), a mid-wife (22:9), a mistress as well as a master (123:2). Deutero-Isaiah pictures God weaning the infant (Isa. 49:15): 'Can a woman forget her sucking child . . .? I will not forget you.' Isaiah 66:13 reads: 'As one whom his mother comforts, so I will comfort you'. Hosea depicts God with a tenderness usually associated with motherhood: 'Yet it was I who taught Ephraim to walk' (Hos. 11:3). The male begetting and female bringing to birth are both pictures used of God in Deuteronomy 32:18: 'You were unmindful of the Rock that begot you, and you forgot the God who gave you birth.'

The New Testament pictures the process of new birth into Christ as involving 'imperishable seed' and 'pure spiritual milk' (1 Pet. 1:23; 2:2). Jesus himself illustrates the maternal tenderness of God in his cry over Jerusalem: 'How often would I have gathered your children together as a hen gathers her brood under her wings' (Matt. 23:37). Christ embodies in himself the 'Wisdom' of God (cf. 1 Cor. 1:30) which in Old Testament Wisdom literature is described as 'She' (Prov. 8:1).

Our understanding of fatherhood and motherhood within the human family is to be drawn from the way God is fatherly and motherly to his Son and to his adopted sons and daughters.

Creativity in Love   The concept of God as creator underlies the whole of the Bible. The concepts of God as Father and Mother bring to the notion of creation a sense of personal intimacy and warmth of love. The Fatherhood of God is frequently linked to his creativity: the begetting of his Son, in Hebrews 1:5 and 5:5; the bringing to birth of the believer in the Johannine literature (John 3:7; 8:23; cf. 1:12).

The prologue of John, in particular, discusses the creativity of God by echoing the creation narrative of Genesis 1: 'In the beginning . . .'. Speaking of the divine Logos we are then told, 'All things were made through him, and without him was not anything made that was made . . . to all who received him he gave the power to become children of God.'

The recreative power of God is described by John as a work of love: 'God so loved . . . that he gave' (John 3:16); and the relationship of Christ to his Church symbolises the sort of love a husband should bestow on his wife (Eph. 5:21f.).

Putting these texts together we have a picture of the Lord through whom all things were made being the Lord who loves his Church as a bride. Human marriage and human creativity are to be patterned on this relationship of God through Christ with his people. In him, and therefore in human marriage, love and creativity belong together. 'Procreation' of course, means to be creative on behalf of another – in this case Him who is Love Himself.

Married love is to be creative. Of course not every marriage can be procreative and we need to be on our guard against suggesting that all childless marriages are necessarily defective. Indeed, there is some evidence to suggest that requests for AID and *in vitro* fertilisation are sometimes caused by socially generated feelings of inadequacy. The person perceives themself stigmatised, as not fully a man or woman because of their inability to have children. In the face of such pressures it becomes an urgent task for the Church to insist that there are equally valid alternative ways of being creative in the divine image. At the same time it must guard against the opposite error of supposing that the presence of children is an optional extra for all marriages, and that their absence does not in turn generate the need to be creative and outgoing in some other direction. Usually, however, mar-riage involves parenthood, and it is because love and creativity belong together in God that the Church has taught that the relational and procreative dimensions to human marriage should not be separated.

This is also a further implication of the phrase we have discussed already: 'one flesh'. In its use in Genesis 2:24, the thought is probably the coming back together again of the complete personal union which was in some way separated in the divine anaesthesia which God caused to fall on Adam. As von Rad puts it, here is an explanation for the powerful drive of the sexes to come together.

> Whence comes this love 'strong as death' and stronger than the tie to one's parents, whence this inner clinging to each other, this drive towards each other which does not rest until it becomes again one flesh in the child? It comes from the fact that God took woman from man, that they actually were originally *one* flesh.[9]

'One flesh' thus points to the relational and the procreative aspects of the personal and sexual union which is marriage.

Such a framework makes readily intelligible the continuing resistance of some Catholics to the severing of love and procreation through the use of contraceptive measures. Their fellow Christians respond by saying that, though love and creativity do belong together, this does not mean that each sexual act must be open to the transmission of life. But the continuing relevance of the principle is shown by their resistance in turn to such practice as AID and the use of *in vitro* fertilisation outside of the context of married love.

At least this shows that disagreement is about the application of a shared principle, not about principles themselves.

Authority for Freedom, Protection for Growth, Revelation for Understanding There are three features of Jesus's use of the concept of fatherhood, as described in the Gospels, which further illuminate the nature of parenthood. The first is *Authority for Freedom*.

Reference is often made to 'the will of my Father' (cf. Matt. 7:21; 12:50) as the decisive direction for what is good. The authority of the divine Father relativises human parental authority, as can be seen in the striking statement in Matthew 23.9: 'call no one your father on earth, for you have one Father, who is in heaven.' But the authority of the divine

Father also gives a pattern for the authority of human parents who, according to St Paul, are to bring their children up in such training and admonition as Christ himself would give (Eph. 6:4). Parental authority is for the well-being of the children. This is the pattern which the Fourth Gospel illustrates. In John 7:17 we are told, 'if any man's will is to do his will, he shall know whether the teaching is from God'; that teaching is from 'the Father' (8:28), and its purpose is our freedom: 'the truth will make you free' (8:32). 'So if the Son makes you free, you will be free indeed' (8:36). The authority of the truth of God is an authority exercised for the sake of our freedom. Likewise, the goal of parental authority in the human family is freedom. Parents' authority aims at releasing the child from their authority.

It is a great pity that in the past the fifth Commandment has often been used to reinforce authoritarian notions, with the growing child never seen as moving at some stage beyond the simple subjection to one authority or another. Thus, for example, the Prayer Book Catechism has been used to legitimate authoritarianism. It expands the Commandment thus: 'To love, honour and succour my father and mother; to honour and obey the Queen, and all that are put in authority under her; to submit myself to all my governors, teachers, spiritual pastors and masters; to order myself lowly and reverently to all my betters.' It is perhaps therefore hardly surprising that the philosopher John Locke found it necessary to offer an alternative theory of parenthood in order to undermine the way in which fatherly authority was being used to bolster contemporary claims to 'the divine right of kings'. Locke offers a much more plausible account when he suggests that parents are there as trustees to ensure that by the use of their authority the exercise of reason comes to take the place of the child's natural wilfulness.

A second feature of the Fatherhood of God depicted in the Gospels is *Protection for Growth*. The Father is one who cares for and provides for his children so that they need not be anxious (Matt. 6:25). Not a sparrow falls to the ground without the Father knowing (10:29). The birds of the air are fed (6:26) and your heavenly Father knows your needs also (6:8,32). He can be asked for daily bread (6:11), for forgiveness (6: 12,14) for direction and for deliverance from evil (6:13). He, much more than earthly fathers, gives good things to those who ask (7:11). It is not the Father's will that any little ones should perish (18:14). The Father offers a place of security and unconditional welcoming love, even to the prodigal (Luke 15:11f.).

Taking this picture as our guide, together with Paul's injunction that fathers should not provoke their children, we can see that parenting involves providing a context of security sufficient for personal growth free from anxiety.

A third aspect of God's fatherhood is *Revelation for Understanding*, as the very title of the Son as 'Logos' (meaning 'reason' or 'understanding') implies.

Part of the meaning of Fatherhood is to reveal truth to and through the Son. Just as in the Old Testament, the family was the primary locus of education in matters concerning God (Deut. 6:1–8), so in the New Testament, the Son who is in the bosom of the Father, he has made him known (John 1:18) – and parents are to instruct their children 'in the fear and nurture of the Lord' (Eph. 6.4). As Eric Berne noted, a parent has done well if the child, on reaching maturity, can say, 'my parents told me the truth about the world . . . I have found out that they were right'.

But just as the exercise of authority must lead finally to free decision-making as an adult, and the provision of security and protection to the growth of an individual who can think and act independently of its parents, so also must the conveying of the truth lead to an independent understanding and appropriation.

The meaning of 'honour your father and your mother' now takes on a deeper significance. For if the responsibility of parenthood is to some degree to represent to the child something of the nature of God, then 'honouring' my parents means my accepting that God has entrusted those self-same parents with me. Of course, parents can be abominably wicked towards their children. Someone who has been 'given' very cruel or abusing parents may need much counselling, therapy or spiritual help to forgive them enough to be able to honour them. Further, as the story of the young Jesus in the Temple illustrates (Luke 2:41ff.), obligations even to the best of parents are sometimes overridden by obligations towards God. But it is seldom, if ever, that nothing of the natural bonds between parent and child survive, and so it remains the case that 'honouring' will retain some meaning even in the most extreme situations of parental neglect. By divine dispensation it is that parent who has been entrusted with me and me with that parent, and so, though society may rightly judge it appropriate for me to be removed for a time from my parents, this cannot sever the natural bonds that will continue to exist nor abrogate me entirely from the responsibility as an adult of attempting to restore the relationship. For under God I retain a special obligation towards that person, just as he or she retains a similar obligation towards me.

Thankfully many children are more fortunate, and to 'honour' parents can be expressed more positively, though its practical expression will change with the transition from infancy to adulthood. For a young child, honouring parents will primarily mean acceptance of their authority. For an adolescent, it will be discovered in the balance between imposed and free obedience in the struggle for identity. For an adult child with elderly parents, it will find an expression both in the child's own responsible freedom from his parents, as well as in respect for the wisdom of the elders (cf. 1 Tim. 5:1) and in provision for their needs (cf. 1 Tim. 5:4,8; Mark 7: 1–13). But it should not be forgotten that even in adulthood the trust given by God remains reciprocal; that not only has the child these obligations, the parent has the obligation to ensure that the child has indeed become a responsible adult and to treat him or her as such.

Partner not Product   It was not an uncommon view in the ancient world – the view of Aristotle, for example – that children have an economic value for their parents. By contrast, St Paul argues that it is not for children to save up for their parents, but for parents to save up for their children (2 Cor. 12:14). Parenting consists in considering the welfare of children, and not merely considering them as economic assets. This incidental remark is consistent with his view that parents have duties to their children to bring them up in the training and admonition of the Lord.

What is it, though, to be a parent? Why should parents

have obligations to their children? And why their children more than anyone else's?

Some see the family primarily in terms of a 'school for character', with the parents as the teachers. Stanley Hauerwas argues that such a view is 'descriptively mistaken and theologically suspect . . . No one gets married or begins a family in order to develop character.'[10]

That is true, but equally true is the fact that our growth in faith and trust is learned first of all not in church, but in the nursery. As Erikson argues, the first critical phase of emotional development is the child's need to work through the question of 'basic trust',[11] and he is helped to do so if the mothering is (in Winnicott's phrase) 'good enough'[12]. Parenting involves providing a 'facilitating environment' which is 'good enough' for the processes of maturation for each member of the family – a process which will be different at different stages of life. Parents can help their children to grow and to grow up; children can also be a means of sanctification and growth in their parents.

But why do parents have a special obligation to their own children? Whence does such an obligation derive?

The traditional Christian answer has been that children are a 'gift' from God. Children were not thought of as the property of their parents, nor of their community. The contingencies of the acts of procreation meant that the begetting of children was understood as part of the unpredictableness of divine providence.

Advances in medicine have drastically reduced the infant mortality rate, an undoubted blessing, but they are also now bringing so much control over our reproductive processes that it is easy to lose sight of the child as a gift of providence. It can easily become viewed instead as simply a product of human engineering. Thus contraception gives us the freedom to decide when to have children and how many, amniocentesis and other means of antenatal testing can give the knowledge of likely physical handicaps while the child is still in the womb and, most recently, with test-tube babies we now have the power to imitate nature in its early stages. What is worrying about such practices is not that they are wrong in themselves, but that they can so easily lead to wrong attitudes, with the child now seen more as a product than as a partner, as something subject to human will and human disposability, rather than someone who exercises a moral claim to be treated as a neighbour. The danger is that we shall all want the perfect 'product', rather than accepting that for example the mentally and physically handicapped are just as much entitled to life as anyone else, or that adopted children can be just as much *our* children as those that are genetically ours (a religion that calls us all to become adopted children of our heavenly Father could scarcely say anything else). At the same time we should be wary of thinking that this problem of the child as product is simply a creation of advances in medicine. Precisely the same phenomenon is in evidence whenever parents see their child simply as an extension of themselves, or use it for their own ends. Unfortunately there is no shortage of examples of this. One observes it in the pressure on the child to accomplish what the parent in his own life has always longed to do, but been unable to achieve. One sees another side to this in the ever-growing problems of child abuse (particularly in the apparently rapidly growing problems of incest, which, though complex, may often involve the use of the child as an object).

The development of the concept of 'children's rights', as in the 1959 United Nations Declaration, is a reaction against the view that parents 'own' their children, and is instead an affirmation that children own themselves. What this ignores is that it is not a question of ownership at all. The concept of personal rights, a necessary corollary of Enlightenment individualism (a concept within which the notion of 'family' sits rather uneasily), is some distance from the family as the covenant of care.

The question of parenting is not, 'Who owns this child?' It is rather: 'What sort of people should we be, and what sort of social context should we provide, to welcome appropriately a new human life into the human community, and to help her develop her "being in communion" to the full?'

A Covenant of Care   We can draw together much of the preceding discussion of the fatherhood of God and the suggestion that family life is intended to find its meaning in and be patterned on the relationships God has with his people, with his Son, and with his adopted sons and daughters, by referring to the covenant.

From beginning to end of the biblical story, God's relationship with his people is one of loving promise: 'I will be your God'; blessing: 'You shall be my people'; and obligation: 'Be holy as I the Lord your God am holy.' The covenant is a relationship based on mutual trust, mutual acceptance and mutual obligation, and provides the context for the growth of personal relationships through time which are based on that promise and that obligation. The keywords of God's covenanted relationship with his people are 'steadfast love and faithfulness'. The ethical question of family life then becomes: What does it mean for us as parents, for us as children, to give expression to love and faithfulness? Part of the task of the Christian Church is to help people grow characters which are capable of faithfulness.

It is in the covenant that a sense of corporate solidarity is fostered. It is in the covenant that individuals find their place and can be helped to grow, and held accountable. The covenant is a dynamic system within an institutional framework but centring on relationship. Family is, to use Kegan's phrase, a 'culture to grow in', the sort of social institution which is needed to assist psychosocial development (cf. Erikson). Sometimes the story is of struggle and pain and discipline; sometimes of blessing and joy. As with the New Testament reference to Christ who 'though he was a Son learned obedience through what he suffered', so it is sometimes through responsible confrontation with the constraints of family life that 'faculties are trained by practice' (Heb. 5:14). The covenant community is open, outward looking and inclusive. The covenant is both a means of grace and a means of service. Furthermore, the covenant of God with his people points beyond itself to the 'being as communion' of God himself. And so it is the divine covenant which sets the pattern for all the human covenants we make with one another, and so perhaps best illuminates the various characteristics of Christian family life which we have been seeking to identify.

A family, then, is a group of people bound together in a covenant of care – the focus of which is marriage, parenthood and shared residence. But blood relationships do not themselves create family. Merely living together under the same roof does not create family. What binds people together as a family is the covenant of loyalty to one another. Some family loyalties are freely chosen (as between husband and wife). Others are loyalties over which we have no choice (who my parents are). But to *be* family is to recognise a covenanted obligation within this particular group of those who are united by blood kinship or shared residence or both. And to be *family* in a way that is consistent with Christian understanding is to pattern those covenanted obligations and relationships on the nature of God's covenanted love to us.

(c) Disorders in Families

C. S. Lewis's essay, 'The Sermon and the Lunch',[13] exposes the hypocrisy and sentimentality of much Christian thinking of family life, by illustrating the contrast between the vicar's sermon about family on the Sunday evening, and the reality of his family interactions at Sunday lunchtime.

We now need to earth our theological norms in the harsh realities of a disordered world in which the results of sin disrupt relationships, in which the image of God in people is tarnished, and covenants sometimes remain mere external structural frameworks of obligation with no growing personal life within them. There are some families 'in name only', where all personal commitment has died. There are few which fully exhibit the covenant qualities of steadfast love and faithfulness. Most move uneasily somewhere in between. The reality of living in the tension of the 'aeons' between the resurrection of Christ and the final consummation of all things under his rule, is that we are all exposed to the disordering effects of 'the world, the flesh and the devil', and family life here is only ever on the way towards being family in the normative sense.

In a highly individualised and isolationist culture, the sad fact is, that many so called families – even 'close nuclear families' – are mere aggregates of individuals sharing the same roof and the same television set, but living their own lives. Lack of real intimacy is a major problem of our age.

Part of the Church's task is to help people develop the sorts of characters which are capable of making relationships, honouring obligations, of showing love and being faithful. The nature of those commitments and obligations changes with time, from childhood dependence and parental authority, through the years of mature interdependency, to elderly dependency on adult children.

Another of the major effects of the shift in industrialised societies from extended to nuclear family patterns has been the abandonment on a large scale of care for the elderly. This is a growing problem not only in the West, but also for those left in the villages of newly urbanised Third World cultures. The Church may be required to take a stand against the prevailing culture at this point, and remind Christians of the strong New Testament stress on care for one's kin (1 Tim. 5:8. Mark 7:9f.).

There are many disorders within families which could be discussed. In the following paragraphs we outline four of the areas which seem to us to need more Christian attention.

(i) The sins of the fathers   One of the disordering effects of family life is related to the fact that, in group dynamic terms, the family is a 'system' of interacting relationships. Disorder, sin or selfishness in one member of the family inevitably disorders the family as a whole. Emotional hurts and burdens can be carried within family systems, as much of today's work in family therapy illustrates. Pincus and Dare wrote *Secrets in the Family*[14] to demonstrate how patterns of emotional response, of basic group assumptions and attitudes, of resentments, guilt and fear, can be perpetuated within family systems, often unconsciously.

One example is the recurring pattern of authoritarianism. Compensating for his own insecurities, a parent may rule his home with a rod of iron. Parental patterns of insecurity may then be taken over by children – or by certain children within the family configuration – who, at a loss how to act outside an authoritarian context, perpetuate precisely the same family dynamics in their turn.

Another example is the controlling grandmother who still has such an emotional hold over mother that the subsequent mother-daughter relationship is affected, with daughter being caught up into the disordered patterns of an earlier generation.

In theological terms, 'the world' exercises its crippling power through such often unconscious patterns of disorder. When parenting is not 'good enough', when the environment of early learning experience does not facilitate normal growth in the child, then 'cycles of deprivation' (to use Sir Keith Joseph's phrase) are activated. 'The sins of the fathers are visited on the children to the third and fourth generation.' The ministry of the Christian Church to families includes the provision of opportunities for other, more satisfactory, forms of relationship than depriving ones. If the Church can instead facilitate what Jack Dominian has called 'cycles of affirmation', then some of the disorders of family life can be rectified, and some of the bruising patterns of family life healed. It is of interest that at the same time David Cooper writes of 'The Death of the Family', arguing – rightly in some cases – that the emotional hurts carried in families can be crippling to the mental health and well-being of individual members, the growth of family therapy is escalating. It is a judgment on the Christian Church that some people find more help through secular family therapies than they do within the family of God.

(ii) Disordered roles, boundaries and hierarchies   Some of the disorders within families can be traced to an unclarity concerning the roles adopted by different members within the family system. Where, for example, is authority in any particular family? Sometimes it resides with the parents. Sometimes actual power is located in a weak family member who manipulates the others to serve his interests; sometimes a tantrum-prone three year-old or a moody teenager 'rules' by requiring everyone else to tread warily round them. And who cares for whom? Sometimes it may be that an emotionally deprived mother can want a child in order that the child will care for her. How are patterns of authority, responsibility and care negotiated between family members? Is there an unspoken collusion, leading to unspoken resentments and frustrations? How are sexual roles handled within families? Sometimes the presence of children in a family can disrupt the parents' sexual relationship with each other. The

sexual dimension of the relationships between fathers and daughters, mothers and sons, and between parents and children of the same sex can be unclear, or unacknowledged, or inappropriately expressed.

Some of the feminist critique of family is rooted in the conviction that family perpetuates a patriarchal structure in which men rule and women serve. It cannot be denied that some Christian teaching has tended to foster such a view of the family. Neither of us wishes to endorse a patriarchal and authoritarian understanding of male/female relationships. We recognise that many Christians interpret the New Testament references which speak of the husband being 'head' of his wife (1 Cor. 11:3; Eph. 5:23; cf. also Col. 3:18f.; 1 Tim. 2:9f; 1 Pet. 3:1ff.) as a 'creation ordinance', and argue from this that the complementarity of male and female, and therefore husband and wife, is to be expressed in hierarchical terms of male leadership and female subordination. There is ongoing debate within the Christian Church on the meaning of such texts, and it is worth giving a little space to discuss this.

The argument is sometimes based on Adam's naming of Eve as his helper, just as he had authoritatively named the animals. However it seems to us that the Adam and Eve story points primarily to sexual complementarity in diversity, and the question of female subordination to male domination is raised *descriptively* in Genesis 3 as a *consequence* of sin, not normatively in Genesis 2. The notion of Eve as 'helper' does not require the sense of subordination, for the word is used many times of the help that comes from God (cf. Ps. 33:20). Not until Genesis 3:20 does Adam use the standard naming formula for his wife; in 2:23 the 'naming' is more delight than domination.

The New Testament texts clearly have to be interpreted in the light of the cultural assumptions of the age. One of us argues that the Church of today is entitled to go beyond their teaching, both in virtue of the critique inherent within the Bible itself (cf. Gal. 3:28 and 1 Cor. 11:11–12) and our better understanding of the social determinants of human psychology. The other of us believes that a 'hierarchical' exegesis is not the only, or the best, mode of interpreting the texts. Indeed, a number of factors militate against such exegesis.

The Ephesians 5 text turns on the analogy between the mutual 'completion' of Christ and the Church in their relationship with each other, and the mutual completion of husband and wife in 'one flesh' union. This section has to be seen in the wider context which begins in Ephesians 4:1: 'lead a life worthy of the calling to which you have been called'; 'be imitators of God' (Eph. 5.1); and, 'be subject to one another out of reverence for Christ' (Eph. 5:21). In other words, let the gospel of grace dictate the pattern of your relationships within the Church (chapter 4); within marriage (5:21–33); within the home (6:1–4); within the sphere of employment (6:5–9). In that sense, Ephesians 5 can be seen as a sort of reversal of Genesis 3:16. There the man is said to 'rule over' his wife. In Ephesians 5:25, he is rather to 'love' her (a revolutionary teaching!) as Christ loves, that is, put her interests first. In Genesis 3:16, the wife is said to 'desire' in a selfishly grasping way her husband. In Ephesians 5:22 the wife is to 'submit to' (i.e. respect; not 'obey' cf. 6:1,5) the husband – that is, put his interests first. The husband as 'head' (Eph. 5:23) is to be interpreted in the light of the way Christ is Head of the Church (cf. Eph. 4:15f.) – by providing a family context in which both can be to the other a source of 'completion'.[15]

The paragraph in 1 Corinthians 11 has also been the subject of much debate, the argument concerning primarily the ordering of worship so that no offence should be given (cf. 1 Cor. 10:32). Paul's use of the Old Testament is selective for his purpose (thus only 'man' is in the divine image 1 Cor. 11:7, contrast Gen. 1:27), and his use of 'head' is related to his discussion of head-coverings. Whereas man is described as 'head' of woman, the sense has to be derived from the way 'the head of Christ is God' (1 Cor. 11:3). The commentary of C. K. Barrett on 1 Corinthians shows how this passage may well be best interpreted in a non-hierarchical way.[16]

The idea of mutuality rather than subordination (except in the sense of mutual submission, Eph. 5:21) is also found in 1 Corinthians 7:1f., and is consistent with the 'charter of our humanity' (also from the pen of St Paul) in Galatians 3:28. That the context is baptismal does not affect the fact that Paul is arguing that in Christ discrimination based on race, status or sex is to be set aside. Such, surely was the attitude of Jesus towards women.

For the Church to perpetuate an authoritarian style of hierarchicalism in its understanding of family life is, we believe, both to misread the New Testament, and to open itself to the just rebuke of some feminist critics of family, that the Christian faith discriminates against women. The truth, we believe, is rather that women and men are equal and complementary within the Church and within the family. Indeed, given our earlier account of parental trust as the responsibility of bringing the child to a capacity for independent decision-making, it is perhaps scarcely surprising that we should view the relationship between the sexes in marriage as requiring a similar degree of independence within the admittedly overarching framework of mutual interdependence and complementarity. How that complementarity is expressed is more a matter of preference, temperament and gifts than of normative structures.

(iii) Abandonment of authority Perhaps a more common problem, at least in modern Western society, is the exercise of too little authority rather than too much. One reason for this is a hangover from the 1960s, the false libertarian assumption that all forms of authority are bad, with the resultant failure to distinguish between legitimate use of authority and authoritarianism. But, as child psychologists are increasingly acknowledging, there is little prospect of a healthy child without the considerable exercise of parental authority. For not only does the failure ever to say 'no' result in a spoilt child unable to see anything except from the perspective of its own selfish interest, but it is also true that clear boundaries are essential to the growing child and that in fact he will constantly test the limits until he discovers the secure borders beyond which he may not go.

Normally, however, the reasons why parents do not intervene will not extend quite so far as the suspicion of authority *per se*. Sometimes it will just be a matter of pure selfishness, e.g. such a strong desire to pursue one's career that little or no time is left for one's children. This can become a particularly acute issue in situations where both parents work, in a society in which free education is provided by the

State from an early age, and in which television can easily be used as a substitute for family interaction. This is not, of course, to say that any of these things are of themselves bad. However, they can be open to the potential abuse of encouraging a selfish abandonment of parental responsibility.

There are also more insidious ways in which even deeply committed Christian parents can be tempted to abdicate their authority. This may be illustrated by common attitudes both to sex and religious education. In the former case, it is widely acknowledged that parents often find it difficult to discuss sex with their children. They are therefore content to leave the matter to schools, ignoring the problem that, while the schools may be excellent in conveying factual information, they are less suitable contexts for dealing with the inseparable emotional and relational dimensions, where the differences in personal psychology become more pertinent, and where, therefore, some discussion in the home must be seen as ideal.

Less widely acknowledged is the fact that a similar problem can also plague religious education. Many parents fail to pass on their faith to their children, not because they themselves do not regularly pray or go to church, but rather because this remains an entirely private activity. It is left to the Sunday School to give such instruction as it can, but the parent is too embarrassed to share his faith either by teaching his child to pray or by raising religious issues. This reluctance is perhaps induced in part by fear that the child may in turn raise questions to which he does not know the answers. Here the Church itself must surely bear a large measure of blame, both through encouraging too private and personal a view of religion and secondly in cultivating too much the notion of priest as the professional expert to whom such tasks ought therefore to be left.

The longstanding and widespread assumptions of Western culture that all education is only the task of professionals and hardly if at all the task of parents, is thankfully now beginning to be questioned (cf. the parent-teacher partnerships of 'community education'), but there is still a long way to go and many questions still to be resolved.

(iv) The idolatry of the family   Disorder within families can arise when the family is thought to exist for its own sake.

Some of those who speak of the family as a 'school for character', says Stanley Hauerwas, can 'too easily turn the family into an idolatrous institution'. He continues, 'Too often the church is supported because people care about the family. They assume the church is good because it produces a good family. God is worshipped as a means to help sustain what we really care about – the family.'[17]

When the family is turned into that kind of god it spells disorder. For when family is asked to carry such supreme moral significance, it is asked to carry too much. 'When the family is invested with such significance, it cannot but be morally tyrannical.'

Part of the temptation to idolatry comes from the temptation to isolate the moral significance of the family from other aspects of the meaning of family life. This was not the case in ancient Israel. One of the intriguing facts of Old Testament family life is the interplay between economic, social and religious factors. In the holiness code of Leviticus 19 for example, there are regulations concerning worship, agriculture, social honesty, property, justice, sex, farming, religion, hospitality to strangers, and so on. And throughout, the refrain 'I am the Lord' indicates that the people's relationship to Yahweh was the unifying dimension in all this diversity, and the people were to express in all these diverse areas of life the fact that they were the people of God. It is not possible, therefore, to separate out a book of Old Testament religion, another of Old Testament ethics, and a third of Old Testament economics. In the family, moral, spiritual, economic and social concerns are all inseparably linked. The family in ancient Israel stood at the centre of a series of connected relationships: to God, to Israel and to the land. The family was the locus for the primary covenant relationship of the people with God; the family was the basic unit and beneficiary of Israel's system of land tenure, because the land was ultimately owned by God, and was given to families as an inheritance.[18]

Family solidarity was therefore very strong. But the family did not exist as a moral community in isolation from its social or economic context.

One of the difficulties of some modern Christian concern for wholesome family life is that it fails to address the social conditions within which family cohesion is economically viable and socially worth while. It is much easier to be 'family' in the stockbroker belt with the sun on our backs than on Merseyside weathering the storms of urban deprivation and long-term unemployment. Easier also than among the 'parking boys' or child prostitutes on the streets of Nairobi; among the abandoned rural kinship groups in the country while the husband seeks his fortune in one of Africa's new towns; easier than in the vast high-rise apartments of Hong Kong. To isolate the moral concept of 'family' from its social and economic context, and from its true meaning within the convenanted purposes of God for human well-being, is to come very close to idolatry.

So in supporting family life, the Church cannot disengage itself from wider social issues such as quality of housing, unemployment, the scale of social security or welfare benefits. Nor can the Church in the West distance itself from the pressing political and social questions being forced on the Churches of Africa in the rapid changes in family life through 'Westernisation'. The Church must also be on its guard against romanticised versions of marriage and family that raise absurdly high expectations of the nature of the relationship or which assume that they must substitute rather than complement other social relationships such as friendship.

(d) The extended family in the Holy City

One of the surprises the Bible holds is that despite the essentially agrarian character of Jewish society, its future vision, apart from a few exceptions (e.g. Mic. 4:4; Isa. 11:6f.) is concentrated on a city. Thus the Jerusalem that is the focus of Old Testament aspirations (Pss. 48, 122, 137) is taken up and enhanced in the New (Gal. 4:26; Heb. 11:10,16). One could scarcely have a more effective endorsement of the essentially social character of the Christian vision. But the city can also have negative connotations, as with the use of Babylon in 1 Peter and Revelation. So it is important to qualify the image in the right kind of way and this can perhaps best be achieved through thinking of that holy city as an extended family. Our Lord on the cross can himself be seen as beginning this process when in John's Gospel he enlarges his own natural family by committing his mother to his 'beloved disciple's care. Symbolically this can be read as inviting all his beloved disciples, that is all of us, into his family since the other half of the declaration implies that equally John has now become fully part of Jesus's family ('behold, your son! . . . behold, your mother!' John 19:26–7). We are thus called to a relationship at once as deep as the family can be at its best, and at the same time one in which all natural ties are clearly transcended.

The ultimate purpose of the divine covenant is pictured by the apocalyptic writer of Revelation 21 as 'the holy city, new Jerusalem . . . and God himself will be with them'. It is here that the covenant of God, the focus of much of our earlier discussion, comes to its consummation. For the covenant is the story of a people on their way home. It is in the holy city that the covenant promise is spoken once more: 'I will be his God and he shall be my son' (Rev. 21:7) It is this picture of the ultimate family of God which gives meaning to, and also relativises, human family life. M. Moynagh calls this the 'eschatological family', rightly noting that the question of the purpose of family life is thus taken outside the family itself.[19] This challenges contemporary tendencies to justify the family in terms of what it achieves for its members. It shows that the eschatological family of the people of God can challenge contemporary families to make God's kingdom more present in the world. Above all it emphasises the fact that family life is only one way, though the most basic, of our being conformed to the divine image as social and personal, with which these reflections began.

NOTES

1 Brigitte and Peter Berger, *The War over the Family* (Harmondsworth, 1983), p. 45.
2 Alvin Toffler, *The Third Wave* (London, 1980), p. 208f.
3 Jessie Bernard, *The Future of Marriage* (Harmondsworth, 1972), p. 281f.
4 Edmund Leach, *Social Anthropology* (Oxford, 1982), p. 182.
5 e.g. C. C. Harris, *The Family* (London, 1969), p. 87f.
6 J. D. Zizioulas, *Being as Communion* (London, 1985).
7 O. M. T. O'Donovan, *Marriage and Permanence* (Bramcote, 1978).

8 Jack Dominian, *Marriage, Faith and Love* (London, 1981).
9 G. von Rad, *Genesis* (London, 1961).
10 S. Hauerwas, 'The Family as a School for Character', *Religious Education*, vol. 80/2 (1985), p. 272.
11 Erik Erikson, *Childhood and Society* (Hythe, 1951), chap. 7.
12 D. W. Winnicott, *The Maturational Processes and the Facilitating Environment* (London, 1976).
13 C. S. Lewis, *Undeceptions* (London, 1971).
14 L. Pincus and C. Dare, *Secrets in the Family* (London, 1978).
15 cf. M. Barth, *Ephesians 4–6* (New York, 1974).
16 C. K. Barrett, *The First Epistle to the Corinthians* (London, 1968).
17 S. Hauerwas, *A Community of Character* (Indiania, 1981).
18 C. Wright, *Living as the People of God* (Leicester, 1983).
19 M. Moynagh, 'Home to Home', *Anvil*, vol. 3, No. 3 (1986).

BIBLIOGRAPHY

On the Family

Ray Anderson and Dennis Guernsey, *On Being Family* (Grand Rapids, Michigan, 1985). *A theologian and a sociologist together explore the convenantal nature of family.*

Brigitte and Peter Berger, *The War over the Family* (Harmondsworth, 1983). *Two sociologists outline the current social scene.*

O. R. Johnston, *Who Needs the Family?* (London, 1979). *An Evangelical Christian assessment.*

Michael Moynagh, 'Home to Home: Towards a Biblical Model of the Family', in *Anvil*, vol. 3, No. 3 (1986).

Onora O'Neill and William Ruddick, *Having Children* (Oxford, 1979). *Philosophical and legal reflections on parenthood.*

On Marriage and Divorce

David Atkinson, *To Have and To Hold* (London, 1979). *Arguing for the permissibility of divorce in certain circumstances.*

David Brown, *Choices* (Oxford, 1983). *This criticises the previous book (!) and is a general survey of specific issues in Christian ethics; see especially chapter 4.*

J. Dominian, *Marriage, Faith and Love* (London, 1981). *A very practical approach from a Roman Catholic psychiatrist.*

W. Heth and Gordon Wenham, *Jesus and Divorce* (London, 1984). *A conservative Evangelical, historical and biblical approach.*

E. Schillebeeckx, *Marriage: Human Reality and Saving Mystery* (London, 1965). *A very full Roman Catholic theology of marriage.*

H. Thielicke, *The Ethics of Sex* (Grand Rapids, Michigan, 1979). *A Lutheran theological survey of human sexuality.*

On Homosexuality

D. Atkinson, *Homosexuals in the Christian Fellowship* (Oxford, 1979).
D. Brown, *Choices*, op. cit., pp. 102ff.
Board of Social Responsibility, *Homosexual Relationships* (London, 1979). *Church of England Report not endorsed by the General Synod.*
P. Coleman, *Christian Attitudes to Homosexuality* (London, 1980).*A full survey of recent debates.*
N. Pittenger, *Time for Consent* (London, 1976). *A careful liberal approach, affirming homosexual relationships.*

DISCUSSION QUESTIONS

1 Identify the main 'threats' to family living in your area (e.g. housing, unemployment, changing sexual behaviour . . .).

2 How can your Christian community help people 'grow characters' capable of making commitments? (How often do you discuss moral issues with each other, and with younger members of the congregation?)

3 In what ways can your local church be more of a healing community (e.g. with pastoral care for the divorced)?

4 In what ways might your church load family life with too many demands? (How many demands does it make on family time?)

5 Can your church improve ways of ensuring that all feel part of the extended family of the Church (the divorced, the single . . .)?

6 Can you think of particular ways in which your church could strengthen right patterns of family living?

NOTE We are grateful to Dr Janet Martin Soskice, tutor at Ripon College, Cuddesdon, and to Miss Elizabeth Sheddon, Director of Care and Counsel, for acting as consultants to the authors of this essay.

7

MISSION AGENDA FOR THE PEOPLE OF GOD

NINE THESES

The terms 'mission' and 'people of God' belong inescapably to one another. For God's people are a people in mission, sent into the world by God, for God and with God. Indeed our mission is his mission. He gives us the great privilege of sharing in his concern for the world, both for personal salvation and for the justice and peace of world communities, as we look forward to the day when all things will be redeemed and united in Christ.

Yet many Christians are perplexed, and even offended, by the vocabulary we tend to use in this context. Words like 'mission', 'evangelism' and 'conversion', and especially 'crusade', may seem to smack of a triumphalism which is inappropriate in the present age of uncertainty. The foundations of our world are crumbling; is this the right time for confident assertions?

On the other hand, people are increasingly turning to the Church for answers. It would be tragic if, just when the world is asking questions, the Church should be too diffident to speak.

We believe the time is ripe for Anglicans to join other Christians in that kind of evangelism which combines boldness with humility. We hope that the 1988 Lambeth Conference will issue a call to mission, and that perhaps it may be initiated by leaders of Third World churches, which are often now more committed to mission than the older churches of the West. To this end we propose the following theses:

THESIS 1: THE PEOPLE OF GOD HAVE GOOD NEWS TO SHARE

There can be no evangelism without an evangel. This is why every discussion of evangelism must include the clarification of our message. What is the good news according to the Scriptures? What is the good news for men and women in different cultures and contexts today? These questions must be asked, and the answers we give must be related to one another.

There is a sense in which God's good news embraces the whole message of the Bible from the creation to the consummation. Often our gospel is too small, and people reject it because they perceive it to be inadequate to meet their needs. Paul told the leaders of the Ephesian church that he had not hesitated to proclaim in their city 'the whole counsel of God' (Acts 20:27). There was a breadth and depth to the apostolic gospel which are sadly missing in much of our contemporary proclamation.

At the same time, the apostles focused on Jesus Christ, and in particular on his death and resurrection. It has often been pointed out that, if the basic message (*kerygma*) of the apostle Peter, as Luke summarises it in the early speeches of the Acts, is compared with Paul's survey in 1 Corinthians 15:1 ff., a common framework emerges. Both apostles spoke of the death and resurrection of Jesus of Nazareth, (a) according to the Old Testament Scriptures and their own eyewitness testimony, (b) as inaugurating the long promised new age or kingdom of God, (c) as being the ground on which God bestows on penitent believers the gifts of forgiveness and of the Holy Spirit, and (d) as issuing in the exaltation of Christ as the Lord of all life. These are essential elements of the good news, which Paul declared to be both the original and the universal faith of the Church (1 Cor. 15:3, 11). They have been revealed by God and given to the Church. So we have no liberty to stray from this core of the gospel.

Nevertheless, when we ask what the 'salvation' is which is offered in the gospel, we find in the New Testament itself a rich diversity of formulations. This is not at all surprising when we remember how widely different were the contexts in which the Word of God came to people as good news. Jesus himself concentrated on the breaking into the world of God's kingdom, with all the blessings and demands which his rule entails. In John's Gospel, 'kingdom' language has largely been replaced by 'eternal life', which is the personal knowledge of God (17:3). In his letter to the Romans Paul develops his gospel of 'justification by faith', the free acceptance of guilty sinners by the Judge, on the sole ground of the atoning death of Christ, by faith alone without any human merit. But the apostles also wrote in their letters of redemption, regeneration or new birth by the Holy Spirit, re-creation, resurrection, reconciliation, adoption, the lordship of Christ, his victory over the powers, purification and sanctification, the new covenant and the new community, and the final restoration of all things. Modern scholarship is tending to emphasise this diversity, for the facts are plain. No one image of salvation may claim to be dominant in the New Testament, let alone exclusive, even if some receive more prominence than others.

It is not enough, however, to seek to define the good news in a way that is faithful to Scripture. We have also to struggle to present it in a way that resonates with modern men and women in that area of the world in which they live. Different cultures demand different emphases. In the West, where many have been led into the despair of meaninglessness and intellectual alienation, there is a great hunger for personal significance, so that we need to speak of God having created us in his own image, and loving us in Christ, as the grounds for a new self-respect and self-affirmation. To people where 'traditional religion' dominates, whose world seems teeming with spirits, often feared to be malign, what appeals is the message that Jesus Christ has overthrown all principalities and powers, and can deliver us from them today. Yet others are burdened with some kind of oppression (poverty, discrimination or the denial of human rights, in addition to the universal tyrannies of guilt, self-centredness and fear): they need to hear of Jesus Christ the liberator. 'Salvation' is an archaic word of traditional religious vocabulary, but 'freedom' rings bells, especially if we are able to unite its positive and negative aspects, and clarify what Christ frees us 'from' and 'for'. He challenges our mediocrity and summons us to a fulfilling life of adventure and service.

Another longing of modern men and women is for love, for authentic human relationships, for genuine community: we need, therefore, to remember that the Church is an essential part of the gospel, as the new community of Jesus. For he gave himself for us, not only 'to redeem us from all wickedness' but also 'to purify for himself a people that are his very own, eager to do what is good' (Titus 2:14). The gospel is good news of reconciliation with each other as well as with God.

Yet another search in which many are engaged, whether consciously or unconsciously, is for a truth which will explain and integrate all their knowledge and experience. Is this not Jesus himself the Logos of God, the Light of the world, under whose headship one day all things will be unified (Eph. 1:10)?

Here, then, are two diversities – the diversity of the New Testament formulations and the diversity of felt human needs. The exciting (though demanding) task of the Church is to absorb the richness of these diversities, to explore and clarify them, especially in relation to each other, in order sensitively to relate divine revelation to human need. We believe that Jesus Christ is the fulfilment of every human aspiration, but in order to authenticate this we have to penetrate more deeply both into the fullness of Christ and into the predicament of human beings today. Then our message will be heard as good news.

THESIS 2: THE PEOPLE OF GOD CONFESS JESUS CHRIST AS THE UNIQUE AND UNIVERSAL SAVIOUR AND LORD

When the 1910 World Missionary Conference in Edinburgh ended, the delegates dispersed in a mood of great euphoria. The reports from different regions which had taken two or three years to compile, and which were submitted to the Conference, predicted the imminent collapse of the ethnic religions and declared the time ripe for the final evangelisation of the world. Two devastating world wars and a period of theological uncertainty supervened, and both the situation and the mood are entirely different today.

Today many countries (especially in Asia) are dominated by a Hindu, Buddhist, Moslem, secular or Marxist culture, while the Christian percentage of the population may be one per cent or less. In Africa during recent years there has been enormous church growth, although there has also been a resurgence of African traditional religion. In addition, there is the phenomenon of thousands of Christian (and sometimes semi-Christian) churches, each seeking to develop its own African expression of Christianity.

In Latin America, the Roman Catholic Church is experiencing spiritual renewal in some places (especially in its 'base communities'), in others a continuing mixture with pre-Christian superstitions, and especially in Brazil the rivalry of Afro-American spiritualistic cults. The Protestant (especially, though not exclusively, Pentecostal) churches have witnessed quite remarkable growth which, however, has often been marred by both intellectual and spiritual shallowness.

In the 'Western' countries of North America, Europe and Britain's former 'dominions' two processes have been at work. On the one hand, secularisation has eroded the influence of the churches. On the other, a liberal post-war immigration policy has resulted in substantial ethnic and religious pluralism. This new phenomenon presents a challenge not only to the country's social cohesion, but also to its churches. Previously, the other religions, being conveniently far away, could be ignored or dismissed; but now Christians meet their adherents daily in their neighbourhood or at work.

Is it still possible in these various situations to speak of the 'uniqueness' and 'universality' of Christ? We are convinced that it is not only possible, but essential. What is sometimes called his 'uniqueness' (because he has no peers), sometimes his 'finality' (because he has no successors) and sometimes his 'supremacy' (because he has no superiors) arises from the facts of his history. The Church must continue to affirm not only that he 'was born of the Virgin Mary, suffered under Pontius Pilate, was crucified, dead and buried, and on the third day rose again', but that in no other person but Jesus of Nazareth has the Word become flesh and dwelt among us, died for our sins and been raised from the dead. The Incarnation, Atonement and Resurrection are all, both historically and theologically, without parallel. We must not therefore be ashamed of the exclusive phraseology of the New Testament, for example the 'no other name' and the 'only one mediator' (Acts 4:12; 1 Tim. 2:5). It is a natural development from the Old Testament affirmations about Yahweh, the Holy One of Israel, that 'there is no other', and that apart from him there is no God, no Saviour (e.g. Isa. 43: 10f.; 45:5 f.). He is the Creator of the world, the Sovereign Ruler of the nations as well as the Covenant God of Israel, the people he chose to be his own.

The corollary to uniqueness is also the same in both Testaments: it is universal lordship, on account of which God calls his people to be his witnesses. For whatever is unique is universal. The Lambeth Conference of 1958 quoted William Temple that 'if the gospel is true for anyone anywhere, it is true for all men everywhere'. To Israel who had experienced his mighty deed of redemption, God said, 'you are my witnesses' (e.g. Isa. 43:10–13, 44:8). To his apostles whom he had chosen to be 'with him', Jesus said, 'you will be my witnesses' (Luke 24:48; John 15:27; Acts 1:8). We ourselves have not known the historic Jesus first-hand, as they did. Nevertheless, we too have come to know him, and must testify to him out of our experience.

In bearing witness to Jesus Christ as the one and only God-man and Saviour, we recognise that there are several pitfalls which we need to avoid.

First, the common humanity which we share with men and women of all races and religions must never be forgotten. We must never affirm the unity we enjoy by redemption in such a way as to deny or overlook the unity which all people have by creation. Scripture forbids all disrespect to human beings, since we all share equally in the image of God (e.g. Gen. 9:6; Prov. 14:31; Ja. 3:9). Zealous evangelists are sometimes guilty of arrogant attitudes; indeed all of us need to repent of lingering racial and religious pride. If God has redeemed us through Christ, it is due to his mercy alone.

Second, in claiming uniqueness for the person, work and salvation of Christ, we are far from denying that God is also present and active in the non-Christian world. We believe that the eternal Logos of God, who became flesh in Jesus, is also the agent of all creation, the source of all life, and the light of all people (John 1:3, 4). Long before he 'came' to the world, he 'was coming' into it as 'the true light that gives light to every man' (vv. 9, 11). Christians therefore claim that everything in human experience which is good, beautiful or true derives ultimately from Jesus Christ, God's eternal Word. This does not mean that we should think of those who make no Christian profession as 'anonymous Christians' (many are themselves offended by this term), but rather that they are beneficiaries of the anonymous or incognito Christ, since they receive from him the life and light of God-given human experience.

The story of Cornelius, a Gentile 'god-fearer', who had probably already embraced monotheism and Jewish ethical standards, has sometimes been misused to teach that sincere and god-fearing non-Christian people are on that account 'pleasing' or 'acceptable' to God (Acts 10:34 f.). What Peter who used that expression meant by it was rather that God has no racial favourites. It is also clear that God was active in Cornelius' life, before Peter's arrival, leading him towards salvation. But these things did not inhibit the apostle from proclaiming the gospel to him and his household. On the contrary, he preached to them, in order that they might believe in Jesus and so receive the forgiveness of sins through his name (10:43). What happened to Cornelius and his household when they believed was that God gave them his Spirit (10:44 ff.), 'saved' them (11:14), granted them 'repentance unto life' (11:18) and 'purified their hearts by faith' (15:9).

The third question people ask, whenever exclusive claims by or for Christ are mentioned, is whether this dooms all those who have not heard of him or believed in him. Probably very few Christians draw this rigid conclusion. For one thing it is not given to human beings to read hearts or pronounce about destinies. This is God's prerogative, who alone 'knows those who belong to him' (2 Tim. 2:19). We must continue to affirm that none of us is fit to enter God's holy presence in our own righteousness, that our religious and philanthropic works (whether Christian or non-Christian) cannot make us fit, and that Christ crucified and risen is the only Saviour through whom God forgives and welcomes sinners. What has not been disclosed to us (and what we do not therefore know) is what degree of Christian knowledge and faith there must be in a person before God saves him or her through Christ. Speculations about this may help us to live with the problem; they neither diminish the uniqueness and universality of Christ, nor reduce the urgency with which he must be proclaimed throughout the world.

The uniqueness and universality of the Lord Jesus raise the dilemma of multi-faith activities. We fully agree that there are a number of good causes in which adherents of different religions can and should work together. We also recognise that some religions can make a common affirmation of monotheism. Nevertheless, any attempt to equate the different 'Scriptures' inevitably compromises the uniqueness of God's revelation through Christ, while equating different ways of finding him inevitably compromises the uniqueness of his redemption through Christ. Zeal for the glory of God in Christ motivates the Church to worship him, to make him universally known, and to avoid any activity which would detract from his incomparable majesty.

THESIS 3: THE PEOPLE OF GOD ARE CALLED TO PROCLAIM AND TO CONVINCE

There is, in fact, a cluster of six words which need to be defined and disentangled, namely evangelism (or proclamation), argument, persuasion, conversion (and baptism), proselytism and dialogue.

At its simplest 'evangelism' means 'sharing the evangel', and both the main New Testament verbs which are used for it (*euangelizesthai* and *kerussein*) mean the same thing. The

English equivalents 'evangelise' and 'proclaim' have unfortunately acquired through the years (doubtless through Christian malpractice) overtones of superiority and triumphalism which the Greek originals do not have. 'Proclamation', for example, conjures up the image of a government official announcing an edict at the top of his voice. No such picture necessarily attaches to the Greek verb *euangelizesthai*. On the contrary, the emphasis is not on the method of announcement, but on its contents. It is significant, for example, that Luke uses the verb to describe both the apostles' public preaching and Philip's private witness to the Ethiopian in his chariot (Acts 8:25, 35). The same is true of the other word; the emphasis is not so much on the activity of proclaiming (*kerussein*) as on the message proclaimed (*kerygma*). It is contrasted with the wisdom of the world and is declared to be the means by which God saves believers (1 Cor. 1:21), even though to unbelievers it is both foolishness and a stumbling-block.

The word 'proclamation' must also not be understood as a dogmatic, take-it-or-leave-it announcement. For at least among the apostles, proclaiming and arguing, evangelism and apologetics went hand in hand. When sharing the gospel with Jews, Paul 'reasoned with them from the Scriptures, explaining and proving that the Christ had to suffer and rise from the dead', and went on to argue that this Messiah was Jesus (e.g. Acts 17:2, 3). When proclaiming Jesus Christ to Gentile audiences, however, he did not argue from the Old Testament Scriptures, which they did not know. At least in Lystra (Acts 14:14 ff.) and in Athens (Acts 17:22 ff.), when preaching to superstitious pagans on the one hand and sophisticated philosophers on the other, he began rather with the visible phenomena of creation and the consequent folly of idolatry. It was still an argument. Paul did not regard the use of arguments as in any way incompatible with his trust in the Holy Spirit. On the contrary, it was through his apologetic that the Holy Spirit cleared away the mists of misunderstanding and led people to faith. We too have to begin where people are, whether adherents of another religion or ideology, or steeped in irreligious secularism. Too much modern evangelism is proclamation without argument. We need more

Christian scholars who will develop a rational apologetic, related to both biblical text and cultural context, which evangelists can use.

'Persuasion' is the next word. The purpose of argument is to convince people the truth is being presented. Paul summed up his whole ministry in the three words 'we persuade men' (2 Cor. 5:11), and Luke describes him in the Acts as doing so. Many times at the end of his missions Luke says that people were 'persuaded' or 'convinced'. We are not implying by this that people are brought to Christ only by linear logic. For teaching and apologetic can take different forms. Jesus himself preferred story-telling, and thus appealed to both mind and heart. Although in all decision-making the will is active, it can be persuaded by reason and emotion, preferably by both in a fully human response.

'Conversion' follows naturally. The apostles were seeking to convince in order to convert. Conversion is a turn from idols to the living God (e.g. 1 Thess. 1:9) and from sin to the Saviour (e.g. 1 Pet. 2:25); it is therefore a compound of repentance and faith. It is not identical with regeneration, although the Holy Spirit is the author of both. 'Conversion' is our turning to Christ as Saviour and Lord, which only the Holy Spirit can enable us to do. 'Regeneration' is his work of rebirth, imparting new life to the soul.

It is sometimes said nowadays that our objective should not be to convert Hindus, Jews or Moslems to Christ, but to help them become better Hindus, Jews and Moslems. This betrayal of the Christian mission should hardly need refutation. If Christ and his apostles had believed it, the Church would never have come into being, since all the first converts to Christ were Jews. And their conversion was publicly expressed in baptism, which dramatised both God's grace, in cleansing and bestowing the Spirit, and the convert's faith, as he submitted to baptism in the name of the Christ he had previously rejected (Acts 2:38). Baptism also marked the transfer from the old order to the new community of the Messiah (Acts 2:40, 41).

Those who dislike the notion of 'conversion' often denigrate it by dubbing it 'proselytism'. But in the last twenty or so years a lot of useful ecumenical thought has been applied to these words, which has been summarised in the two World Council and Roman Catholic documents entitled *Common Witness and Proselytism* (1970) and *Common Witness* (1980). In these reports witness itself, proclaiming Christ and testifying to him, is accepted as a legitimate Christian activity. It becomes 'unworthy witness', and therefore 'proselytism' as opposed to 'evangelism' (a) when the motive is human prestige rather than divine glory, (b) when undue pressure of any kind is used to induce conversion, and (c) when the message includes untrue or uncharitable references to the faith of others.

'Dialogue' is the fifth word for consideration. We do not put it last because we think it is a separable activity. On the contrary, all evangelism must be to some degree dialogical, in the sense that it engages with the minds and hearts of people, responds to their questions and evokes a further response from them. This has been so from the beginning. *Dialegesthai* is another word Luke uses to describe the work of the apostles; it may mean no more than to 'conduct a discussion', but in the Acts it refers to Paul's debates with people in the market-place as well as in the synagogue.

Dialogue takes many forms, and in recent decades a great deal has been said and written about it. It may be defined as a serious religious conversation between two or more people of different faiths, in which each participant listens as well as speaks. For Christian participants such listening will involve the struggle to enter deeply into other people's worlds, in order to understand them and appreciate their cultural riches. It will demand great humility and love. It is also an activity in its own right. It can certainly never be a substitute for evangelism, although this is how it has sometimes been presented.

Another reason for the hostility some Christians express towards dialogue is the proposal, which has on occasion been made, that each side must enter the dialogue with complete openness. If by 'openness' is meant the openminded desire to listen and to learn, there is no problem. This is essential. But some advocates of dialogue demand the kind of 'openness' which suspends all previous convictions. This would not only be an inauthentic gesture by Christians (and others), but would actually render the dialogue impossible. Dialogue is a frank exchange between people holding different views. A proper commitment on both sides, and not the suspension of commitment, is therefore indispensable to the development of dialogue.

THESIS 4: THE PEOPLE OF GOD MUST REACH OUT TO ALL WHO SUFFER INJUSTICE

The most lively ecumenical debate in the sphere of mission during the last quarter-century has been variously expressed as concerning the relationship between the vertical and the horizontal, love for God and love for neighbour, evangelism and social action. The tension surfaced at Mexico in 1963 and again at Uppsala 1968, but was not resolved. Bangkok 1974 ('Salvation today') and the development of liberation theologies have attempted a solution by defining both 'mission' and 'salvation' in largely socio-political terms.

We are in full agreement that the Christian mission has a social as well as an evangelistic dimension. Our difficulty lies in deciding how to relate them without confusing them. Two fruitful possibilities which merit further exploration and which should not be controversial are the demands of God's kingdom on the one hand and of love on the other.

It is evident from the Old Testament expectation that the kingdom of God, to be ushered in by the Messiah, would be a rule of justice and peace (e.g. Isa. 11:1 ff.; 42:1 ff.; Jer. 23:5 f.). In the New Testament fulfilment these concepts are enriched to include the new relationship which through Christ God's people enjoy with him: 'having been justified by faith, we have peace with God' (Rom. 5:1; cf. 14:17). Yet the Old Testament social dimension has not been lost. Those who belong to the kingdom must exemplify its high standards of justice and peace in their own community life, and cannot be indifferent to any situation in which they are absent. Sometimes the values of the kingdom may be discerned even where Christ is not known or named. At other times these values are publicly contradicted, whether by moral permissiveness, social injustice or corruption in high places. In such cases the

Church has a prophetic as well as an evangelistic responsibility, namely to denounce the evil, commend the good and call rulers to repent, thus witnessing to the law of God, as well as to his gospel. Moreover, faithfulness to God's law and gospel, including the call to personal and social repentance, often arouses opposition (even within the Church) and so commits the people of God to walk in the footsteps of the Suffering Servant.

The 'works' of Jesus were more than signs of God's kingdom; they were also signs of his love. He performed them when he was 'moved with compassion' towards people in need. We, too, should be similarly moved; otherwise God's love is not in us (1 John 3:16–18).

Thus justice and love combine to demand action on behalf of the poor and the oppressed. The followers of Jesus should always be deeply ashamed when some followers of Marx exhibit a stronger commitment to the exploited than they. There would be a fundamental anomaly in proclaiming the gospel of God's love to Indians in Latin America whose land is being expropriated, to fishermen in Kerala whose ancestral way of life is being threatened by big business, or to the victims of the neglected inner cities of the West, without identifying with them in their sufferings and their struggles.

All people, whether poor or prosperous, need to hear the Christian message. Yet much has been written in recent years about the gospel as 'good news for the poor' (especially based on Luke 4:18; 6:20; 7:22) and about the need in mission to establish a 'preferential option' for the poor, while at the same time remembering the spiritual poverty of many who are rich and powerful. In this discussion we consider it important not to polarise those who stress the 'spiritual', and those who stress the 'economic', aspect of biblical poverty. For 'the poor' in the Old Testament are both the deprived and the oppressed on the one hand, and on the other the meek who look to Yahweh alone for help. We believe it is God's purpose to combine these, since his kingdom is both a free gift of salvation to those who acknowledge their spiritual bankruptcy (Matt. 5:3), and the good news of justice in the Messianic community in which material poverty should be abolished.

We believe that the most effective Christian outreach is the kind which is committed to the holistic vision of mission. Whenever evangelistic, educational, medical, agricultural and developmental concerns are brought together in a comprehensive care for whole persons and whole communities, the love and justice of God shine brightly.

THESIS 5: THE PEOPLE OF GOD MUST BE SEEN TO BE WHAT THEY CLAIM TO BE

Many Christians seek to glorify Christ by testifying to what he has done for them. In this situation those who do not make a Christian profession have the right to ask for evidence from those who do. If we claim that Christ has saved us and made us his people, in what ways do we manifest salvation in our common life?

In a world of ideological claim and counter-claim we desire to stress the need for Christian authenticity. Our light will shine, as Jesus put it, and people around us will give glory to God, only when they see our good deeds (Matt. 5:16). The invisible God will be seen to live among us only when we love one another (1 John 4:12). Nothing commends the gospel more eloquently than Christlike lives, whereas nothing hinders the spread of the good news more than a community life which contradicts it. The people of God must embody the gospel they proclaim.

We select two characteristics of consistent Christian living which seem to us to be particularly important today.

The first is Christian unity. 'Brokenness' characterises the contemporary world. The East-West nuclear confrontation shows little sign of abating, racial conflicts continue, nations threaten or fight one another, tribal and ideological rivalries become more violent, the class struggle manifests itself in industrial disputes, the debate over sexual identities and roles leads to bitterness, marriages and families disintegrate, and individual personalities fall apart. The tragedy is that many of these same conflicts are to be found in the Christian Church itself. Racism, nationalism, tribalism, casteism, denominationalism, classism and sexism, not to mention personal and family tensions, have not yet been eliminated from the community which claims to be God's 'single new humanity', his 'family' of reconciled brothers and sisters (Eph. 2:14–20).

It is the quest for structural unity which has preoccupied the churches during the past forty years. And we still believe that Christian unity must be made visible. Indeed, we welcome all ecumenical efforts (like the consultations which have produced the BEM and ARCIC documents), which seek to promote doctrinal agreement as the necessary basis for unity. We also know both that some churches feel able to co-operate in mission before they are united, and that church union schemes do not necessarily lead to a fresh impetus in mission. Further, we are not advocating the replacement of our colourful Christian differences with a dull monochrome. What is essential for the Church's witness is that, even while we share with others the same human fragility and even brokenness, we provide some evidence that the Heavenly Potter is at work among us, mending our fractured lives and communities.

The second necessary characteristic of consistent Christian living seems to us to be Christian integrity, especially in moral standards. Religious experience which does not issue in ethical transformation must be declared spurious. 'God is light . . . If we claim to have fellowship with him yet walk in the darkness, we lie and do not live by the truth' (1 John 1:5–6). The world has a right to expect us to live by the values and standards of the Jesus we profess and proclaim. Lack of integrity brings discredit on the gospel. Some churches mar their witness by litigation with fellow-Christians, in defiance of the teaching of the apostle Paul (1 Cor. 6:1–8), and by bribery and corruption, even in elections to Church office. Others are lax in the business honesty and sexual purity they expect in their members, while in affluent countries Christians often seem to be marked more by covetousness than by contentment.

Hence the need for Church renewal. This does not mean that, before we can engage in mission, we have to wait until we are perfect. In that case we would wait for ever. It does mean, however, that the spread of the gospel is hindered when it is contradicted by inconsistent Christians and churches, and advanced when it is adorned by Christlike living.

THESIS 6: THE PEOPLE OF GOD MUST BE MOBILISED AND EQUIPPED FOR MISSION

Of all the Lambeth Conferences, whose reports have referred to aspects of mission, that of 1958 was notable for its insistence that evangelism is a responsibility which rests on the *laos*' the whole people of God. The Encyclical Letter included this affirmation: 'The worldwide task of evangelism is not an "optional extra": it is the high calling of every disciple'. The bishops also wrote in their 'Missionary Strategy and Appeal': 'Evangelism is not to be thought of as the task of a select few . . . It is for every Christian to do what Andrew did for his brother – to say "we have found the Messiah", and to bring him to Jesus.' What this means is not that every Christian must be a preacher, teacher or missionary (for God calls and gifts different people for different ministries), but that each of us should be a witness, and avail ourselves of opportunities to share the good news with others.

'Mobilisation' may be too military a metaphor for some, but at least it has the merit of laying the task of mission on all Christian people. The biblical basis for this is unequivocal. Although the risen Lord's great commission was given to the apostles (e.g. Matt. 28:16), it was not limited to them, since others were with them at the same time (e.g. Luke 24:33). The early Church clearly understood this, for when the believers were scattered by persecution and 'preached the word wherever they went', Luke specifically adds that he was referring to 'all except the apostles', since the latter remained in Jerusalem (Acts 8:1–4). True, the Pauline doctrine of the Body of Christ emphasises the *variety* of ministries to which its members are called according to their gifts, and not all are 'evangelists'. Nevertheless, the Church itself is 'apostolic', sent out into the world to witness and serve, and every member is to share in its God-given apostolic mission.

Several attempts have been made in the second half of this century to make the 'mobilisation' of God's people for

mission a reality. We think, for example, of interdenominational programmes embracing whole nations and regions like
'Evangelism in Depth' in Latin America and 'New Life for
All' in West Africa. Some Anglicans have been involved in
these. We hope that the bishops who assemble at Lambeth in
1988 will remind the Anglican Communion that the Church is
both 'a holy priesthood', called to offer to God the sacrifice of
worship, and 'a people belonging to God', called to declare
his praises throughout the world (1 Pet. 2:5, 9). In other
words, God intends witness to be as continuous and universal
a function of the Church as worship.

Once the people of God catch the vision of their evangelistic calling, they readily acknowledge their need for training. It
has also been widely recognised in recent decades that
training is one of the chief responsibilities of clergy, since
'pastors and teachers' are given 'to equip God's people for
their ministry' and so to 'build up the body of Christ' (Eph.
4:11, 12).

We believe that every local church should either develop its
own lay training programme or join with other local churches
in providing one. In some parts of the Anglican Communion
(e.g. some dioceses of East Africa) lay training centres have
been established, to which people come for courses of six to
twelve weeks. Theological Education by Extension courses
have also been prepared, which include practical as well as
doctrinal instruction in evangelism. Indeed the best way to
learn evangelism is to begin doing it. Some parachurch
organisations also produce useful training materials. In our
view 'church' and 'parachurch' should not be viewed as being
in competition, provided always that parachurch groups
undertake specialist ministries on behalf of the churches and
accept accountability to the churches. It would be helpful if a
descriptive list of training materials in use in different parts of
the world could be compiled and made available to Anglican
churches.

The 'equipment' for mission which the people of God need,
however, is not just training in apologetic and methodology.
Even more fundamental is our maturing in worship, fellowship and holiness, so that God's grace may flow through us
with ever greater freedom. It is above all at the Eucharist that

his grace is renewed in us and that we are sent out again into the world to serve.

When seeking to increase in Christian people a missionary consciousness and concern, and particular vocations, we believe it is important to fuse local and global horizons. That is to say, it would be anomalous for any congregation either to be become committed in prayer and giving to the Church's world mission, while neglecting any outreach into its own parish, or to become preoccupied with parochial mission, while forgetting what Jesus called 'the ends of the earth' (Acts 1:8).

THESIS 7: THE PEOPLE OF GOD MUST BE SENSITIVE TO DIFFERENT CULTURES

Culture is an amalgam of accepted beliefs, values, customs and institutions, which has been inherited from the past and which gives a people its sense of cohesion and identity. All human beings are creatures of culture. Having imbibed our own cultural inheritance from childhood, we are not always conscious of it, until perhaps travel to another country obliges us to compare its culture with ours and to evaluate each critically. This is particularly true if our cross-cultural travel is undertaken in the interests of the Christian mission.

Each culture has its own authenticity and deserves respect. This does not mean, however, that we should approve every aspect of every culture. Since culture is man-made, it reflects our human ambiguity, both our createdness and our fallenness. What is good in human cultures should be thankfully and joyfully celebrated, while what is evil has to be rejected. In particular, at the heart of every culture a religion or ideology is enthroned, which may not be compatible with Christ. He is the judge of every existing culture, and, when his lordship is acknowledged, he refines and ennobles it. In this sense he is himself trans-cultural, for his standards of truth and righteousness can be expressed in many different cultural forms.

Cross-cultural messengers of the gospel need to develop such self-awareness that they discern the difference between the gospel itself, which like Christ himself is trans-cultural, and their own inherited ways of understanding and expressing it. Missionaries have often unconsciously exported a culture christianity, which has then been rejected not as false but as foreign. Or, if it has been accepted, it still looks alien. In the past Anglicans have been particularly insensitive in exporting Gothic architecture, medieval clerical robes and an Elizabethan liturgy.

In addition to a humble willingness to leave behind their own cultural prejudices, missionaries have to develop a respect for all those aspects of their adopted country's culture which are compatible with the lordship of Christ. This will lead to the task of translating the gospel into appropriate words, concepts and symbols, that is, 'contextualising' it. As the national church grows, it should also be encouraged to use the art forms of the local culture in its architecture, music, pictures, dress and customs. This principle applies equally when the cross-cultural situation is within a single country. Inner city, suburban and rural cultures differ so widely from one another that it would be impossible for evangelism, church development, worship or leadership to be the same in them all.

Cultural imperialism involves the double blunder of seeking to impose one's own culture and despising the other person's. Cultural sensitivity, on the other hand, involves the humility of respecting the other's culture and not clinging to one's own. No more striking example of cross-cultural identification can be found than the incarnation. For the Eternal Son both 'emptied himself' and 'humbled himself' in order to take human flesh and become a servant. Now he sends us into the world, as the Father had sent him (John 17:18; 20:21). True incarnational mission does not resemble those occasional raids into enemy territory which commandos make, only to withdraw again; it is rather a deep, prolonged and transforming penetration of society for Christ as its salt, light and yeast.

We must not assume that national Christians are always friendly to the process of indigenisation. In some countries the older generation of Christians, who have inherited an imported culture-Christianity, resist the tendency to develop an authentic national expression of the gospel, since this would damage and even destroy their sense of identity. The younger generation of national Christians in developing countries, on the other hand, want to absorb those elements of Western culture which they think would benefit their culture (e.g. modern technology), and resist any attempt, in the name of indigenisation, to deny them such gains.

THESIS 8: THE PEOPLE OF GOD NEED THE SPIRIT OF GOD

We cannot discuss evangelism without raising the issue of power. For the apostolic commission involved turning people 'from darkness to light, and from the power of Satan to God' (Acts 26:18), while conversion is to be rescued by God 'from the dominion of darkness . . . into the kingdom of the Son he loves' (Col. 1:13).

Jesus and his apostles clearly believed in the real existence of spirits both good and evil. Paul in particular wrote of the 'principalities and powers', 'spiritual forces of evil in the heavenly realms', whom Jesus had dethroned and disarmed at the cross, whom the Father had placed 'under his feet' at his exaltation, and with whom we continue to struggle, clothed in the whole armour of God (cf. Eph. 1:20 ff.; 6:10 ff.; Col. 2:15).

Influenced by the call to 'demythologise' Scripture, many Anglicans have given up their former belief in the devil and in personal powers of evil. Many others, however, refuse to do so, not only because of the New Testament's teaching, but also because of the resurgence of occult practices in the West and the continuing hold which 'the spirits' have over the adherents of 'traditional religion' (previously called 'animism') in many parts of Africa, Asia and Latin America. In such situations Christian conversion takes the form of a 'power encounter', in which the superior power of Jesus Christ is demonstrated, the spell of evil forces is broken, and human beings are liberated from idols and sin into the service of God (1 Thess. 1:9f.).

The idols of the post-Christian West are just as gruesome and powerful. Demonic forces may be detected not only in the covetous materialism which has gripped many individuals, but also in the secular technology which dispenses with God and demeans persons, and in structures of social injustice. Only the power of Christ can set people free.

Certainly the New Testament attributes the whole process of conversion, from beginning to end, to the powerful work of Jesus Christ by his Spirit. It is the Spirit of truth who convicts us of the realities of sin, righteousness and judgment (John 16:8ff.); who witnesses to Christ, opening our eyes to see him and our mouths to confess him as Lord (John 15:26; 1 Cor. 12:3); who regenerates us, since the new birth is a 'birth of the Spirit' (e.g. John 3:8; Titus 3:5); who witnesses with our spirits that we are now God's children (Rom. 8:16); and who gradually transforms us into the image of Christ (e.g. 2 Cor. 3:18). We need to repent of the proud self-confidence which imagines that we can by ourselves convert souls, and to humble ourselves to acknowledge the indispensable necessity of the work of the Spirit.

Anglicans should be grateful that the Pentecostal Churches and the Charismatic Movement have obliged the Church to re-examine the person and ministry of the Holy Spirit, who was often previously the neglected member of the Trinity. Although we cannot accept the doctrine of a two-stage Christian initiation (first regeneration, then 'the baptism of the Spirit'), as taught by classical pentecostalism and by some charismatics, we nevertheless affirm our need both of the fruit of the Spirit to make us Christ-like (Gal. 5:22 f.) and of the gifts of the Spirit to equip us for service (e.g. Rom. 12:3 ff.; 1 Cor. 12:4 ff.).

THESIS 9: THE PEOPLE OF GOD NEED STRONG INCENTIVES FOR MISSION

Being rational creatures bearing God's image, we need to understand not only what we are supposed to be doing, but also why. So incentives are important in every area of life, and the Church's comparative indifference – even indolence – in the sphere of mission suggests an absence of the necessary motivation. Mission can be both demanding and discouraging; only clear, strong incentives will induce us to persevere. They are not wanting.

The first is the nature of God himself. According to the biblical revelation, he is love, and in love is ever reaching out to give himself. It is in the context of his love that his 'sending' makes sense. God sent the prophets to his people. Then the Father sent the Son, and the Father and the Son sent the Spirit, while Father, Son and Spirit together send the Church. This outgoing of love has prompted some Christian writers to use the adjective 'centrifugal' in reference to God. Jesus himself likened the Holy Spirit both to a spring of water welling up within us and to rivers of water flowing forth from us (John 4:14; 7:37 ff.). As William Temple commented, 'no one can possess (or, rather be indwelt by) the Spirit of God and keep that Spirit to himself. Where the Spirit is, he flows forth; if there is no flowing forth, he is not there.'[1] Indeed, this is precisely what we see in the Acts. Once the Spirit had been poured out on the Day of Pentecost, the outflow began. We speak of the early Church's spontaneous witness, but the 'spontaneity' was due to the ceaseless activity of the Spirit, driving his people out in concentric circles, from Jerusalem through Judea and Samaria to the ends of the earth (Acts 1:8).

Second, there is the nature of the church. Jesus spoke of his disciples as equally given to him 'out of the world' and sent back 'into the world' (e.g. John 17:6, 18). These truths have been preserved in two of the Church's four 'marks' or 'notes', namely that it is both 'holy' and 'apostolic'. Throughout the centuries of Church history God's people have found it hard to maintain the balance between sanctity and apostolicity, and have tended to oscillate between the extremes of withdrawal from the world and conformity to it. Yet in either case the Church denies a part of its essential identity and renders its mission impossible. Mission arises from the doctrine of the Church in the world, in it but not of it, immersed in its life, yet transcending it by a God-given life of its own.

Third, there is the nature of love. We have already written of God's love. Now we note that the love to which we are called has the same self-giving, outgoing quality. God's love was uniquely revealed in the Son's sacrifice on the cross and is constantly being poured into our hearts by the Spirit (Rom. 5:5, 8). If therefore we have what others need (whether material or spiritual wealth), and do not share it with them, we cannot claim to have God's love within us (1 John 3:17). Good things are worth sharing, because of their intrinsic value; and love moves us to share them. It would be a mistake therefore, to reduce motivation for mission to the Great Commission of the Risen Lord. To be sure, we must obey it. Yet the great commandment to love our neighbour is more comprehensive than the great commission to preach the gospel and make disciples. It is unfortunately possible to share without loving; it is not possible to love without sharing.

Fourth, there is the nature of worship. We have already mentioned that the Church in God's purpose is both a worshipping and a witnessing community. It is not enough, however, to bracket worship and mission as twin responsibilities of the people of God; we have to see how each necessarily involves the other. For if worship is our acknowledgment of the infinite worth of God, it will inevitably lead us to make his worth known to others. And the reason why we want them to know him is that they may come and worship him, too. Thus worship leads us to witness and witness into worship in a perpetual cycle. Only so could the apostle Paul speak of his evangelistic ministry in priestly terms; it was because thereby the Gentiles became 'an offering acceptable to God' (Rom. 15:16).

SUMMARY

God calls his people to share in his own mission in the world. It is in relation to this task that we have stated our nine theses about what God's people either are or should be.

The people of God
(1) – have good news to share
(2) – confess Jesus Christ as the unique and universal Saviour and Lord
(3) – are called to proclaim and to convince
(4) – must reach out to all who suffer injustice
(5) – must be seen to be what they claim to be
(6) – must be mobilised and equipped for mission
(7) – must be sensitive to different cultures
(8) – need the Spirit of God
(9) – need strong incentives for mission

We conclude with a quotation from the report of Section 3 of the last Lambeth Conference (1978):

Since we have been commanded by our Lord to proclaim the news of salvation to all nations, and since there are over two billion persons in the world who need to know Christ crucified and risen, Anglicans are called upon to commit themselves afresh to the work of evangelisation, in co-operation with their fellow-Christians of other Communions wherever possible[2]

FOOTNOTES

1 *Readings in St John's Gospel* (London, 1945), p. 130.
2 *The Report of the Lambeth Conference* (London, 1978), p. 111.

Note. We are grateful to the Rev. Kobina Quashie (Ghana and UK), the Rev. Dr Peter Pytches (UK) and the Rev. Dr Christopher Wright (UK and India), who met with us as a group. We also thank the following consultants who read our nine theses in draft and made helpful comments: the Rt Rev. David Gitari (Kenya), Mr Alan Milton (UK), the Rev. Professor John Pobee (Ghana and Geneva), the Rev. Dr Viney K. Samuel (India), and Dr Mary Tanner (UK).

BIBLIOGRAPHY

David J. Bosch, *Witness to the World – the Christian mission in theological perspective* (Basingstoke, 1980). *The biblical foundations, history and theology of mission, including socio-political involvement, by a deeply concerned South African professor.*
John C. Chapman, *Know and Tell the Gospel: the why and how of Evangelism* (London, 1981). *Canon Chapman of Sydney, Australia, explains the biblical basis of evangelism, and gives many practical guidelines.*
Kenneth Cragg, *The Christian and Other Religions* (London, 1977). *The well-known scholar-bishop, whose special expertise is in Islam, sets the distinctives of Christ's claims within religion and not simply between religions.*
Timothy Gorringe, *Redeeming Time – Atonement through Education* (London, 1986). *A young theologian with first-hand experience in South India argues imaginatively about God's redemptive work 'rooted in Christ's solidarity with us, continued through the Spirit'.*

Michael Griffiths, *What on earth are you doing? Jesus' call to world mission* (Leicester, 1983). *The Principal of London Bible College, who had many years as a missionary in Asia, gives a colourful description of missionary life today.*

Lesslie Newbigin, *Foolishness to the Greeks* (London, 1986). *An analysis of the Church's failure to engage properly in mission at home, by one of the most ecumenical of missiologists this century.*

René Padilla, *Mission Between the Times: Essays on the Kingdom* (Exeter, 1986). *Nine essays by a Latin American Evangelical leader, focusing on the relationship between evangelism and social action.*

Vinay Samuel and Christopher Sugden, *Evangelism and the Poor – a Third World Study Guide* (Exeter, 1982). *A collection of study material for groups planning and reflecting on their witness to the poor.*

John R. W. Stott, *Christian Mission in the Modern World* (Eastbourne, 1986). *An examination of the words 'mission', 'evangelism', 'salvation', 'dialogue' and 'conversion' in contemporary debate.*

David Watson, *I Believe in Evangelism* (London, 1976). *The gifted evangelist, who died in 1985, discusses the motives and methods of evangelism.*

DISCUSSION QUESTIONS

1 Share with one another as a group what the good news has come to mean to you.

2 Granted that Jesus Christ is both the only Saviour (e.g. John 14:6; Acts 4:12; 1 Tim. 2:5), and 'the true light that enlightens everyone' (John 1:9), how would you relate these two truths to each other?

3 What are the major hindrances in your local church (a) to evangelising its parish or district, and (b) to being more committed to world mission?

4 What practical steps would you wish to recommend to your church leadership in order to 'mobilise and equip' your church membership for mission?

5 What are the elements of your local culture which seem to you to be (a) barriers to, and (b) possible bridges for, the gospel?

6 If you had to add a tenth thesis, what would it be?

CONCLUSIONS

There has been a remarkable and pleasantly surprising agreement between the authors of each of the essays. This has encouraged members of the group to hope that some positive stepping stones to further theological progress may be found in our agreement; and this not only between our two traditions, but also between other groups of Anglicans as they prepare for the Lambeth Conference.

There are several ways in which this book might be used. Theological gourmets may be interested simply to sit and read the essays, for they offer fresh thinking in a number of different fields. Study groups may wish to take an essay at a time (and not necessarily in the order we have printed them!), for each of them offers sufficient material to form the basis of several study sessions. To help them with this, we have suggested questions for groups to consider, and further books on each subject which they may like to consult. Some people or groups may well wish to give their attention to one or two topics which are of special interest to them, and leave the rest until a rainy day! Whichever category you fall into, these few conclusions may help you to continue your thinking.

Is the Anglican Communion having an identity crisis? One might not think so, to see dozens of bishops packing their cases in preparation for the pilgrimage to Lambeth, showing much confidence in the Communion and a real sense of belonging. But a deep desire to share mutual problems and blessings, even a common liturgical tradition will not hold us together unless there are other factors which also bind us to one another more strongly than we are bound to the other

Christians of other Communions in each of our separate nations or continents. For there is a real sense in which the Anglican Communion is the most absurd of all the Christian denominations; a national church which went international providentially and/or by accident rather than by design. Nevertheless, we do belong together, at a practical level if at no other. So the essay, 'In Search of an Anglican Identity', with its clear historical bias, is intended not only to inform interested readers of the issues which gave rise to this amazing church, but also to provoke in us the question, 'What is it, beyond the grace of God which holds us together today?'

This question struck me with new force, when I was teaching in a school for catechists in the Sabah Anglican interior mission in Malaysia. I was commissioned to give a brief history of all the churches; when we arrived at the Reformation the students were much inspired by stories of Luther and Calvin and some of the other reformers whose faith had set them on fire. 'And who,' they asked, 'began the Anglican church?' Never had the familiar tale of royal divorce and pressure to maintain the inheritance seemed so ridiculously incongruous as it did that day in the jungle. I was forced back to the theological platitude that the power of God can bring good out of unlikely circumstances. But the question remains; '*Do I* believe that the power of God *has* brought good out of unlikely circumstances in the case of the Anglican Church?' And if I do believe it, and if you do, we must ask the further question: 'Was the Anglican Church created to fulfil a temporary purpose in a little bit of Europe, or has it a future in the kingdom purposes of God in the world of today and tomorrow?' Then we shall need to ask, 'Can God again bring good out of the unlikely contemporary circumstances of our Communion today?'

Since these essays give rise to such important and big questions, I hope that our essays may inspire some to dream dreams, and to see visions, for the future of any part of God's mission has rarely emerged from study groups and discussion sessions; it has more often come about when women and men have been open to the future with God, as they wait on him in the present. This is especially important in a large and scattered Communion, for a sense of common purpose will weld us together more strongly than any other of the things we have in common.

The difficulty about forward planning is that it is easier to do when we imagine that we are starting from scratch or from some other place! The reality is that we can only set out on a journey if we know our departure point. Individuals, groups, dioceses, bishops and the Lambeth Conference itself may need to undertake a kind of 'mission audit', an assessment of our present position, if our plans to move forward are to be any more than make believe.

One of our attempts to take stock will undoubtedly be a reassessment of the good news which has been committed to us. That is why we have included an essay on 'Jesus – God with us', for this is the epitome of our 'good news'. Unless we start with him, we have no foundation at all. Starting with Jesus does not primarily mean going back in history; for his resurrection makes him our contemporary and our goal before he is our predecessor. But the essay about Jesus shows us that his universality means that he is not only 'our' Jesus; he is Lord of all those who confess him in many different ways, in the other denominations and in none. So any attempt to understand ourselves in relation to him, will have to take that into account: relationship with him brings us into relationship with many people whom we do not understand, nor even normally encounter. Our vision for the Anglican Communion of the future must take seriously our *working* as well as our *talking* relationships with other Christian people. It is to these and to other questions that our essay on the Church addresses itself, for it reminds us that we need to know both what vessel we sail in, and where it is heading.

But the universality of Jesus extends beyond the Christian group, however we number or define it. This Jesus knows no bounds: 'without him was not anything made that was made' (John 1:3). Our attempts to understand our Anglican selves and our mission must therefore take into account all those who were made by him, although they may neither know nor acknowledge it. It is for this reason, and out of this conviction, that our essay on the 'mission agenda for the people of God' sprang. This topic falls at the end; 'the best wine kept to last' because it is precisely this motivating paper which may help those working through the volume to renew their vision and their efforts before Lambeth even begins.

Any who rush fervently into the world will encounter many problems which reach beyond what has traditionally been understood as the 'spiritual' realm. We have taken the family as our one example of such problems because it touches us all, whatever our nationality. This is not an Anglican statement on the family: rather it is two Anglican scholars, who share a common conviction and way of doing theology. They address themselves to an ethical issue, with a double aim in view. First, this essay should be of interest to every thinking Christian, Anglican or otherwise, who is concerned with the place of the family in society, with relationships within their own family grouping, and within the family of the Church. Second, it is a model of doing theology which well illustrates our first essay: in its use of Scripture and tradition; its reference to contemporary research, and its practical outworking. Those who find the theoretical discussion of our first essay hard to grasp, might well turn next to that on the family, where illustrative examples abound.

The Anglican Communion has not been renowned for its theological expertise. There are few Anglicans among the theological giants of our own or earlier times. However, this does not signify that Anglicans do not hold it to be important. It is the reverse conviction which has led us to make our first essay, 'on doing theology'; for those who do not know how to drive a car or how to paint a portrait may occasionally succeed in the task, but the experienced driver and the skilled painter are more likely to be effective. Anglicans do not only share a common history, and a common liturgy; they share a common conviction about the way in which to make progress in theology. The question which remains is whether they can work at theology together in a way which makes a common vision possible for their future together.

Our third essay undertakes precisely this task in an area which is perhaps *the* most contentious in our Communion today. This essay should help those who wish to look not only at the issues which surround ministry, but also to consider how we can be Anglican in a way which does not jeopardise the integrity of other members of our church; while at the same time remaining true to our own convictions. Often our way of being Anglican in these circumstances is to ignore those who do not agree with us; practically very easy in our separate churches and churchmanships, agreeing to worship together in words which are common, but which hide contrary convictions. Alternatively, we have in the past sallied out to do battle against those who do not think or worship like we do. But to us is committed a ministry of reconciliation. The challenge of the essay on ministry is: can we learn to work together in a way which respects the other more than it considers itself? Can we listen to the hard questions which we need to hear from those who are different from us so our discipleship can be deepened? For do not our own traditions often confirm our prejudices and mask our weaknesses? Can we resolve never to do separately what we could do together, even though it will always be harder to work with those unlike us than those we feel closest to? We have claimed our Anglican ministry to be not only a symbol of unity, but to be an effective symbol which enables these questions to be answered 'YES!' If that ministry truly extends from Christ to all his members, then it is to everyone, not just to our bishops (or priests, or deacons) to which a final searching question comes: Are we all participating fully in this ministry of reconciliation?

THE CONTRIBUTORS

The Rev. Dr David Atkinson (Evangelical) is Fellow and Chaplain of Corpus Christi College, Oxford, author of *To Have and To Hold* and *Peace in Our Time?*. Lecturer in Ethics and Pastoral Theology at Wycliffe Hall, and Theological Consultant to Care and Counsel.

The Rev. Professor James Atkinson (Evangelical) was Head of the Department of Biblical Studies at the University of Sheffield, and is now Director of their Centre for Reformation Studies. He is well known for his work on Martin Luther.

The Rev. Peter G. Atkinson (Catholic) studied theology at St John's College, Oxford; Westcott House, Cambridge; and the Venerable English College, Rome. He is now parish priest of Tatsfield, Surrey. He is married, with one son; and is the brother of fellow-contributor David Atkinson.

Dr Richard Bauckham (Evangelical) is Lecturer in History of Christian Thought in the University of Manchester. He has written extensively on New Testament, historical and modern theology. His most recent book is *Moltmann: Messianic Theology in the Making*. He is also an Anglican Reader.

Dr Christina A. Baxter (Evangelical) is Registrar at St John's College, Nottingham. A member of General Synod, and its standing committee, she is an Anglican Reader.

The Rev. Roger Beckwith (Evangelical) warden of Latimer House, Oxford, and lecturer on liturgy at Wycliffe Hall, Oxford. Author of *The Old Testament Canon of the New*

Testament Church (SPCK) and contributor to *The Study of the Liturgy* (SPCK). Member of the Anglican-Orthodox commission.

The Rev. Dr David Brown (Catholic) is Fellow and Chaplain of Oriel College, Oxford, and author of *Choices* (Blackwell, 1983) and *The Divine Trinity*. Member of the Doctrine Commission of the Church of England, and University Lecturer in Ethics and Philosophical Theology.

The Rt. Rev. Colin Buchanan (Evangelical) has been Bishop of Aston (Birmingham diocese) since 1985, following 21 years at St John's College, Nottingham. He helped to create the ASB. He was joint author of *Growing into Union* (1970), and writes on liturgical, sacramental and ecclesiological subjects, editing *News of Liturgy* and other Grove Books publications.

The Rev. Dr George Carey (Evangelical) is Principal of Trinity College, Bristol, and formerly Vicar of St Nicholas's, Durham. He is unashamedly committed to the *Renewal* and *Unity* of the Church. He is author of books on Church, Christ and Man. He is the new chairman of the Faith and Order Advisory Group of the Church of England.

The Rev. Martin Dudley (Catholic) is Vicar of Weston in Hertfordshire. A member of the Church Union Theological Committee, he also teaches on the St Albans Ministerial Training Scheme, and is co-editor of the new journal for Catholic renewal, *Living Stones*.

The Rev. Canon Roger Greenacre (Catholic) has been Chancellor of Chichester Cathedral since 1975. He studied at Cambridge, Mirfield and Louvain and has taught at Ely, Paris and Chichester. Since 1979 he has served as Chairman of the revived Church Union Theological Committee.

The Rev. Canon John Hind (Catholic) principal of Chichester Theological College after 10 years parish ministry in London, is a member of the Faith and Order Advisory Group and of several ecumenical dialogues. He believes mission and unity to be inseparable and that reconciliation between Anglicans and the wider ecumenical task are closely related.

The Rev. Canon James S. Robertson, O.B.E., formerly Secretary, United Society for the Propagation of the Gospel.

The Rev. Dr John Stott was Rector of All Souls Church, Langham Place, London, from 1950 to 1975, and is now President of the London Institute for Contemporary Christianity. He has led university missions on five continents. His books include *Christian Mission in the Modern World, Issues Facing Christians Today*, and, most recently, *The Cross of Christ*.

The Rev. Dr Rowan Williams is Lady Margaret Professor of Divinity in the University of Oxford, and had written several books on theology and spirituality. He is a member of the Inter-Anglican Theological and Doctrinal Commission, and of the Doctrine Commission of the Church of England.

OTHER STUDY GROUP MEMBERS

The Rev. Dr Gerald Bray, Lecturer in Christian Doctrine, Oak Hill Theological College, London.

The Rev. Alan Walker, Chaplain to the Polytechnic of Central London. Secretary to the Church Union Theological Committee.